RESILIENCE & THE CITY

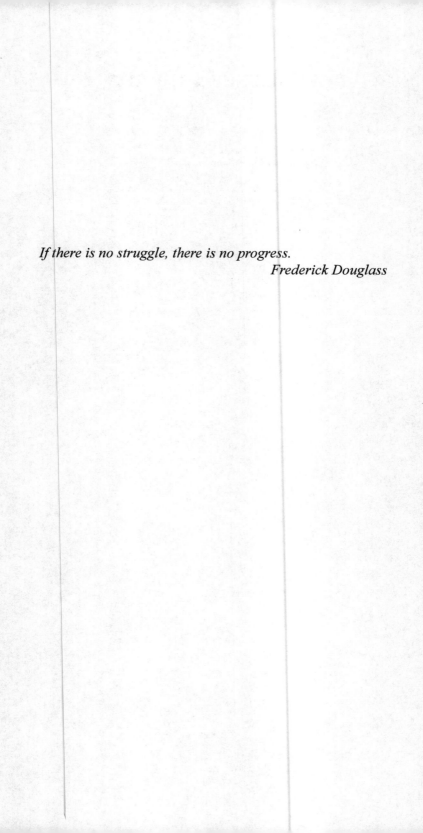

If there is no struggle, there is no progress.
Frederick Douglass

Resilience & the City
Change, (Dis)Order and Disaster

PETER ROGERS
Macquarie University, Australia

Routledge
Taylor & Francis Group

LONDON AND NEW YORK

First published 2012 by Ashgate Publishing

Published 2016 by Routledge
2 Park Square, Milton Park, Abingdon, Oxon OX14 4RN
711 Third Avenue, New York, NY 10017, USA

Routledge is an imprint of the Taylor & Francis Group, an informa business

British Library Cataloguing in Publication Data
Rogers, Peter.
   Resilience & the city : change, (dis)order and disaster. --
   (Design and the built environment series)
   1. Crime prevention--Great Britain. 2. Urban policy--
   Great Britain. 3. Urban ecology (Sociology)--Great
   Britain. 4. Lefebvre, Henri, 1901-1991.
   I. Title II. Series
   364.4'9-dc23

Library of Congress Cataloging-in-Publication Data
Rogers, Peter.
   Resilience & the city : change, (dis)order, and disaster / by Peter Rogers.
      p. cm. -- (Design and the built environment)
   Includes bibliographical references and index.
   ISBN 978-0-7546-7658-4 (hardback) -- ISBN 978-0-7546-7659-1 (ebook)
   1. Cities and towns--Social aspects. 2. Cities and towns--Growth. I. Title. II. Title:
   Resilience and the city.
   HT119.R64 2012
   307.76--dc23

2012021693

ISBN 13: 978-0-7546-7658-4 (hbk)

Contents

List of Figures and Tables

Figures

Tables

Acknowledgements

There are many, too many to include everyone, who have informed or influenced my life during the preparation of this book. I would like to thank those friends and family who put up with me, and those colleagues around the world who have provided proofreading on some parts of the end result, some kind words, a place to sit and quietly write away from the hubbub, or an audience for the papers that spun out of this or related work; these include Gavin Smith, Stephen Graham, Nick Vaughn-Williams, Alison Wakefield, Pat O'Malley, Amanda Elliott, as well as my friends and colleagues at Macquarie University – especially Harry Blatterer and Justine Lloyd for reading some of the more impenetrable drafts. I should also acknowledge the Economic and Social Research Council and Macquarie University for funding elements of the applied research that I've been involved with over the last few years, these projects have often guided both my reading and research focus. I would like to thank the team at Ashgate for their patience in the long road to getting this up and running in its current form, especially Val Rose, Carolyn Court and Caroline Spender. Also thanks to Dale Harrison, Andrew Elliott and David Shervington for their last minute suggestions on the cover images, I wish we could have used them all (maybe next time!). Two last acknowledgements, then 'on with the show'. To my partner, you bring order to my days and fend off disaster in so many ways, thank you, for everything. Finally, to those who are reading it, thanks for taking a risk and looking at things in a different way, I hope you find it interesting and maybe even useful.

Chapter 1

Introduction

Be not astonished at new ideas; for it is well known to you that a thing does not therefore cease to be true because it is not accepted by many.

Baruch Spinoza

What's the Idea?

This book seeks to offer, if not a totally new idea, then perhaps a new way to approach a very old one. This study grew out of several years reading the work of Marx, Lefebvre and Foucault, both their own work and what others have written on them; but it is not a book of theory. This study also grew out of several years of research on the topic of security, resilience and the city, but this is not a case study of empirical research. This book seeks to apply a novel reading of social science to both the theory and empirical study of the city as a 'resilient' phenomenon. In this book, an argument is made that (1) the concept of resilience is of growing importance to enquiry, and (2) this importance can be enhanced and meaningfully grounded in a project of spatial history. The point is that resilience is not a new idea – it is not an innovation springing into the world fully formed. It is a very old feature and characteristic of how we go about living, surviving and thriving. The goal in this book is to find a way to theoretically inform and empirically ground how this idea has emerged, has changed, and is informing the change happening around us in the city today. What we think about it, how we know what to do and how we then act out 'resilience' in the city can give us some real insight into this idea.

As the struggle to bring order to risky times, spaces and places appears increasingly disordered, there is much interest in how we can change, adapt and become more resilient. Change and adaptation over time affect the similarities and differences in the beliefs of different groups (e.g. theology, rationalism), the abstract knowledge of how to do certain things (e.g. worship, masonry, scientific method) and how everyday lives are acted out (e.g. preying, building a house, running an experiment). Change can create fear and uncertainty, as adaptation acknowledges that new ways of thinking, doing or acting are possible or may become necessary as the world changes around us. Change creates cascade effects, meaning one change that triggers others in both negative and positive ways. A change in beliefs can affect the interests of a group, which alliances are made or broken, the groups or coalitions that individuals, tribes, nations choose to be members of. When looking at changing cities, a tipping point can affect whom particular spaces of the city belong to, or change what a place means to the different groups that use it. How authority is used to manage or govern the changing city informs the way that people think, the knowledge of how to do things and the way they act out their everyday lives. Change demands adaptation; those who adapt become more resilient, those who do not may not, but change and adaptation are two sides of the same coin. This complex interplay can be aligned in different ways at different times, shaping individuals, locations, cities, societies and civilisations to become more or less resilient. Some alignments persist, are adaptable and resilient, others falter, decay, fall prey to war, disaster or are absorbed by other ways of thinking, of doing or acting and fade away as times change.

This book uses the city as a crucible. Its key contribution is the use of the city to explain the features and characteristics of resilience. The key questions are how did cities happen, where did they come from, why did people come together to make settlements, villages, towns and cities? What were the agreements made that allowed people to cooperate to raise houses, walls or temples? How did technologies help them to progress? What institutions and organisations underpin the creation, destruction and recreation of an urban everyday life? This might seem like a lot of questions, and it is. These questions overlap in so many ways as to make up delightful contradictions. They shift and oscillate to shape our understanding of the world, of each other, of time, space and place in different ways at different times. Sometimes we are resilient through our positive adaptation to change. We are able to learn from our exposure to danger, shift and transform our ways of thinking, doing or acting to come out stronger than we were before. Sometimes we are resilient because we refuse to yield to change. We resist and remain obdurate and unchanged despite the damage or danger faced. This book seeks to open up the debate on positive and negative forms of resilience by using the lens of change in the city to crack open the old questions of who we are, and how safe we are in the face of dangerous and ongoing change.

In order to get to the city of today, though, we must first make an effort to open up the debate. To such an end this book is split into two parts. The first uses the method of spatial history to develop a deeper understanding of change. If we can assume in broad terms that religion is the seed of philosophy, and philosophy is the seed of science, then none in their current form could exist without the interplay they have had with each other. Very simply put, could the modern scientific method exist without the combination of Persian mathematicians, the European philosophers and the tipping point where reaction against religious dogma triggered the Enlightenment? Could modern democratic government exist without the interplay between the corruption of the aristocracy and the economic poverty and decades of disease that created the ripe conditions to trigger the English Civil War or the French Revolution? These oversimplified points suggest that there is an ongoing interplay between different theories, different knowledge of how to do things and different ways of acting upon that knowledge. These three (theory, knowledge, action) constitute beliefs (as ways of thinking), rules (as ways of doing) and norms (as ways of acting). Through their interplay and alignment, order and disorder emerge, the features and characteristics of which can be traced to highlight the trajectory of change over time. The term 'trajectory' is used here loosely; inferring the alignment of beliefs, rules and norms as they interact is a process of fluctuation, of oscillation and realignment across complex and interdependent forms. These forms create and destroy systems as they realign, the thread of which coalesces into a particular way of thinking, of doing and of acting at a particular time. Using this theory to identify evidence allows an analysis of the 'meta-stable equilibrium' as it goes through the process of becoming something else. Civilisations adapt as the interplay between forms of beliefs, rules and norms are perturbed and disordered, and reordered again. Tracing the trajectory of change throughout history can show how resilience and the city are (re)constituted through a process of struggle between order and disorder that stimulates adaptation and transformation in those resilient orders that survive, and often helps to show how those that are too rigid or unable to adapt can struggle, decline or fall foul of the conflicts that result from a lack of resilience. The second part of the book extends this theory to look at mapping out the present in more depth. This engages with the features and characteristics of a democratic, entrepreneurial and capitalist social order, and the challenges to that order that are posed by ecological, technological and human hazards, risks and threats.

Concepts and Context

In order to achieve this end there are some difficult concepts that need to be unpacked along the way, first amongst them: order, disorder and resilience, but also authority, risk, disaster, hazard, security and more. These are far from simple or uncontested concepts. Indeed, a large part of the discussion that follows is taken up with unpacking (in Part I) what these concepts mean and how they can be unpacked differently at different points in history, and (in Part II) what they mean today and how or why they are important. There is almost always a struggle at the heart of defining a concept, and more struggle involved in turning that concept from raw knowledge into a form of thinking, doing or acting that has an effect on the world around us. This struggle runs throughout the discussion, but it should always be remembered that this definition and categorisation are a means to an end, not ends in and of themselves.

The analysis emerges from a personal struggle with the increase in cross-disciplinary research on disaster and security in recent years. An intellectual explosion of sorts has seen contested ideas come forth over how we should understand the next world order, or in sociological terms what the next meta-narrative is to be used for bringing the current global (dis)order into focus. Of course, this has far-reaching implications for those studying core concepts in crisis, disaster, catastrophe and the urban. Such an approach requires that the analyst touches upon and cuts across the 'world risk society' (Beck, 1999), the social science of disaster (Rodriguez et al., 2006), climate change and environmental hazards (Pelling, 2003; Vale and Campanella, 2005), the search for urban resilience (Coaffee et al., 2008) and attempts to model the urban as complex systems (Fujita et al., 1999; Bretagnolle et al., 2003; Batty, 2008).

Many crossovers emerge across such diverse approaches to the study of urban space. The topics blur and cut across urban security, emergency or crisis, muddying the analysis across scales of territory, place and networks as the urbanising world struggles to be prepared for the worst.

One of the central features of such crossover is the integration of 'resilience' as a useful concept in theory, governance policy and the management of urban space (Coaffee and Wood, 2006). What we understand as risk, hazards and threats are now being reconstituted within new theories, taxonomies and typologies to bring the ongoing process of change into debate. Any effort to clarify the muddy waters of this complex discussion must now take into account both the real and imagined crises, emergencies, disasters and catastrophes – be they urban and rural, anthropogenic and technological, legal or cultural and so on. At the same time there is a growing fragility inherent in the increasingly urban, capitalist and democratic social order. In a world of 'shocks', 'clashes' and 'tipping points', numerous approaches can be useful, but in amidst all the competing arguments order can easily become disorder. One must not lose sight of change as a contested process of becoming something else.

One might easily make assumptions to bring order to this chaos. One might assume that 'security' and 'order' are two sides of the same coin. One might say the same about 'disaster' and 'disorder'. However, when we dig deeper there are subtle and important differences in how we know or think about, understand, do and act in orderly or disorderly ways. Security can create disorder, as shown by the Western investment in paramilitary groups used to secure the Middle East during the Cold War, many of which have since been radicalised by geo-political extremism into terrorist organisations. Equally, disaster can stimulate positive growth, as the chain of recent disasters in the twenty-first century have stimulated both economic growth in reconstitution of affected locales, regions and nations and in new ways of thinking about disasters around the world. There are also fluctuating interdependencies between different forms of knowledge, of thinking, of doing and of acting on knowledge linked to customary beliefs, traditional rules and established norms, themselves idiosyncratic to a given moment in time. Any analyst will find complex typologies and taxonomies of sometimes contradictory, sometimes complementary, ideas on what we know, should be able to do, the best way of doing it and enacting that as a course of action. Our efforts to better deal with danger appear differently at different moments, and it seems that, no matter how deep one digs, change over time is the only constant.

Aims and Outcomes

The aim here is ambitious. The aim is to rethink urban history as a process of struggle that creates different forms of order and disorder. From the particular alignment of the orderly and disorderly in everyday life change can be traced, identifying which resilient features and characteristics emerge as positive and progressive adaptations or negative and regressive resistance to change at different times. Order is the alignment of the pattern towards a meta-stable equilibrium, disorder towards perturbation, crisis or even catastrophe; resilience emerges as analysable features and characteristics of change sliding between these poles. A very basic definition of resilience is the struggle to adapt within complex, interdependent systems in order to survive, and to thrive. Resilience is a process rather than a subjective or objective 'thing'. As such, the study of resilience in the urban is the study of interplay between different forms of thinking, doing and acting to understand the process of change in space and place over time. Now, in fulfilling this aim and reaching this outcome one must engage with some dense philosophical notions, and even more dense theoretical language, but the end result will be a much richer understanding of the process of change and the importance of the struggle for practical resilience of use to academics, researchers, policymakers and practitioners.

Understanding change as a process of interplay harnesses ideas around 'mapping the present' (Elden, 2001) to show how diverse categorisations of knowing, doing and acting are an elaboration on the existing content of what is already concrete in life around us. Resilience is something built on the interplay between the real and the imagined. As such, it is interplay between our knowledge about the world and the lived experience of that world over time. As the world in question is increasingly urban this discussion takes place in a predominantly urban context. It will provide a toolbox for the future analysis of the concrete in everyday life, drawn from the interplay of the concrete with the abstract – i.e. what we know, what we do and how we act. It is, as such, less a *repackaging* of previous theoretical, political and economic frameworks and more a *reconstitution* of philosophical and sociological enquiry alongside a spatial history of urban social change. In short, this book will look deeper, further back, and with a more critical eye unpack the antecedents of contested discourses of the resilient city. This is overly simplistic, and the detail is unpacked throughout the book, but at its most basic, *time* is the lens for understanding how change occurs, *space* is the lens for understanding where it occurs and *place* is the lens for unpacking the meaning of change for those who experience it. By reconstituting change over time–space–place we thus redefine our dialectic understanding of traceable patterns that (re)constitute 'everyday life' (Lefebvre, 2004 [1992]). This can help to chart the resultant 'discursive formation' (Foucault, 1970) of given 'truths' and how they inform the decision-making that leads people to settle in a location; we chart some applications of this method through the city in history (Part I). When this is reapplied to the city of today (Part II) it gives the analyst a way into unpacking urban order or disorder and the emergence of challenges posed by emergency, crisis, disaster and catastrophe in more detail and with more depth.

Now, it might be possible for this discussion to bring some clarity to muddied waters, but given the complexity of the project it could equally stir up more confusion for some readers. For example, throughout this discussion questions are asked on how authority is linked to both order and disorder. The analysis addresses the 'conditions of possibility' for the creation of order and the potential for it to be changed – sometimes by forms of thinking, sometimes by forms of doing, sometimes by dangerous events that are beyond human control. The increased focus on the interplay between different 'forms' draws out the character of a given order but also the perturbations of the disorderly that both inform the trajectory of change. The forms of influence are diverse and can include particular types of knowledge – *theology, philosophy, scientific method* – specific technologies or functional practices – *writing, construction, computing* – social relations between individuals or groups – *exchanges, conversations* – the environmental conditions of a space or location – *temporary or permanent, rural or urban* – as well as the institutions – *forms of politeness, religious doctrine, code of laws, democratic elections* – and organisations – *church, army, judiciary, civil government*. All of these forms are a part and parcel of ordering everyday life. Who has access to them and what they do with that access is also important for the complexity and adaptability of the system. Understanding the interplay between these forms will enliven the understanding of the anthropological context through which our everyday lives are ordered and enacted. This helps to elucidate the impact of change in the present, enabling analysis of the current trends in policy and practice. As an aim and outcome of the book it is hoped that by reflection on these trends a more positive sense of how resilience has developed and can be understood will be used to build cyclical adaptations into the ordering of everyday life. This will stimulate debate over the need for more meaningfully democratic forms of urbanism. It *is* possible for a deeper meaning to underpin urban resilience. One that draws together the themes of disparate research, highlighted above. Rather than simply a passive 'bounce-back' to a pre-existing stable or steady state, we can adapt, we can change and we can transform. Contributing to this debate as it evolves is a central aim of this book.

Themes and Questions

There have been a number of influential arguments in the discussion of a dominant archetype or 'meta-narrative' of our contemporary social order, from 'risk society' to a 'clash of civilisations' or the 'end of history'. These often define not just the topic or theme of enquiry, but also the kind of questions one can ask in empirical research. Rather than more prosaic research questions (RQ1, RQ2, etc.) this book operates across these themes to draw out questions for further debate. First, the book offers a way into theory and practice, stepping away from a history of the political and economic towards a spatial history. This does not refute the utility of political economy, but rather seeks to avoid reducing analysis *ab initio* to political and economic processes. The political and the economic are vital forms to include, but they are not the only way to get at the meat and bones of complex change over time. For example, what effect does a location or site have on what people do there? What other forms of beliefs, customs, habits or traditions are enshrined as institutions? Which coalitions combine into authoritative organizations? How do these deep roots develop? Of special interest are the patterns emerging over time, whereby individuals gain or lose in the range of choices available to them; how the beliefs, rules and norms underpinning choice link with particular locations, institutions, organisations. Is there a trend in the trajectory of change that allows us to trace these shifts over time in the alignment of beliefs, rules and norms as schools of thought, as laws or ways of behaving?

The well-intentioned, but oft misguided, treatment of such discussions in policy and practice has set up a context for enquiry in which the analysis of technique and actuarial tools (e.g. risk assessment, risk management and risk mitigation) too often take precedence over 'making sense' of the everyday world around us. The result of such an approach is a more pragmatically defined and efficiently managed series of governance techniques, struggling to match the territoriality and organisational capacity of the nation-state with the needs of global capitalism, and leaving the individual citizen behind subject to the whims of choice in a market of indecision. Such a view potentially omits the experience of people on the street, being more focussed on the 'space of flows' through which capital and information now move, or with the nuance of institutional and organisational wrangling for the best way to meet the requisite obligations of government – to create, ensure and maintain order. It also misses the chance to draw on characteristics of people, society or civilisation that underpin these techniques, mechanisms and institutional or organisational processes. Notions of persistence, durability, recovery, efficiency, adaptation can be drawn on to give a much more positive view of the future than a bleak, paranoid, disaster-ridden quagmire of dangerous people, risky places and alienating markets. The interests of experts and citizens *can* be moved back together, but doing so requires a better picture of how we choose to live – or perhaps are *encouraged* and *ordered* to live in the best way. Such knowledge is vital to improving practices of security, emergency and other government professionals because it informs our understanding of what it is we are trying to make secure, which is not always as clear as one might assume.

Using a more sociological vernacular, one can say that by reconstituting our key concept of 'resilience' in the city we gain a broader context and a clearer focus. The understanding of social change as an ongoing process with a mappable trajectory brings together theory and practice in a more nuanced discussion of how we have got to where we are today. Following this logic, this book seeks to interrogate how patterns emerge through the *interplay* of 'forms' over time. The 'sociology of forms' (Lefebvre, 1978 [1966]) is used because it helps to clarify how the conditions of possibility for change both generate and emerge from the 'social order' of the day. 'Genealogy' (Nietzsche, 2003 [1913]) is used because it helps to interrogate time–space–place in more depth, looking back with a more forensic intent at the process of change over time. This approach sets up an operative understanding of how organisational techniques, practices and processes are informed by (and likewise inform) the rhythms and patterns that direct the orderly flow of everyday life through 'institutionalised' beliefs, rules and norms. These 'institutions' inform the relationships between individuals, groups of individuals in coalition and even formal groups such as 'organisations' with a common role, cause or purpose. The combined forms are at once material, cognitive, spatial, processual, etc.; as such, the forms interplay differently at different times to contextualise our understanding of everyday life. It is from the 'interplay of everything' that the resultant knowledge emerges from logic, languages, systems, codes and, as such, 'ways-of-thinking', 'ways-of-doing' and 'ways-of-acting' that can be mapped out, both in quotidian and circadian patterns of daily routine but also over longer periods. This is not an attempt to rework a comprehensive history of ideas, but rather to offer a different insight into the potential gains of a genealogical method harnessed by the sociological imagination. Using genealogy helps to bridge the gaps between forms of social ordering as they develop, flex and change. It helps to identify the particular pressures on the trajectory of change over time. It helps to draw out the patterns of interplay between order and disorder that inform the everyday life of the city in the struggle for theory, the struggle for history, but also in the struggle for the city of today. To develop this empirically, the city is used as a key to unlock the theory of change in applied examples of the ongoing interplay.

Summary of the Book Structure

To summarise, it is the argument of this first chapter that one can trace knowledge, practice and action as ways of thinking, doing and acting over time in useful ways. Undertaking this project will offer a different alignment of theory and practice, using tools out of the box – from genealogy to rhythmanalysis – to unpack the history of the present and demonstrate the struggle for resilience in the city. Part I (Chapters 2–4) offers a very wide historical focus for the development of the theory, genealogy and the city in history. This establishes the framework of analysis in more depth for Part II (Chapters 5–7), with a narrower focus on the post-industrial global city as a history of the present.

Chapter 2 develops the theoretical framework for understanding change, tracing particular epistemic and discursive formations of knowledge and philosophical issues underpinning the tools chosen for analysis (i.e. the struggle for theory). Chapter 3 will then unpack the concepts of authority that inform the creation of an urban order in different forms at different times (i.e. the struggle for history). Chapter 4 identifies the major types of danger that have created crisis or posed challenges in the discursive transformation of urban orders (i.e. the struggle for the city in history). Chapter 5 offers analysis of the alignment of particular forms into the social order we might call the 'entrepreneurial' city in modernity (i.e. the struggle for the city of the present). Chapter 6 enhances this overview of modern urbanism by linking the city with risks, hazards and threats to highlight challenges faced in maintaining this order (the struggle for security). In Chapter 7, the development of 'all hazards' approaches to resilience is placed in the genealogical context of the democratic city, revisiting the dangers of war, disaster and disorder (the struggle for resilience). Lastly, in Chapter 8, some final points on the lessons we can learn from where we have come from and what we are doing are turned to teasing out the interplay and interdependencies in the city of today. This will draw to a close the discussion but not end the debate, offering potential topics for future study, and calling for a refinement and improvement of the tools used in this work. The end goal is to take the lessons of history and use them to help us better understand both the range of forms that need to be included in the discussion today, but also the formative framework of theoretically informed and empirically grounded research used to critically unpack the interplay between them as change continues in the resilient city.

One must accept that in this book the net has been cast very wide; however, the issues to which this discussion relates are of critical importance and deserving of a more coordinated and in-depth treatment. It is my hope that this will be of interest and use to commentators, researchers and practitioners alike. By developing a reconstitution of the issues along theoretical and empirical themes, such as offered here, the analyst can begin to link together some of the philosophical questions with a practical operative sense of what we are doing, why we are doing it and perhaps, even, what we expect to achieve once the impact of ongoing change has been rolled out. It is sometimes too easy to lose sight of the impact on everyday life between the different fields of activity in which we are operating, and by bringing the focus back towards both notions of interplay and impact through the rhythms of security in the democratic city, perhaps some of our actions can be both individually and collectively questioned and redirected towards a more constructive and inclusive approach to the everyday lives that we would like to lead.

PART I
Theory, Genealogy and History

There is a theory which states that if ever for any reason anyone discovers what exactly the Universe is for and why it is here it will instantly disappear and be replaced by something even more bizarre and inexplicable. There is another that states that this has already happened.

Douglas Adams

Chapter 2
The Struggle for Theory: Interplay, Poiesis and Change

Whenever a theory appears to you as the only possible one, take this as a sign that you have neither understood the theory nor the problem which it was intended to solve.

Karl Popper

Chapter Outline

The bulk of this chapter will deal with unpacking and reconstituting theoretical foundations by giving some inner coherence to the definition, use of and links between key concepts. This effort is made in order to adhere to the notional framework suggested by Lefebvre (2008 [1961]: 1), insofar that the two-fold imperative of enquiry must (a) reflect the coherence of thought and concept, but also (b) take into account the emergence of new and unforeseen insights. This follows Popper's assertion that the use of multiple theories is essential to enhancing our understanding. Avoiding adherence to any one meta-narrative opens up debate by drawing on a little of many theories in good proportions to reach a better overall understanding of the topic. One can from this point of departure begin to move both backwards (regressively) and forwards (progressively) to uncover genealogical connections, root out the antecedents of change and apply them to everyday life today.

To begin with this requires expansion on some first principles – in particular, the concepts of *praxis* (briefly) and *poiesis* (in more depth). The discussion of praxis and poiesis informs the wider sense of what it is that is being studied when one discusses interplay and change. It also gives a better theoretical basis for informing and reinterpreting everyday life, time, space, place and history as addressed by Henri Lefebvre and Michel Foucault – two key scholars underpinning the approach of this book. These will be drawn together to offer a perspective on the process of change in order to form a foundation for the critical reappraisal of some lessons learned, or perhaps forgotten, throughout history.

Developing the Interplay of Forms: Praxis, Poiesis and Change

The emphasis on interplay and poiesis is intended to draw out the implications of a different approach to change. It is argued that one can understand change in the patterns of order that permeate the everyday as the interplay between 'forms'. A narrow example of this method would bring together the forms of *ethos*, *mythos* and *nomos* as 'layers' in the particular alignment of human understanding at a given time [episteme]. Each epistemic layer acts as a 'field of knowledge' for understanding everyday life – for example how humans or the world was created, what is right and wrong, who should be in charge, etc. Each field informs our internal world (what we know, how we think), frames the mediation of our external world (the right way to worship, farm, hunt, build) and gives technical know-how to human actions in the context of the everyday (the process of praying, planting, skinning a kill, building a house, etc). One must, however, also move beyond the thinking, doing and acting and incorporate into the analysis where a thing happens and how long it endures. The articulation of layers is thus permeable; they run through each other, change in meaning, and are contextualised by both the prevailing alignment and its resilience or adaptability in a given time, space and place. None of these forms can be properly understood without reference to the others, but each gives a different lens through which to view why we do what we do, how we do it, what is the right way to do it, how it has been done before and so on. Forms are linked, yet malleable and amenable to change through the space and time of everyday life throughout history. Change can happen through repetitions, but also divisions or ruptures, and in different ways at different times. Forms are thus reflexive and self-referential, but also interpenetrate and crossover and informing each other. They are a means of interrogating the experience of individuals, coalitions, institutions, and organisations.

This makes historical context very important to consider. Knowing, doing and acting on the knowledge of how to do are reflected upon through the idiosyncrasies of the time in which the individual is situated. That is how each individual is able to make sense of, and thus understand, the world in flux, by making reference to the dominant paradigm. As such, everyday life is best analysed by identifying examples of these forms and tracking how our understanding, use and performance of them changes. We can track the presence of these forms across history, tracing the genealogy of their influence over time, not as specific subjects or objects but as concepts restated differently through different alignments, realised in productive performance in everyday life. From these concepts our knowledge, our forms of thinking, our sense of 'truth' is realised. This resonates with Mannheim's view:

> If we are to arise to the demands put upon us by the need for analysing modern thought, we must see to it that a sociological history of ideas concerns itself with the actual thought of a society, not merely with self-perpetuating and supposedly self-contained systems of ideas elaborated within a rigid academic tradition. (Mannheim, 1936: 65)

This approach to the study of interplay does not really subscribe to a given school of thought, a canon of thinkers or static ideology. Reality is developed here as a multi-layered *interplay* to be *experienced* as change, that is, the *sense* of change is to be understood as an adaptive *poietic continuum*. The aim here therefore becomes to embrace the evidence of the empirically verifiable – the meat and bones of history – in locations (buildings, artefacts, geology, etc.), alongside that which is harder to trace, the ebb and flow of concepts, values, ways of thinking, ways of doing and ways of acting as 'forms'. In rather grand, if abstract, terms the inclusive genealogy of change is treated here as an analysis of the creative destruction of urban existence – the city being the primary location of the analysis. In slightly simpler terms the genealogy will trace the trajectory of change over vast periods of a spatial history. The theoretical framing of an ongoing interplay between forms is a foundation for empirical evidence of the continual transformation in how we understand everyday life, with the city as the crucible. The theory discussed here is thus more of an attempt to 'open the door' to a *reconstituted* critique of long-standing staple 'facts' of enquiry. An exhaustive study of concepts such as praxis, poiesis, space, time and knowledge, should such a study even be possible, would involve more texts and theorists than one can possibly include here; a task for another time. This chapter is used to clear some of the confusions that might clutter the conceptual foundations at the outset. The main thrust, therefore, is to demonstrate that such an approach can in fact deepen our understanding in ways hitherto glimpsed, but not yet fully developed.

Reconstituting 'Poiesis': Some Thoughts and Thinkers

Introduced above was the idea of poiesis, or rather of poietic continuum. The concept is a difficult one and needs to be explained in more depth. The concept of poiesis arguably has roots in the work of Plato, with reference to *Symposium*, but is also developed by Aristotle in *Poetics*, and these roots cannot be ignored in any meaningful application of the concept. The etymology of the term refers to the Greek ποιέω as *poieo*, 'to make', and the verb form ποίησις as *poiesis* meaning 'an act or process of creation'. The Platonic use, as voiced in dialogue by Diotima, and evoked by Leo Strauss (2001), makes reference to the act of creation regarding poetry, and indeed the term is the etymological root of the modern term poetry, but for Plato it also evokes a sense of rhythm and metre as constituent elements of the 'act of producing' poetic works (Ibid.: 201). What is useful to be drawn from this early form is the distinction between the scientist–philosopher and the artist–poet in the creation of two different types of knowledge. This emerges again in a division into three interrelated concepts in both the poetry of Neoptolemus and the philosophy of Aristotle. In a critique of Neoptolemus, the suggestion was made by Greenberg (1961) that there is a division between the art of poetry (as a form of doing and potentially appreciating or understanding), the poem as the artefact thus produced (as *ars-artifex*), and the poet as the producer (Ibid.: 265). In this way, a distinction is created between the *technique* of producing [*techne*] and the *act* of producing [*poiesis*].

The Aristotelian use evokes a related distinction that serves us better in developing interplay and social change. Here, it is suggested that there is a distinction between *theoria* (as theory, evoking the sense of an art), *praxis* (as action) and *poiesis* (as the act of production). As a result there is a need to clarify better what is meant here by praxis as 'action' and poiesis as 'act of production'. For Aristotle, praxis is the province of craftsmen: through science and scientific methods, it is 'framed' – and thus contextualised – by the technologies surrounding it. By contrast, poiesis remains in the realm of artists and artistic production. It belongs to the artist and relates more to the knowledge as produced or rather the end product of poetic production. Whilst similar, insofar as the activity also has a technical dimension (perhaps thought of as artistry as opposed to a scientific method), the outcome of the activity is not determined by technology or the technical process. The poetic product or artefact is seen as a form of thinking which prioritises existence – which 'dwells' in existence. Poiesis thus evokes a sense of thinking about the world that can be used more broadly, but draws on the root meaning depicted by Plato and Aristotle as a fluid, artistic and therefore poetic endeavour at its heart. There is an uncomfortable crossover, or blurry edge, to these forms when thinking about art as a priori knowledge [*theoria*] and the skills used to produce artefacts [*techne*]. One can argue that the distinction between praxis and poiesis has captured a lot of attention. Heidegger appears most useful for our purposes in trying to clarify the blurry edges between them.

Heidegger qualifies the two concepts differently, but does so through a 'temporal disposition' of the concepts.[1] One can read Heidegger as framing praxis in action, or rather the potential for acting correctly. It is deliberative and therefore it is internalised. There is no intent beyond a sense of acting appropriately, in the proper fashion – i.e. to act 'well'. Praxis is what it is exactly because it is made up of the 'fields of *knowledge*' [*savoir*] of a 'way-of-*doing*' rather than the productive *process* for a 'way-of-*acting*'. Making sense of the world, understanding it, comes into focus through the disposition of 'practical wisdom' in the internal world, or *phronesis*, which might be seen as 'knowing-how-to-do'. This means that the potential disposition of praxis happens over time, time is a priori a condition of knowing. Praxis does not create an external artefact or an external impact, praxis enables the individual through *phronesis* as knowledge of 'how-to-do' to take actions that affect the external world, but is not predicated upon the external world for its existence.

There is a complex contradiction here: in order for the abstract layers of thought to manifest in human action (for them to become 'concrete') praxis must be linked to an external 'way-of-acting' or more specifically an 'act-of-doing'. The knowledge of how to act cannot create, it cannot produce. Logically it can only

---

1   An interesting appraisal of Aristotle and Heidegger can be found in McNeil (1999).

inform one of how best to do so. Poiesis resolves this difficulty by giving space for acting to occur, and allowing the internal knowledge a concrete application in the external world. It supplies an operative action of fabrication that produces as a 'way-of-acting' [*techne*], where praxis supplies only the abstract knowledge of a correct 'way-of-doing' [*phronesis*]. The disposition of poiesis can therefore only be realized through reference to a technical skill set that is external, in resources to manipulate or through spaces and places of production. Praxis can be self-referential and internal but poiesis cannot. The technical skill set is disposed through the operative 'way-of-acting' which can also be translated as a sense of 'know-how' [*savoir-faire*] through which the 'act-of-doing' is realised. Poiesis is a productive knowledge that is at the heart a 'way-of-doing' reflecting a form of knowledge. They refer to each other to have meaning – however, the disposition of poiesis both is, and has, an external affect. This affect results in the production of an artefact that exists in physical space in a way that praxis does not.

In reading this through the eyes of Tamineaux (1992), the end result of an Aristotelian approach suggests that poiesis is, at its core, limited. One can never produce and have produced at the same time; as such, the poietic action is limited to the act of producing, through the disposition of poiesis as a 'way-of-acting', i.e. the making of 'things'. In this sense it can only ever perform the functional delivery of a means-to-an-end by production of a product – the 'act-of-doing' – and therefore cannot form a basis for knowledge of a 'good life'. It is inherently limited to being a process for making things in the external world. However, praxis can form a philosophical basis for a 'good life' through its self-referential disposition as *phronesis*, i.e. thinking about as knowing the right way to do things. The disposition of praxis forms a practical wisdom that enables realisation of a good life as knowledge of 'how-to-act' properly (i.e. what should be done); for one can intend to produce and have the knowledge of production simultaneously and use this as a basis for correct action. Here, Tamineaux's reading suggests that: 'praxis is oriented to living well, free, because it liberates desire from necessity and utility and renders an individual existence worthy of being remembered or taken as an example' (Ibid.: 193).

There is perhaps another contradiction here as the slight overlap of praxis with poiesis identified earlier remains, but now taking on a different emphasis. In the act of creative production the knowledge of how to produce is often changed, in some cases symbolically destroyed by the act of creation (production) itself. Tension between production and destruction is resolved in use of sublation [*aufheben*] to describe the moment of creation. This draws on a reworking of *sublation* – where sublation is 'becoming something else' through creative-destruction – insofar that new things take up elements of the old and reform them, in doing so absorbing that which was before. In 'becoming something else' this means that becoming destroys that which came before in the process of creating (producing) that which is new. In the end, the difficulty of a contradictory overlap depends on the analyst, as many commentators 'discussing this distinction often fail to face the real difficulty, that actions often or always are productions and productions often or always are actions' (Akrill, 1978: 595).

Change that results from creative-destruction is ongoing and must by its very nature draw on the knowledge that exists to create something different, be that an idea, a process *or* a product. Heidegger gives an applied grounding to the Hellenistic foundations of these concepts but does not fully fix the contradictions in applying them to everyday life. He in fact raises more questions with regard to the temporality of ways-of-thinking, ways-of-doing, technical practices which seem to evoke both *techne* and acts-of-doing drawn out of operative ways-of-acting. In this sense it is difficult to see how the creative act of production avoids the act of destruction. Change appears necessarily painful and fraught, with conflict between that which is and that which is coming into being. It also means that, particularly in the earlier Heidegger, there is a privileging of time over space, because time is the a priori condition of experience. He also allows for us to draw the conclusion that time and space are required components of how we make sense of and gain meaning from our internal and external experiences in everyday life.

Poiesis and Time–Space–Place

The concept of poiesis can thus be set up as a nexus for understanding change, but this is only in the relative context of time, space and place. A logical link to the interplay of forms allows for the analysis of time (processually becoming something else), space (geometrical/material dimensions of the existent world) and place (as experiential concepts, perceptions, and reactions *in situ*) as forms to be incorporated as a lens through which our experiences are made legible. There is a key point that is useful in developing this premise. The sense of poiesis in Heidegger when read as a moment of moving away from one thing and becoming another realigns the 'act-of-doing' *in ecstasis* or more accurately as the *ecstases* of temporality (Ibid.: 375–377). The lack of clarity between the knowledge which forms our understanding of how to act, the act itself, the creative-destruction required by the act of producing and the end product (or artefact) causes endless headaches. In an attempt to resolve this one can suggest that the knowledge (or concept), the act and the artefact are all linked to both time and space to gain meaning, and thus attain meaning through discursive formation (see the discussion of Foucault below). Neither time nor space is privileged a priori as they are not linear preconditions to understanding, but reflexive points of reference to be understood in a historical context. History is thus not a linear chronology but understood as the past, the present and the future combined in the 'moment' as a perspectival point of reference for understanding the here and now through forms of thinking, doing and acting. Such an approach makes the 'moment' of creative-destruction pivotal in clarifying poiesis. By making the 'moment' the point of collision in which all comes together (an 'eternal return', to reference Nietzsche) then a 'perpetual act of creation' is drawn through a finite (re)thinking of our definitions (Nancy, 2003). This can be applied here only so far as it has roots in a notion of 'the moment of becoming' as the nexus of sublation; i.e. the destruction of infinite possibilities and the creation of a finite reality.

As Hegel suggests: '"To sublate" has a twofold meaning in the language: on the one hand it means to preserve, to maintain, and equally it also means to cause to cease, to put an end to' (Hegel, 2010: 81–82). From this position we can suggest that the 'perfect' knowledge of the best way to act that is evoked by praxis is thus maintained, but rendered into something less immediate, less pure, less perfect or ideal by the poietic act of creative production. Praxis and poiesis are both destroyed in their original form and reconstituted; they are transformed through their re-creation as something else. To close the loop of this discussion we might suggest that humans mediate abstract knowledge as thought (theoria) which when translated into knowledge of how to act (praxis) creates the conditions in which the knowledge of how to produce is turned into creative action (poiesis), and is thus rendered concrete. When one moves from the discussion of art to discussing the art of government this becomes even more relevant. Any artefact is produced as a new totality. When the product is the political subject the totality produced is the citizen at the nexus of complex interplay between forms. Interplay is thus creative-destruction in the production of the total, or perhaps ideal type, of political subject. But most importantly that which existed is transformed into something new. The whole process is a cycle of rendering the abstract concrete; it is a 'processual cycle' of becoming something else. To achieve this, praxis and poiesis necessarily make reference to that which they are (or were) and that which they are not (or have become) and emerge with a new totality, or unity, through the perpetual and ongoing moment of creative-destruction.

The philosophical, alas, most often remains at the layer of the abstract. To apply this discussion is to try and grasp the concreteness of everyday life, not just its abstract forms as they (re)inform each other in this 'cyclical' way. To do so we must understand both the abstract and concrete as discussed above and how they interplay with each other. We must also shift emphasis from the artefact as perpetually produced, destroyed and reproduced in each perpetual moment, to the perceiving subject themselves placed in an appropriate historical 'moment'. This draws another contradiction from the 'moment' as a nexus of forms. The past, present and future in the presence of the perceiving human at a moment of creative-destruction must always be changing, never static. A movement in time cannot be limited to that perceived by the senses, or given perspective solely by a priori knowledge or hermetic externality of products and production. All of these, if taken alone, are both perceived and yet imperceptible as roots of meaning. The sense of 'being-in-time' brings together the infinite with the finite, the unknowable with the knowable. It is a moment of perpetual creation that (re)occurs. This temporality requires a deeper understanding of the 'perpetual' moment as a nexus point between senses, knowledge and actions in time and space. It is seen, then, as a movement away from the past into the future through the determination of our presence in the present in constant flux, through the interplay of forms in context.

It is, to some extent, apparent that the distinction between praxis and poiesis is only relevant insofar as it helps us to unpack the interplay between these constituent forms, giving us insight through reflection on the context of thought, action and experience. We must move beyond reflection, however, to practical understanding of how thought, action and experience are reconstituted as a perpetually sublative continuum. The individual is made manifest not through any of the singular components, but through the process of interplay that renders the abstract *and* the concrete meaningful. The interplay is between praxis/*phronesis*/ *savoir* as 'ways-of-*being-in*-the-world', though this process must also be seen to emerge from and through reference to *poiesis*/*techne*/*savoir-faire* as 'ways-of-*doing-things*-in-the-world'. Specifically for this reason I have chosen to focus on unpacking the 'moment' further as a lens through which to view the continuum of interplay, i.e. the history of moments is an attempt to trace the ebb and flow of mediated forms as they come together in becoming something else. Investigating the history of the present becomes an attempt to analyse any patterns in the rhythms of such interplay between these (re)constitutive forms over time. This allows for solid links to be made from the more abstract theorising to the concrete forms of/in everyday life.

Space, Time and Rhythm: Lefebvre, Spatial Production and Forms

There is reference to 'forms' made in the above that is not fully explained. To do so requires a more in-depth engagement with the work of Henri Lefebvre. The concepts of space, time, rhythm and spatial production in Lefebvre's work can help to ground the idea of interplay in what is referred to here as the sociology of 'forms', emerging from a re-reading of Marxist theory. Lefebvre (re)constitutes the dialectical project of Marx in such a way that no one force, topic or issue is given precedence, but in some of his works a strong interest in space and time is also clearly apparent.

First, it is useful to look at Lefebvre's insistence that contradictions in our understanding are not always problematic. They in fact enhance our understanding of interplay and help to trace the patterns, rhythms and productive processes through analysis. To tease out this contribution one can look to Lefebvre's work on everyday life (2005 [1981], 2008 [1951], 2008 [1961]), which is essential to his wider project. Secondly, in developing the foundations of a 'sublative becoming' offered above one can link understanding the sociology of forms which runs through this work with Lefebvre's approach to spatial production and finally extend this reading of everyday life towards a historical analysis of the city.

Situating Everyday Life

Lefebvre is especially useful when he moves beyond a canon of thought into an appreciation of links between forms of thinking. A good example is his reading of the contradictions inherent in dialectical materialism as emerging from a Hegelian reading of Marx. In *Dialectical Materialism* (Lefebvre, 2009 [1940]) one might say that Hegelian dialectics are shown to try, but inevitably fail, to transcend the limitations of an early historical materialism. For dialectical materialism:

> The transcending is located in the movement of action, not in the pure time-scale of the philosophical mind. Wherever there is conflict there may – but it is not inevitable – appear a solution which transforms the opposed terms and puts an end to the conflict by transcending them. (Lefebvre, 2009 [1940]: 93)

For Lefebvre, what we can draw from Hegel is valuable, but only in so far as dialectical materialism once developed brings to full flower Lefebvre's reading of Hegel. Transcending the conflict and struggle between terms is here a dialectic mediation that allows the analyst to transcend the 'one-sided' definition of concepts in Kantian reason (e.g. form or content but not both) and harness the ambiguity of language to demonstrate the transformation of that which was into that which is now. Hegel opens the door to an analysis that allows thought and reality to be merged with form and content, in becoming something else. It throws up the contradictions of formal logic and replaces them with dialectic logic. For Lefebvre, it was the analysis which should determine the solution to a given problem, it was through experience that this solution can be realised as a part of the social world, and as such it was the thought combined with the actions (or *thought-action*) of decision-making agents that allows us to transform our everyday lives. To transcend the limitations of an overly rational, motionless and formal logic, one must embrace the dialectical logic that allows us to appreciate the movement of thought and action as transformative. This logic can tease out the historical – not seeking to resolve all contradictions, but to acknowledge them as necessary to understanding. For Lefebvre, in re-reading Marx, the subtlety of dialectic logic allows for an analysis of movement, of change and of becoming where a formal philosophical logic falls short.

In applying this to the social, Lefebvre also recognised that there are clearly times where there are problems faced by a given social formation that cannot be transformed or 'solved', giving the example of the economic and political contradictions at the heart of the Roman Empire (Lefebvre, 2009 [1940]: 94). These conflicts persisted until its downfall, and some might say were the seeds of its eventual destruction.

If we want to understand the importance of contradictions, they cannot be treated as 'static' or determined logically to be found in reproductions of that which already exists, or even that which has been destroyed in the transcendence of a new formal unity (i.e. society as a whole). Contradictions are living relations 'experienced in existence' in the 'everyday'. Understanding what is meant by 'everyday' and 'everyday life' is thus vital to the analysis. Everyday life is not to be reduced by theory to an abstract or a trivial thing, even though the banal aspects of living do reside within the everyday. It is better viewed as *potential for transformation* that exists in all that constitutes our view of life and of living. It is an adaptive moving on from the acceptance of contradiction to the acceptance of the paradox of 'knowing' and 'comprehending' inherent in 'becoming-something-else'; 'only to this extent is there anything like "knowledge", i.e. a measuring of earlier and later errors by one another' (Nietzsche, 1968: 281). Importantly, one must acknowledge that that which exists is never truly destroyed, it leaves a residual legacy in the institutional memory of culture, it creates stickiness and resistance to change as much as the conditions of possibility for adaptation. Everyday life is at its best the potential for a process of transformative change, of becoming something else, that resides in the struggles that are all that constitute social life, social beings and society as a totality. Indeed, for Lefebvre: 'Everyday life [is] the terrain of struggle just as production is broader than that of things and encompasses all of social life' (Elden, 2004: 111).

Whilst this statement is made by Elden with the concept of alienation in mind, it is also a means to link Lefebvre's critical Marxism to the goal of his analysis of the everyday. For Lefebvre, alienation is more than economic. For Lefebvre, the 'total man' is thought and action transformed into creative activity, thus creative activity transforms the everyday. The total man is at once a contradiction, being in body *of* Nature and yet embodying an inhuman internal conflict as separate from Nature. The separation of the total man from nature is social. The example given by Lefebvre in *Introduction to Modernity* (1995 [1962]: 145–149) is spring and the cyclical becoming of the Eternal Return to springtime in which the days, weeks, months, seasons, the planets and suns are repeated, and yet in this repetition are changed, becoming something else. The evolution of the harvest through the seasons in basic agricultural subsistence creates the uncertainty of scarcity in the spring as stocks run low, the last grains held back for the seeding of crops in the year to come. This scarcity evolves solutions through better tools for increased surplus in the harness, the plough, the threshing machine, and new systems of producing in the rotation of crops replaced by enclosures or the storage of food in the granaries. The rediscovery of the springtime reduces the uncertainty and new signs, new symbols, new poems and art embody this rediscovery. A new Nature replaces the old signs and significations. The separation is thus compounded in the realm of the social; through the institutions of everyday and the cultural appropriation of Nature becoming less fearful, a new meaning emerges. In this case cultural productions evolving concurrently with the technical, economic and social 'progress' emphasises a new, more linear, cycle, a new totality, distinct and different from that which came before. The combination of an embodied Nature with the social 'other' of the thinking self allows the human to constitute itself as a whole or 'total man', but this is a whole that is at heart a contradiction. The contradiction is reproduced and becomes more severe as order is imposed on Nature by thought focused into creative action, praxis and poiesis in full flight. In simple terms, by imposing order on the everyday the human becomes separate from Nature, gains authority over it and transforms both Nature and themselves. The experience of everyday life is a process of divisive rendering by which all we know, all we see and all we do is transformed in an ongoing cycle of becoming something else.

This gives us a sense of the importance of the idea, but it needs to be applied if it is to be useful for analysis of the key forms of knowledge and experience, as well as the topics of order, conflict and change addressed in the next two chapters or risk, security and emergency later on. If the everyday is a struggle to transform, and a process of transformation, then we need to understand how this is experienced over time. We need to acknowledge that whilst there are processes of active change inherent in human action and agency, there are also the institutions and organisations of ordering that place limits on what can be mobilised as right knowledge, corrects forms of doing and righteous ways of 'being-in-the-world' at any given time. The active and passive interpretations of the forms present in the everyday need to be contextualised according to time, space and place. We need to develop a sense of the temporal, of the spatial and of platial context.

Everyday Life and the Sociology of Forms

The first part of this chapter outlined a background of praxis and poiesis as conceptual tools. We can use these tools to help us achieve, first, a sense of the temporal by reading praxis and poiesis from a more Marxist perspective. The reconstitution of Marxist theory in Lefebvre's reading of praxis and poiesis in *The Sociology of Marx* is useful again here. In this case, praxis is taken as the basis of society in social action, but this draws not only on the Aristotelian reading but on that of Marx, whereby praxis is seen as meditative social practices for ordering groups with specialised social roles. It arises out of the division of labour as more than a pure knowledge of how to act; it is translated as the meditation of *pragmata*, 'the matters actually deliberated by members of a society' (Lefebvre, 1978 [1966]: 45). Praxis is formative of religious, cultural and political 'functions', where poiesis is formative of labour or of religious, cultural and political 'work'. This addresses a contradiction, in so far as neither praxis nor poiesis can be understood without reference to each other, yet praxis is self-referential and therefore appears to subsume poiesis, taking precedence. The division positions poiesis as a productive and creative action, as the sensuous thought-action of the human agent in relation to Nature, but which must make reference to a mediated social praxis to be meaningful. Poiesis is the creative action that transforms the materials of an external world *and* the internal human subject into something else. It is, however, always shaped to some extent by a divisive and functional ordering that draws on the knowledge that presupposes transformation [praxis], thus in this reading praxis determines the forms by which creative activity is undertaken and understood.

For a Marxist 'sociology of forms', praxis is still a self-referential functional knowledge because it is made up of the human relationships, the managerial activities and the functions of order that are embedded in the mediation of the everyday by the 'state'. Whereas poiesis is at once the devalued productive labour of the farmer and also the creative activity of the craftsman or artist – a distinction that allows value to be attributed differentially to the end products, be they beans or sculptures. Such distinctions inform also the mediation of privileged status attributed to 'work' as undertaken by those with free access to specialised knowledge and skills, the traders, teachers, orators or political leaders, and those no or limited access. Importantly, this places new emphasis on the institutionalisation of relations and informs the creation of new conditions of possibility for formal coalitions to emerge as credible organisations for managing, moderating or mediating those relations. There is a corresponding tendency towards formalisation of institutions and organisations that creates an ordered set or series of processual relations manifest as stories and myths, values and virtues, codes of practice, formal laws and so on and so forth. For Lefebvre, in his reading of Marx, this gives new importance to the 'sociology of forms' (Lefebvre, 1978 [1966]: 56), which allows us to trace the struggle between determined repetition and imitation of forms from the past, that influence the order of the present and the innovation of new forms (often in transgression) that can transform the present. This struggle is an ephemeral interplay between a normative linear continuity (order) and transgressive and transformative discontinuity (disorder) which reconstitutes beliefs, rules and norms. It can be analysed dialectically to allow us to grasp the totality of change as movement in, through and of, time–space–place. The struggle of praxis with poiesis is thus an ongoing mediation of forms in the becoming of 'everyday life'. For this work, this needs to be linked back to that dominant urban form, and how we can tie the sense of beliefs, rules and norms directly into a spatial framework.

There is a sense of renewed concern at the nature of acceptability and morality in the normative moral landscape of the individual, as a sole entity and as a member of a coalition of individuals (in the most simple terms a social 'group'). This is, of course, subjective to differing particular ideological perspectives, each perception on the problems (and solutions to those problems) adding another layer to the interplay underpinning social order. Reframing the perception of rights and responsibilities is a key ideological and political question inherent to the balance of social ordering in the governance of the everyday life of a democratic city (see Part II). Here, perception is used to give a sense of the fine-grade analysis that is required at the level of personal interactions in local urban spaces, as sites or locations of everyday life and of change. At this fine level of interplay, change can be unpacked critically to shed more light on the separation of particular 'use-values' in the production of local spaces, be they attributed through the creation of a logical typology of spatial resources or by the active engagement with a location by an individual or group in the real-time experience of a given location. By unpacking the rhythms of interplay between such intricate social forms, everyday life can be broadened to give a bottom-up insight into the texture of a discursive (trans)formation *in situ*. A brief and simplified example can be drawn from the complex interplay of forms surrounding urban unrest in England at the cusp of the nineteenth century (e.g. the Gordon Riots in London, later Peterloo in Manchester – see Chapter 4). By tracking back the interplay of forms we can trace the institutionalisation of industrial relations, the formation of the police as a social ordering organisation, the shift to science from religion as a dominant knowledge base for thinking, doing and acting (i.e. social ordering) in Western capitalist democracies – or as it rolls out in the entrepreneurial democracy of urban space (Chapter 5). This changing and flexible interplay aligns the sense of a socially constructed urban order at a given time, with the interpretive perceptions and experiences of specific locations in a given moment – what was seen as a protest by some was a riot to others, and in the case of Peterloo this led to violence and death. It has been suggested that:

> There is no uniform set of rules across society regarding the use of space, as different social groups have differing interpretations of what is appropriate. However, one group is usually in a dominant position to dictate which people and behaviours are deviant. These ideas of right and wrong are transmitted through space and place, creating a *normative landscape* (Creswell 1996). The behaviour of a person in a particular place generally reflects their interpretations of this place. When these meanings are normalised they appear as common sense, which in turn reinforces the established order (1996). (Nolan, 2003: 317, emphasis added)

If this is so, then it suggests that there is a codified system of morals informing a certain level of acceptability that is maintained in the behaviour exhibited by an individual when in the company of others, but that this is not and cannot be comprehensive or universal, only (contradictory though it may be) broad yet individually specific. When in public, for example, morality can be represented by the strongest collective beliefs and norms shared across the majority of people in that specific space at that specific time. This notion is derived in part from Durkheim and his work on the '*conscious collective*' (Durkheim, 1893), but is more flexible and individualised than Durkheim's rigid, mechanical approach when rolled out in practice:

> The totality of beliefs and sentiments common to average citizens of the same society forms a determinate system which has its own life; one may call it the *collective* or *common conscience*. (Durkheim, 1893: 79, original emphasis)

This 'conscience collective', or normative 'moral code', is implicit in each individual citizen but the smaller idiosyncrasies vary within individual mental realms – i.e. the cognitive judgements/decision-making of individuals. This can be linked to their individual concept of personal identity as constructed through consumer culture or conceptual demographics applied to other users of a given location – a single person or a person as part of a group of like-minded individuals (e.g. an organisation or a sub-culture). The combination of individual and group perceptions forms a morally opinionated reservoir which is subject to change over time, hence 'conscience' (of appropriate morality exhibited in appearance, behaviour and activities) 'collective' (forged from the group as they interact in public). The collective perceptions of morality and appropriateness set an informal understanding between the users of public locations and participants of urban life as to what to expect on the streets and in the public locations of the city in which they live. It forms a codified system of conscious and unconscious judgements/decisions by which the individual can draw meaning from the *'realm of strangers and acquaintances'* and understand the activities of these different 'others'. It is a reflexive engagement with the beliefs, rules and norms embedded in the *nomos*, *ethos* and *mythos* of the wider civilisation in a specific time–space–place. A sense of *nomos* can be used to tease out the spatial sense of an appropriate order embedded in the community.[2] Rather than left as an abstract connection of thoughts in the mental realm, this takes on a role in the changing interplay of rules as laws, and the administration of them through governance organisations and actors within particular organisational coalitions – each with specific roles to play in the construction and maintenance of order. This spatial connotation gives a grounding of morality to the specific locations, but we must recognise that different locations reflect different balances. There is a different nomic sense of order in the 'common law', for example, than in 'Sharia law', informing different behaviours, or in the houses of Parliament than in a church or school room, but moulded into different imbalances within each location by the end users. Much of the concern over the current trajectory of security in the urban realm is concerned with the imbalance at the nexus of relations between the body, security and the time–space–place of the city. The balance of rules and spatial order is different in a private office building to that of a semi-public, privately owned shopping mall, and again this is different in a public park or city street, where the balance is mitigated and managed in the public trust by local governments. Commentators have suggested that 'contemporary security policies permeate the production and management of everyday urban spaces' (Klauser, 2010: 326). Such examples can be used as analysable case studies that enable a direct comparison to be made between different perceptions of what is appropriate in different spaces and how different groups can be perceived as more or less appropriate on a sliding and permeable scale defined by the poietic fluctuations in

---

2   A very good integrogation of the origins and uses of *nomos*, through the work of Carl Schmitt, can be found in Legg (2011).

specific locations as the interplay of distinct forms is enacted and lived. What this enables is a counterpoint to the top-down prescriptions of the dominant positivist sociology and governance policy of the day, making the form of thinking, doing and acting of people on the ground more central and drawing on our paradox of becoming more directly when building comprehensive analyses of the everyday.

Michel Foucault's appreciation of public punishment and execution can be used to demonstrate a historical shift in this normative public morality through time and space; though typically his work is applied to concepts of power, space and the body (Driver, 1985).[3] In *Discipline and Punish* (1975), Foucault demonstrates effectively the extent to which change can affect this public code of morality over long periods of time. He achieves this by explicitly describing public punishment and the spectacle of public execution in the seventeenth century, charting the change in morality, law and social justice which thus affected the perception of the public spectacle and, over time, the moral perception of public execution:

> By the end of the eighteenth and the beginning of the nineteenth century, the gloomy festival of punishment was dying out, though here and there it flickered momentarily to life … it leaves the domain of more or less everyday perception and enters that of abstract consciousness; its effectiveness is seen as resulting from its inevitability, not from its visible intensity … the publicity has shifted to the trial, and to the sentence. (Foucault, 1995 [1975]: 8–9)

The shift of public spectacles of punishment from the public eye to the more sanctioned punitive courts (and thus leaving the awareness of punishment within the collective conscience) is one of many significant changes to the use and perception of public locations in cities, and demonstrates the ability of the 'conscience collective' to reflect the normative public 'moral landscape' of an epoch. Equally importantly it represents the dynamic connections between the spatial public with the social public and the mental public:

- The physical space in the form of architecture and environment itself, the geographical and symbolic boundaries of the space. *E.g. a plaza.*
- The mental realm as the changing perception of what is an appropriate form of public spectacle and the way in which people deconstruct the meaning of a spectacle. *E.g. the widely accepted understanding of appropriate ways in which to use the plaza.*
- The social relations that take place between the physical bodies of individuals within a space, the actual act of 'use' in a public space and actions engendered by their mental perceptions. *E.g. the reaction and interaction of users and managers to and with each other.*

---

3   Another interesting issue not brought into the discussion here is the ethics of Foucault, a good argument towards this end can be found in Bernaur and Mahon (1994).

- Extending this through Lefebvre's work on the much-discussed 'production of space' (Lefebvre, 1974) gives us a spatial framework to extend this method of separating the 'physical', 'mental' and 'social' (Ibid.: 1–9) as layers added to the interplay of time–space–place. Lefebvre theorised the 'means of production' spatially, effectively integrating a sense of lived experience into the critique of capitalist society. This contrasted significantly with previous research, which had been largely dominated by Marxist 'critical political economics'. Lefebvre thus attempted to transcend this economic determinism:

> What can be said without further ado is that the concepts of production and the act of producing do have a certain abstract universality ... They were taken over in the past, admittedly, by specialised disciplines, especially by political economy; yet they have survived that annexation. By retrieving something of the broad sense that they had in certain of Marx's writings, they have shed a good deal of the illusory precision with which the economists had endowed them. (Lefebvre, 1974: 15, original emphasis)

As a part of Lefebvre's approach to the 'production' and the 'act of producing', the physical design of the space (referred to above as the geographical boundaries, but which also includes the architectural design of the whole space) is 'deployed' as a mediator between the mental and social activity that occurs within space (Ibid.: 27), and the synergy of these three creates a 'conceptual triad' between the 'perceived', the 'conceived' and the 'lived' (Allen and Pryke, 1994: 454).

What is offered through the 'conceptual triad' is one treatment of a complex system of creative-destruction through the interplay between diverse actors, architectures and (often competing) interests. This has been applied widely in critiquing the potential for conflict between the commercial concepts of space, the perception of problematic user groups and the uses to which they put particular types of space when there is imbalance in the interplay between elements of the (re)productive process (see Allen and Pryke, 1994; Stewart, 1995; Gottdeiner, 2000; Borden, 2000; Kipfer, 2002). A point of friction emerges between representations of space and representational spaces in particular as connected but distinguishable features of the conceptual triad (Lefebvre, 1974: 33–46).

'Representations of space' have been interpreted as 'rationality of planned urban locations or the meticulous design of architectural projects' (Allen and Pryke, 1994: 454). Simply put, it is not the physical geography of the space but the conceptual processes from which knowledge of that space is produced. It is the conception of purpose (hence use-value) inherent in the strategic policies of investors, managers, designers and controllers (Stewart, 1995: 610). 'Representations of space' are the formal economic and political identities of a space conflated with the economic and political managerial tactics through which it is produced, maintained and controlled. This is very important in discussions of design and renaissance, but more so in discussions of bio-political interventions and security as the conceptual spaces of the city are increasingly aligned with security priorities in design and management (see Chapter 5).

The second form, that of 'representational spaces', is seen as the 'lived' space. By 'lived', what is referred to is the perception of users as they interpret the space in action (Allen and Pryke, 1994: 454), or rather, the significant, almost territorial, meaning underpinning their activities. There seems to be an almost ethereal imagination of reality behind this that is very difficult to unpack. The imagined experience of living in a space seems to feed the meaning of what that space is, for the user. In this way, 'representational space' can at times be confused with 'spatial practice' because it links strongly with activity and performance. Representational spaces are sometimes seen as informal spaces of resistance or locally specific ways of (re)interpreting space through activities performed by a particular minority group (Stewart, 1995: 611). The key is that these are spatial meanings derived through activity, and they often differ between coalitions (be they categorised as subcultures, demographics, organizations, etc.).

The 'spatial practice' forms the 'meat and bones' of this theory, binding together 'representations of space' and 'representational spaces' at several levels of analysis. It is also one of the themes in Lefebvre's theory that suffers most from translation, making it subject to interpretation as a loosely defined notion of 'common sense' or assumed knowledge that appears to underpin other elements of spatial production (Shields, 1992: 162–163). 'Spatial practice' is more than this assumed normative communal 'sense' – though this is a part of it. When the connection between individuals as 'common sense' or nous is framed through the emphasis of the perceived then perception itself becomes the connection underpinning spatial practice. It appears not as a series of isolated inputs of sight, sound, scent, touch and taste; perception in spatial practice is the *perception of* and *reaction to* the creative or performative activity as a 'moment of communication' (Lefebvre, 1974: 369). This moment gives form and coherence to the interactions of each individual with each other (Allen and Pryke, 1994: 454), on the one hand as individuals but also as coalitions with potentially oppositional commonalities in the beliefs, rules and norms they share. Spatial practice thus differs from representational spaces as well. It represents the framework of perception that is produced out of every action that takes place within space, rather than specific actions as the word 'practice' implies. This is not the meaning of the action for the actor, but the perception (as a response) by the observer through abstract and differential spaces; through this interplay the spatial triad is connected as a singular process of production. It connects everything from the policy of the governing body to the performance of the skateboarder on the street, from the policeman on his beat to the street artist or busker in the creative production of time–space–place. It is *poietic*, emerging from the mental and social actions and reactions of these individuals and coalitions within the physical architecture. Spatial practice is then the perception of different 'Others' within a space and potentially the reaction to their activities as they occur in what can be called a singular moment of 'reactive perception' grounded in, but distinct from, the normative moral or social space.

In the context of specific locations (e.g. street, plaza, shop, office), all actions must have a significant impact on the interpretation of what each location should be as the conceptual triad unfolds through and over time. One of the applications of this concept – in the definition of meaning and the methods by which we draw an experiential understanding from space through this reaction to the perception of others – is through locating the body as a determining factor in the 'architectonics' of experience:

> Bodies generate a space which replicates the structure of the body itself – bilateral and rotational symmetry yield a sense of duality – whereas the physiological closures of the body imply a conceptual differentiation between internal and external spaces, and hence of the distinct body. (Stewart, 1995: 612)

By distinguishing between the external body moving through space and the internal mental 'computation' of action, reaction and assimilating experience reflexively moment to moment, there can be an engaging process through which an *'anthropological stage of reality'* (Lefebvre, 1974: 192, quoted in Stewart, 1995: 612) is created. The temporal and physical-biological is thus an addition to the interplay of the conceptual triad in the production of space through time as *poietic*. The suggestion here is that by looking at different aspects of the production of space from the perspective of the group most dominant within that particular element, we can develop the tensions apparent in the interplay of specific coalitions throughout the poietic processes of spatial production as a complex adaptive system. If the citizen is produced through the 'art of government' as a poietic process of governmentality[4] then the technical disposition of that process is the alignment of the citizen's ability to make decisions with the desired outcomes of decision-making. One cannot simply criminalise an individual or a group, but rather limit the choices they can make through a bio-political intervention into the design, management and use of locations within which people act out their everyday lives. When this is done 'in the best interests' of the citizen it is an attempt to optimise the positive outcomes by aligning decisions with those deemed appropriate, desirable or useful – measured by complex performance indicators, usually with an economic focus or emphasis.

This premise underpins this research and is very important in understanding the full implications of time–space–place as lived experience (as rolled out in Part II). When applying the more abstract theory to concrete empirical situations, Lefebvre's approach can be redeployed to identify empirical data that verifies the general trajectory of change in the characteristics of locations produced, the processes of how they are managed and the framing of problems within those spaces, but also the methods used to deal with those dangers (as hazards, threats or risks). It helps to identify how we conceive, perceive and act as a process of interplay through the framing and tracing of prominent beliefs, rules and norms as

---

4   For an introduction to the concept of governentality see Dean (1999).

institutionalised in the roles and responsibilities of those tasked with managing, ordering locations, as well as the choices of appropriate action in particular categorised location 'types'. The analysis requires an awareness of spatial production, but also of the dimensions and relations of power, treated by Foucault in this case as *dispositif* or 'apparatus', meaning:

> a thoroughly heterogeneous ensemble consisting of discourses, institutions, architectural forms, regulatory decisions, laws, administrative measures, scientific statements, philosophical, moral and philanthropic propositions – in short, the said as much as the unsaid. Such are the elements of the apparatus. The apparatus itself is the system of relations that can be established between these elements. (Foucault, 1977: 194–195)

The analysis of interplay thus draws out the process of contestation between the 'said and the unsaid', both through the everyday ordering but also at the limits of order and disorder through particular time-specific alignments in specific locations. For example, as noted above, the normative public morality surrounding appropriate forms of punishment began to change at the end of the eighteenth century. As such, the perception of torture and execution began to change. This interplayed with the institutionalised concepts of justice and of norms of conduct in public space, amending also the appropriateness of public punishment as a spectacle. The actions and activities deemed normal, the rules underpinning justice, the beliefs of public morality interplay in this example of change as a long slow transformation through time–space–place. The end result is the shift of the public spectacle of punishment into the public imaginary and the limitation of freedom rather than public infliction of bodily torment as the means to instil discipline. In this example change occurs through the widespread acknowledgement of a moral consensus that is prevalent in the perception of both beliefs and norms of accepted social behaviour at that moment in history; this is the dominant morality of underpinning customs and traditions, systems of moral belief, formal laws and the ethical sense of what is a normal way to behave. This can be applied to a social spectrum or civilisation in a broad-brush sense, but it is far more analysable in terms of specific locations (the camp, the settlement, the village/town/city), as we can chart the changing membership and occupancy of these locations – as users enter and leave or conduct their business and activities throughout the circadian limits imposed on the time–space–place of everyday life. The balance of users in a given location has a 'knock on' effect on the balance of a widely accepted normative moral landscape in a specific location which can potentially be traced – with reference to the broad-brush view once more – from the public space to the suburb to the city to the nation-state and back again.

Everyday Life: Towards Urban Rhythms, Time and Space in History

Lewis Mumford, in the opening of his seminal work *The City in History* (1961), alludes to the importance of the human element in understanding why cities began to emerge, by identifying two 'poles' between which life is said to 'swing', these being 'movement' and 'settlement' (Mumford, 1961: 12–13). Movement in this sense is the embodiment of cyclical patterns of the natural world, for example the balance of a stable ecosystem or a natural harmony implied between humanity and Nature in early hunter-gatherer societies. Settlement is a process by which humans divide themselves from Nature by changing the land, for example using tools to shape the environment to their needs. This is a more linear pattern of geomorphic engagement that shapes the ecological balance and implies a drift from *existence on* the world to a *manipulation of* the world. Key forms such as the needs of human survival, relationships with other humans and the capacity to manipulate and shape the external world foreshadow more complex forms that begin to emerge. The relationships with locations, sites and artefacts engage both the sense of space and meaningful relationship with place. The two are necessarily connected through needs, relationships and the capacity of each human group to undertake settlement or movement as an action. The dominant form of social organisation for a given time period can perhaps be seen as unique to a particular historical moment, but it is the interpolation of place within, across and through spaces that is the lens for which meaning is garnered, and such dwelling in locations can gain in symbolic meaning. Identification of dwelling becomes therefore more practically sustainable as we shift from 'existence on' to 'manipulation of' as characteristic of an episteme from which meaning and understanding are developed. As such, each fledgling urban community may grow or dissipate depending on the determined repetitions, imitations and innovations in form that arise in that context. Also, whilst the conditions and relations surrounding each are distinct, some trends and similarities can be teased out of the idiosyncratic context that brought about the initial gathering together of humans around a specific site for different reasons at different times.

This is a difficult point from which to develop our sense of historical change, as the connection between theory and practice here sits uncomfortably within, on the one hand (1) reworking dialectical methods of enquiry in a sociology of forms, and (2) the somewhat abstract philosophy of struggle between *praxis* and *poiesis* (begun above), and on the other (3) the links between a somewhat subjective archaeological anthropology, and (4) 'hard' science and evidence-based research. However, Mumford is a useful point of departure for thinking about change over time and drawing on the topic of rhythms and space in a more applied setting. Mumford's thesis on the *City in History* (1961) has a certain timeless quality in its sociological intent, if not in the veracity of its assertions. In the broadest terms the theme of movement resonates well with Lefebvre's readings of creative action (poiesis) and the natural gestures of the body. Equally, settlement resonates well with social practice (praxis) and the linear, repetitive influence of technical mediations. However, it must be noted that whilst 'movement' in Mumford is aligned with the 'hunter-gatherer' in nature, this hunter-gatherer is romantically unburdened by technology or 'society' as we might call it. The broader meaning of movement in Lefebvre is used to denote a system of programmed acts within a linear time-space, tied to the productive-destruction of capital (an approach perhaps embedded in the social order of modernity). This wider lens of interplay is brought now to a sharper focus on how social ordering occurs in particular spaces and how this changes over time. It is from this that the sociology of forms can be applied to a project of *socio*-spatial history. This is not a specifically spatial orientation of the sociology of forms, nor a specifically historical form of materialism. Rather, it is an attempt to draw together the interplay *between* forms as political, economic, spatial, social, cultural or legal forms that influence the continual remaking of social order along a particular trajectory, over time, towards and through the rhythms of risk and security as they play out in the presence of people dwelling in the moment.

It has been suggested by Elden that the study of rhythms requires that the small details of the everyday are kept in focus to allow for the bringing together of different temporal frames of reference into both personal and spatial narrative. This is achieved for Lefebvre by reflecting upon the linear patterns of technological, mechanical and external forces acting upon the cyclical biological rhythms of the body. Movement can be seen through this lens to take on a different meaning, not as the spatial movement of hunter-gatherers in a cyclical-embodied equilibrium with the natural world, but the metaphor of movement as change, the change which brings together different forms of everyday life, often into a linear ordering of the social world; as such, it has been suggested that the 'rhythm of capital is that of production and destruction. The former is the production of things and human life more generally; the latter is the destruction through war, "progress" and invention' (Elden, 2001: 196).

One can suggest that this spatialising of a Marxist historical materialism is compatible with aspects of Foucault's approach to the bio-political, which we will address below, but it also sets up the framework for applying this theory in more depth. I seek to bring these thinkers together to elaborate on the connection between the top-down excavations of politics of power in time–space–place addressed in Foucault, with the bottom-up analysis of quotidian experiential aspects of time–space–place in Lefebvre. This draws out two key issues; first, in the (re)constitution of order from both sides of the coin, and second in the variations of potential (as conditions of possibility) for creative-destruction to transform that order. For Lefebvre, the productive and destructive connections forge an entry into the analysis of struggle between the natural patterns and repetitions of nature in the cyclical and cosmic time of the embodied life with that of the linear, divisive social practice of destructive progress inherent in the social ordering of capitalist systems. The harmonic and productive embodiment of the cyclical appear as a meta-stable equilibrium or *eurhythmia*; where the linear emerges from the movements of capital in society to create dissonance in this meta-stable equilibrium, creating *arrhythmia*, which sooner or later – if not remedied – becomes a pathologically destructive condition embedded in advanced capitalist modernity. Such a division is resonant of anomie, but in this case the condition is given a softer, more subtle and more insidious feel. The division between and throughout (not within but interpenetrating) the body is a confluence of forces manifest in space-time as experience at the level of everyday life. This situates our discussion of experience in its fuller sense, as the reconstitution of the subject in perpetual interplay – an experiential poiesis. The knowledge produced by the confluence of forces is grounded into the appropriately reconstituted context through the sociology of forms. Lefebvre's Marxism is as such:

> a method that on the one hand, depends upon a certain number of determined concepts but, on the other hand, *is analytic and critical of a certain historical process of becoming*. As a consequence of this movement, the real tends toward the possible while, at the same time, eliminating all other potentialities, though the possible also comes up against the impossible, discernible only in the course of practical action. This attitude implies a triadic analysis of movement and becoming: reality/possibility/impossibility. Moreover, there is a strategic objective: to change the world. (Lefebvre, 1988: 77, original emphasis)

Traces of the process of change (or progress) can be found in many locations (places); this might include the fables and beliefs of religions linked to land settlement around a sacred site [mythos], the influence of land-appropriation linked to juridical boundaries or burgeoning statehood [nomos] and to ethical formation of subjects within a seemingly rational and cogent ordering of everyday life into a way of being [ethos], all as different forms. This layered ordering of the concepts at play advances our understanding in a much more dynamic framework of systemic interplay as it situates a dialectical 'regressive–progressive' analysis of time, space and history through the lens of the body, as empirically analysable experiences of everyday life.

Blending Lefebvre and Foucault as such allows the temporal and spatial aspects of 'everydayness' to operate at multiple levels simultaneously. This places the embodied subject *in statu na'scendi*, in the process of becoming, at the centre of social change, as the nexus of complex systemic interplay. Rhythmanalysis is useful, but only so far as it can be deployed to 'the juxtaposition of the physical, the physiological and the social, at the heart of daily life' (Lefebvre, 2005 [1981]: 130). Lefebvre can be used to underpin the analysis of physical, physiological and social forms as elements, or layers, of a complex system of transformation. As a tool of analysis it can be used to trace the crushing influence of more linear repetitions in everyday life on the cycles of bodily lived experience. In doing so, perhaps links can be made to another discussion on the destruction and domination of the body through capitalism, that in many ways complements the historicity of this discussion, in the work of Michel Foucault.

History, Time and Space: Extending Forms Through Foucault

Why do we turn here to the work of Michel Foucault to help develop and apply these ideas further? Foucault offers first a deeper theoretical grounding for the concept of the social and historical context within which change is itself contextualized (see Foucault, 1977); also offering a different interpretation of the relationships of linear influences upon the individual through his analyses of power and the bio-political (see Foucault, 1979). It is important to note that Foucault suggested that economics provided a good method for the analysis of production relations, whilst linguistics and semiotics were good for signification, but power lacked a method for uncovering its own relations (Foucault, 1982). Foucault saw the need to challenge the existing orthodoxy, and expose through his study of power relations the troubling rational acceptance of the banal in everyday life around him. Unpacking specific epistemic fields (madness, illness, death, crime, sexuality) opened up the potential for a rejection of this implicit trap; that *homo economicus* should be passively accepted. Foucault sounded the challenge, identifying these two key points in identifying the struggle in his work:

> They are struggles which question the status of the individual: on the one hand, they assert the right to be different, and they underline everything which makes individuals truly individual. On the other hand, they attack everything which separates the individual, breaks his links with others, splits up community life, forces the individual back on him-self, and ties him to his own identity in a constraining way. These struggles are not exactly for or against the 'individual' but rather they are struggles against the 'government of individualization.' …
> They are an opposition to the effects of power which are linked with knowledge, competence, and qualification: struggles against the privileges of knowledge. But they are also an opposition against secrecy, deformation, and mystifying representations imposed on people. (Foucault, 1982: 781)

One particularly useful 'form' that can be unpicked is the juridical, of *nomos* (of law), as the principles governing human conduct drawn from culture and tradition and bound as a unity of order in a territory or location. Throughout history there are endless variations over this particular dynamic, the rights to live, and the right to die or, more specifically, to kill and remain righteous. The power over moral right to live has most often resided within religion, overseen by an organisation (the church, priesthood, etc.), and over the legal right to kill with the sovereign as absolute power (king, queen, despot, etc.) or distributed power through organisations (government, corporation, etc.). In the modern world power is different; 'to make die and let live' has been turned on its head and the debate rages over the implications of a ruler that 'can live and let die' (Lentin, 2008). Rather than seizing the right to end life (or 'right of death') through 'sovereign' power, this shift emphasised the technical mechanisms that could be aligned to elicit particular ways of doing, discouraging others, and implicitly order the conditions of possibility for administering, optimising and multiplying the life chances of the population. It is a 'right *over* life' used by the organisations of rule to collectively produce the optimal citizen, for their own best interests, through the technical mastery of social ordering.

The more explicit historicity of Foucault draws our experiential framework of what we do in the moment back towards the genealogic appraisal of how we got here. When developing a sense of movement and transformation in 'mapping the present', an applied 'genealogy' helps trace the spectre of complex patterns in the process of change. Looking at how both Lefebvre and Foucault have drawn on Nietzsche and Heidegger differently to achieve their own conceptual tool box for the interrogation of time, space and experience is especially fruitful. Foucault engages, at times, with the same conundrum of production and destruction that was discussed above through Lefebvre, but perhaps spatialising the latter at the expense of the former. By emphasising the statement of the technological and mechanical, the destructive reduction of the linear is purged of its rhythmic anthropologism. Foucault as such evokes again the importance of understanding change, but doing so in a way that emphasises the operations of power, production and destruction in everyday life in the relationship of the human to the self.

One can read Foucault as presenting the ongoing production and destruction of the self as a struggle, and this struggle for the self should be understood as a 'work of art' within a particular historically situated context. As the self is produced through its interplay with power, the process of change is inherently productive, producing the subject in a particular way. Importantly, this seems to invoke the logic of creative-destruction that is aligned more with poiesis rather than praxis, as they have been described above. Where the praxis of a particular time (as the knowledge of how to act) is manifest in the statement of an 'episteme', this operates as a discursive formation of given truths, forms of knowing, seeing and doing. These forms place limits upon our opportunities to gain control over this process, disciplining the production of the embodied subject through a particular alignment towards a particular form of selfhood. Importantly, as the bio-political is essentially 'creative' it is not a struggle to control praxis, as power is conceived through ideology in more traditional Marxist theory, rather it is the struggle to control poiesis, in the creation of a particular alignment of political subjectivity in the embodied citizen.

The self can be understood, then, as being a form of creative-action in the struggle for actualised 'selfhood', and as a productive movement within history determined by the boundaries, limits and thresholds of a given episteme. This approach better renders the mechanisms and techniques of ordering the 'self' more visible, whilst illustrating their disappearance into the increasingly abstract processes (mediations) of rule (or power). The centrality of power offers a different focus to Lefebvre. It is not an attempt to develop better understandings of an immediate experience, as invoked by Lefebvre's rhythmanalysis, but to better demonstrate the struggle between particular discursive formations of knowledge that establish hierarchies of ordered 'truth', how these create particular technologies and mechanisms of power that act to subjugate the local/personal knowledge of 'what people know' or *can* know in everyday life (Foucault, 2003 [1963]: 7–10). Thus, by amending the interplay between praxis and poiesis to control one's knowledge of how to act, the subjective act of self-creation is disciplined, and therefore realigned. Taken together, these approaches offer opportunities to develop a discursive transformation of time–space–place as a dynamic process of adaptive transformation at multiple levels of complexity. Redeploying Foucault allows space to be treated as a 'part of the conceptual armoury we have for the analysis itself' (Elden, 2001: 151) in relation to the creation of ways of knowing, thinking and acting upon and through 'platial' meaning. The forms of expression, content and action through this integrated approach allow, as Deleuze suggests, the 'sedimentary bed' (Deleuze, 1988 [1999]) of that which can be articulated and rendered visible for analysis to come forward. This is both a history of space and a spatial history of those particular discursive formations, but also the limits of them. By placing limits and breaking limits there is potential for adaptation to result from exposure to conflict, thus potential for transgression of the limits to stimulate change. This is particularly relevant to our discussion of adaptive change from the potentially catastrophic event rendered 'visible as events that can be subjected to different forms of knowledge' (Aradau and van Munster, 2011: 113).

Foucault's use of archaeology and genealogy to unpack change did not reach the exceptional or the disaster event, but it does open up the conditions of possibility for certain changes to occur as triggered and thus (re)constituted by changing interplay between institutionalised epistemic formations and organisations. Reading this creatively also contributes greatly to the sociology of forms that operates upon, within and through the level of the everyday (discussed above). Archaeology can easily be misunderstood in Foucault. It is not used in the same strict sense as that of classical historiography, but rather in the creation of an archive. Again, this can be misread as purely lingual, but in the constitution for Foucault it is possible to draw out the genealogy of more than words, it is the nexus of the logical, the grammatical, the locutory in discursive formations (Elden, 2001: 95–96). This draws on similar roots to those developed by Lefebvre, in so far as it renders pro-spatial the characteristics of knowledge by opening up the overlapping and interpenetrating fields of knowing, doing and acting. This reading of Foucault suggests that one does not need to draw out moments as raw knowledge (aligned to praxis [ways of knowing]) but rather should seek the means to render visible or articulable particular continuities and discontinuities in the formation of knowledge [*conaissances*]. By then asking which knowledge is more or less important at a particular time, one can interrogate the conditions of possibility for that knowledge to emerge as an epistemological field [*episteme*] and thus realign as a historically grounded knowledge-informing agency and potential creative action (aligned with poiesis [ways of acting]). The key here is in setting up the 'conditions of possibility' as a lens through which to view the analysis. Here we are divorced not from knowledge or action but from understanding the implications of acting. This is the key to be turned in constructing a genealogical understanding of complex and adaptive transformations; what is at stake is understanding how historical forms coalesce to create a totality, i.e. the configuration of conditions of possibility in which particular types of knowledge come forth, and how these can be used to analyse change between the epistemological 'breaks' and historical 'tipping points' where systemic transformation is manifest not only in what people know, but how they do things, how they act and by doing so are (re)created as a particular type of 'subject'. This is frequently rendered in research through the lens of 'bio-political' interventions in everyday life; which is itself framed by the reappraisal of the interplay between the disorderly conditions of possibility made manifest by economic, social and biological danger from roughly the sixteenth to eighteenth centuries. The archaeological approach allows the traces in the drift between these changes to be critically analysed over time. It identifies the existence of alignments that manifest as social order, the characteristic 'modalities' of that order in institutions and organisations, the power exchanges and formalisation of beliefs, rules and norms in faith, law and behaviour. In the initial analyses of bio-politics this was framed by the limits of normality in the population through the removal and remediation of the abnormal using spatial paradigms of discipline embedded in particular locations, such as the prison, the asylum, the hospital or school (Driver, 1993; Philo, 2001). As constituent elements of interplay, these spatial treatments of the disorderly (re)create the conditions of possibility for particular forms of knowledge to gain influence, such as 'madness', 'criminality'. These may be 'employed in grammar and philology, in natural history and biology, in the study of wealth and political economy' (Foucault, *Madness and Civilization*, 13; *The Order of Things*, xxi–xxii; cited in Elden, 2001: 97). This is a useful method of analysis to deploy here as archaeology and genealogy of the bio-political can help to deepen the understanding of from whence we came, in a way that is most succinctly put by Foucault himself:

> To put it in a nutshell: *Archaeology is the method* specific to the analysis of local discursivities, and *genealogy is the tactic* which, once it has described these local discursivities, brings into play the desubjugated knowledges that have been released from them. That just about sums up the overall project. (Foucault, 1997 [1975]: 10–11, emphasis added)

As is noted by Elden, the specific focus on local rather than global discursivities helps Foucault avoid one ready criticism, that he is over-privileging space, and it focuses the attention on micro-processes of power. Another criticism on the implicit structuralist sympathies of his work is harder to dismiss outright (Elden, 2001: 99–102). It is also important to acknowledge that this is not a purely historical reading of science. The emphasis on the underlying rules that order forms and formation of knowledge gives weight to the distinctions of the archaeological from the purely epistemological. The archaeological in this sense is an analysis of the order underlying the conditions of possibility from which statements are both made and transformed – these statements are discursive and formative to the order of a given truth at a given time. This also draws the eye to the complementary use of genealogy, which places the analysis of these ordering principles within the circulatory processes of power used to sustain a given form of knowledge, understanding or truth. It is tempting to some extent to then rely on the appreciative reading of Foucault in Agamben's juridical interpretation of 'bare life' (Agamben, 1998; 2005) in order to extend this into the realm of security and exception in the modern world. However useful this is in developing a more abstract theoretical debate in the context of the aim here, which is to extend the temporal, spatial and 'platial' characteristics of ordering and disordering into everyday life, the exceptional is less central to our topics. This debate I leave for another time; it is not central to our topics in this book to reduce humanity *ad infinitum* to its juridical self, but rather to look at how the production and efforts to produce particular alignments of order have been mobilised to maximise the 'citizen subjective' in the alignment of particular conditions and possibilities. The debate over 'bare life', whilst significant in some contexts, is perhaps less central at this stage. The meat and bones of applying this to the present are expounded in Part II.

Sufficient for the purpose here is to say that Foucault, like Lefebvre, draws on the complexities of the whole, both real/imagined and conceived/perceived, as 'abstraction from the more fundamental level of the lived experience' (Elden, 2001: 119). Foucault, however, extends the experiential reading of Lefebvre's critical Marxism, emphasising the micro-processes of power as quotidian. Using a genealogy of the struggle between diverse localised discursive formations of knowledge, Foucault applies the relationship between space and power over time in the embodied 'bio-political' conduct of everyday life. One might argue in the production of embodied subjects that this is again inherently poietic.

By looking at the history of the present with an archaeological method, and a genealogical tactic, the moment of the present is viewed through the lens of knowledge as productive, producing through the discursive (re)formation of knowledge everyday operations for ordering individuals and coalitions of individuals. Logically extended, this helps to unpack the boundaries and limits of the cognitive choices available to perceiving subjects, but also the alignment of the framework of knowing, doing and acting used to decide what is acceptable by both individuals and coalitions, leading to contestation, transgressions and exceptions. These themselves can both enhance stability through order or promote growth through disorder, and vice versa. Foucault might have referred to this differently as the 'optimal average' of conduct and the 'bandwidth of acceptability' within which actions are measured (Foucault, 1977: 6), which gives us access to both the root and the branch of transformative change in complex systems, as this operates at the heart of both actual transformation and the potential for transformation in ways of knowing, doing and acting at any given moment. Such an analysis helps to apply the forms from which order is drawn to the space and time of everyday life in its localised context, but also the positive adaptation of those exposed to the unpredictability of disorder. It is embodied, and thus lived, knowledge that helps to produce ordered subjects and, as such, ordered everyday life, but likewise stimulates the fractures and discontinuities of disorder. Taking this to be so, we can now unpack more critically the origins, evolution, permutations of order and disorder as they interplay through these discursive transformations in specific examples of time–space–place.

From the Struggle for Theory Towards the Struggle for History

Finally, before I move on, I want to finalise the explicitly theoretical framing of the discussion here by a return to the notion of history and of moments. Foucault draws on Nietzsche's three modalities of history (monumental, antiquarian and critical). Following Heidegger, this implies a totality from which a genealogy can be traced, a genealogy of struggle between different forms of knowledge. These archaeological genealogies trace the drifts, ruptures, continuity and discontinuity of formations as historical 'ages' in the broadest sense. Archaeological genealogy of knowledge is thus a mapping of the present through the project of tracing the drifts between particular discursive formations, as attitudes towards a period of history emerging from the knowledge utilised to understand experience of the everyday prevalent at that time. This is a genealogical excavation of the spatial history by which moments are made through the interplay of forms from discursive formations, conditions of possibility and experiences of the everyday. These conceptual tools tease out the application of Nietzsche's 'eternal return' that draws the monumental, antiquarian and critical appreciation of history together into a 'total project' of the 'total man'. It is mapping out our sense of history in informing, reconstituting and transforming the present as it thus becomes, in the moment, *in statu na'scendi*.

There are some problems to relying too heavily on Foucault, and on the insights on a specific framework of juridical or bio-political governmentality – I have discussed some of these issues elsewhere (Rogers, 2011b). An approach too strongly reliant on a Foucault will tend towards an emphasis on the poietic, not just at the expense of praxis, but at the expense of the experience of both *in statu na'scendi*. The production of bio-political subjects developed by Foucault moves the analysis away from the structural emphasis on organisation of rule to the techniques and mechanisms of rule, as the dominant constitutive force is enacted upon the bio-political subject. This approach to the 'art of government' sets the techniques/mechanisms of creating a perfect citizen over the reality of a good life, over the knowledge of how to best live. It is a very negative interpretation of ordering as something that is enforced upon the subject through correct governance as governmentality for their own good, reflecting the tyranny of order over the subject. Whilst this may be reflective of some dominant trends in the organisational power of the current social order that has emerged from Enlightenment rationality, it is not a comprehensive view of the perpetual becoming, and potentially pushes the focus away from the praxis as knowledge of how to act properly towards technical mechanism as the doing thereof – i.e. the poetic 'act' of creation – ergo the creation of the bio-political subject prioritised at the expense of the *interplay between* praxis and poiesis. Is this an attempt to move away from the secular traditions of enlightenment positivism by purging the anthropologism from enquiry? This is perhaps the case, but the discussion of theory above draws on that very complexity not as a vice, but as a prerequisite for taking the next step towards an analysis of the inherent paradox between knowing and understanding. It is one step closer to reintegrating a sense of the anthropological in the discussion differently, through the interplay of forms, and through the patterns of social change that are a part of the rhythm of everyday life. By drawing on the strengths of both Foucault and Lefebvre there is a chance to push further in drawing the experiencing subject back into the discussion. The subject as a citizen is, after all, the root and branch of social ordering and the most important part of securing any social order, as they are the people for whom it is being secured, and they are the people that need to be the most resilient to the negative impact of change, as well as the potential for positive and forward-looking change in the final analysis.

The genealogic appreciation of how the configuration of knowledge can emerge from discursive formations and as historical forms provides a sense of how clearly visible change can be. It can be a change in the understanding of what the best way to do a thing is; it can be change in the technical doing of that thing. What is most important is that these are linked to how people act out their lives. All of these, the 'pure' theory, the knowing of how to do and the creative action of doing are rendered through interplay and combine to create both the meaningful subject and the meaningful object – be it a word, an artefact, a location or a person. In the subsequent chapters of this book this approach will be grounded in historical examples to show that change occurs at once diachronically – via particular epistemic triggers and 'tipping points' – and yet also in a continuum – both progressive and regressive. Such 'forms' of change are analysable aspects of an interdependent systemic interplay through and within the space of knowledge, but also in how people understand doing and acting upon that knowledge differently at different times. Foucault's approach to the 'sociology of limits' is not one that cleanly identifies the breaks and ruptures between forms of thinking as clean divisions in the discursive formation of each episteme, hermetically sealed from each other – to treat it as such is to limit the reading of his work to a history of spaces of knowledge. Perhaps a more useful reading is as an attempt to identify the traces of drift in the *conditions of possibility* for continuities and discontinuities from which change arises through grounded spatial examples. Reading discursive formation to be a sediment for 'each age [that] says everything it can according to the conditions laid down for its statements' (Deleuze, 1988 [1999]: 46) allows only 'a measuring of earlier and later errors by each other' (Nietzsche, 1968: 281). Tracing patterns should not ignore the dynamics of complex adaptation and transformation in time–space–place. One can draw on a theory of moments to identify the trajectory and tipping points in the conditions of possibility which allow the paradoxical to be embraced. Patterns thus emerge through the resilience of particular ways of knowing, doing and acting in the perpetuation of a given civilisation over time–space–place. When this is used to unpack order and disorder then the rationalist understanding of crisis events as points of departure for new forms of understanding can be enhanced, seeing them as contributing forces in the 'tipping points' at the nexus of meaningful change within a wider genealogic 'sociology of forms'. The proposal is therefore that in applying these tools critically one can retain the abstract sense of time and place alongside the applied tools of a spatial history of experience; thus used to chart the importance of particular forms as they emerge in the epistemic discursive formations which operate to balance the schematic of 'living' towards an optimal condition, which appears at the steady-state or stable equilibrium. Both the effort to bring social order from a dangerous world and the understanding of crisis, actual crisis and forms of dealing with the impact of the event on those affected can be drawn together to see the effect of this interplay of the conditions of possibility for change, both in order and in disorder as stimulants of systemic adaptation and/or transformation. Tracing this process through examples is to where we now turn our attention, extending the theory towards history, and (in Part II) towards the present.

Chapter 3
The Struggle for History: Applying Theory to Change

Bound as our lives are to the tyranny of time, it is through what we know of history that we are delivered from our bonds and escape – into time.

A.L. Rowse

Ordering and Disordering the Historical Urban

It might not be apparent at first glance how the broader theoretical project outlined above fits into the schema of this book. That is understandable given that the majority of the above is an effort to realign the emphasis of enquiry from the object, subject or system to the interplay between them. It is this realignment that allows for the process of spatial production to complement spatial history, thus linking genealogy of the past (Part I) to the analysis of the present (Part II). Building on this foundation, the struggle for history begins to unpack the interplay of order and disorder with the urban. When speaking of order and disorder one must engage with concepts of violence and authority to better understand the development of institutions and organisations. This is not an adoption of the Hobbesian 'war of all against all', rather an appreciation of the archaeological evidence that shows clearly that as the level of technology has advanced so has the complexity of the interplay between objects, subjects and systems, and thus human institutions and organisations. At its simplest this can be read as the technological mastery of force, and the authority to use it, that has improved a group's chance to survive and/or thrive.

Through institutionalising particular 'rules of the game' from beliefs, customs and traditions and, in tandem, creating organised coalitions with shared interests or goals, the semblance of cooperative ordering comes into being. In 'natural' societies with more direct personal relationships (e.g. kinship and skills-based hierarchies) order and disorder are necessarily linked with the use of force, and the customs and traditions institutionalised in direct authority are simpler, more direct and easier to trace. In more mature societies, political institutions are more complex, and are generally seen as the vehicle through which particular elite coalitions become organised enough to gain authority over other groups. Importantly, technological development also is an important factor. It raises the complexity as access to technology is often tightly controlled, thus mutually informing specialisation of roles in everyday life, but also the use of technology in both peace and war. In both the more 'natural' or 'mature' forms this complexity is both cooperative and contested. Change can be a direct result of human agency (e.g. competition for access to technology, resources, territory) or situated in external environmental conditions (e.g. unequal living conditions or unstable ecological events).

The analogy of force here is a broad one. At the heart of much social contractarian thinking (from Hobbes, Locke and Rousseau onwards), an individual may fear being a victim of a violent act perpetrated by another individual and seek protection in coalition with others. Equally, the use of force by a given coalition to gain, or maintain, supremacy over a subject population is a regular feature of social ordering – never more so than when a diverse population gathers in large numbers. However, it has been suggested that there is a common mistake in Hobbes, Locke and Rousseau, whereby all three of these thinkers treat humans as isolated individuals in the 'state of nature' (Fukuyama, 2011). Sociability is thus treated as something not natural to human conduct. Fukuyama presents one alternative using the economic model of agency currently in vogue, refuting the liberalism of such social contractarian theory by treating mutual dependence as emergent through immanent self-interest. The formation of coalitions becomes a process enhanced by inequality, emerging in turn from unequal access to technological innovations (e.g. military or agricultural). Through these means cooperation is enforced through mutual self-interest. The problem arising is a lack of historical evidence to support either the 'war of all against all' or the naturally occurring cooperation as formative of social order in the 'state of nature'. Fukuyama attempts to deal with this inconsistency by grounding the 'Hobbesian fallacy' of 'primordial individualism' as a failure to engage with kinship relationships and the cooperative altruism of early human coalitions using an uncomfortable blend of psychology, game theory and biology (Fukuyama, 2011).

If one follows this route, one treats the emotional and biological content of human sociability as a pre-existence condition for living. The picture of our base and basic nature treats humans as purely rational, mechanical and calculating. This has a bearing on the treatment of coalition formation and social cooperation, especially relevant when anthropologically grounded in the analysis of ancient cultures, the role of violence and the socio-historical and archaeological evidence of the use or threat of violence in creating order. When a particular coalition or elite have a monopoly on the use of force we see echoes of social ordering in the institutional and organisational forms of authority used to maintain that power. This is as true of 'Big Man' cultures – seen, for example, in New Guinea – as it is of highly evolved democratic cultures – in the industrialised West, the difference is the level of personal connection between those interacting. In tribal societies, violence is up close and personal; in democratic societies it is impersonal and distant. The control of disorder is in both cases tied to forms of legitimate sanction or reprisal, as well as legitimate violence undertaken by a powerful individual in coalition with others, i.e. 'enforcing' order and thus reducing disruption, encouraging the orderly flow of everyday lives amongst a population. This authority to use violence legitimately can encourage and establish particular alignment of conformance to the beliefs, rules and norms in the rhythms of everyday life. This ever-present facet of social ordering is one that needs to be addressed in more detail to develop the understanding of why we submit to the collective, or even idiosyncratic, will of a ruling body. As such, little discussion here will specifically emphasise the random physically violent act of one individual against another individual in terms of the Hobbesian bellum omnium contra omnes ("war of all against all"), rather the emphasis will begin to draw out *organised* and *institutionalised violence* in the creation of organised coalitions of rule.

Organised violence informs issues such as: cooperation and conflict; war, protection and defence; militarisation and security and, most importantly, some of the variations in the formation of elites, coalitions and the modern notion of a territorial nation-state. Violence features often in discussion of social cooperation and urban development in its earliest incarnations, but also in more complex social orders. It is a feature of how time–space–place can be interpreted to see the discursive formation of particular beliefs, rules and norms, and almost always a guiding principle of the legitimate sanctions used to discipline those who do not adhere to them. This concept of violence is historical. It puts meat on the bones of urban formation as a crucible that can be used to tease out the development of social order. It also helps to highlight the systemic processes of interplay by which order and disorder change – also how and why different epistemic formation of beliefs, rules and norms inform who we are and what we do. By taking this slightly wider lens one can trace the transformation and change in social ordering and disorder as systemic adaptation and transformation over time. This chapter establishes links between movement, settlement, territory and authority as an extension of the theoretical framework of the previous chapter, but as a first foray into the empirical grounding of this theory in data. It builds on the relationships of space and place that are embedded in ordering. It expounds upon the importance of urban formation and the discursive formation of institutional relationships between people, extending the relationships to the processes that coalesce into patterns at particular moments of history, and how these can embed the authority of legitimate force and violence first in coalitions and then later in organisations. This is a first step towards the struggle for history.

Urban Form and Origins

In the previous chapter it was noted that Mumford once suggested (1961) that the initial positions of humanity are those of *movement* and *settlement*. Mumford also suggested that the origins of settlement, at the most primitive, emerged from spiritual links to specific sites and practical needs for increasing the safety of the social group. The marking of caves by painting or carving, as used to indicate a territorial mark of ownership highly significant to the nomadic tribes most typical of the Palaeolithic era is given as an example; another reason for the territorial statement of ownership could be the claim laid to sites of agricultural fertility, with good hunting and few predators, such as the Indus Valley and the Deltas of Ancient Egypt, Sumeria and Mesopotamia. These appear to be logical assumptions but are difficult to prove empirically. Supposing that there is credence to such assertions, it would certainly evoke a time whereby the primitive human was more aligned to the cyclical rhythms and demands of the physical world, but we cannot romanticise this as a 'state of Nature'. The process towards settlement of given areas could equally have emerged from the development of basic needs into traits or characteristics of groups that survive into institutionalised 'forms-of-doing' and 'forms-of-acting' over large spans of time. The repetition of such acts slowly creates knowledge of locations, of forms of doing, which inform survival. This is no different in Nature between the movement of herds of deer and the movement of packs of wolves, as mysterious as the march of the penguins in Antarctica to the nomadic tribes of the Russian steppes. In the human case, over time we have seen such transitions in the knowledge and practices of survival inform Mesolithic territorially based cultivation which sits at the roots of agriculture. Regardless of exactly when or how these changes from nomadic movement to settlement of a specific location or site took place, one thing is certain: that in no two locations or territories did these practices occur in the exact same way. The cyclical rhythms of the natural world could have disastrous consequences for nomadic tribes, early settlements and established urban centres alike. There is no unifying theory that can conclusively demonstrate how and why hunter-gathering cohabitation became territorial *possession*, how that became settlement of a territory rather than nomadic movement, or how settlement became territorial *ownership*. In primitive habitations, from the cave or cairn to the preferred camp site with reliable water and food sources, there is some evidence that settlement had a fundamental impact on humanity's relationship with the land, particularly in relation to our efforts at subsistence agriculture, animal husbandry and the domestication of the landscape (Hooke, 2000).

Despite some variation, the ways in which resources were gathered seems to have developed alongside the specialisation of tasks amongst the group informing, concurrently, specialisation of social roles (i.e. forager to farmer, hunter to warrior). There appears some consistency in institutionalising a specialised task into the organisational hierarchy. Forms of institutionalised knowledge for 'forms-of-doing' and 'forms-of-acting' appear *sui generis*. These necessarily draw on the material specificities of the territory as environment. As the context of a relationship with the land is diverse, the forms that emerge are also diverse in establishing the appropriateness of interactions with others – human, animal, plant, mineral, astrological, ephemeral, etc. In anthropological studies one might find this progression to be described as one where 'culture evolves by the replacement of natural economy (ecology) with a political economy' (Bettinger, 1991: 4), but beyond this we also need to see how rules emerge to provide a normative spectrum of appropriate behaviours in a concrete spatial order, as a shared cognitive system [nomos]. This is complemented by beliefs and stories of right and wrong [mythos] and expectations of how one should behave [ethos] that when combined provide a motivation to follow those rules.

The habits and requirements of survival appear as the earliest drivers of conformance (to established forms of thinking and doing) tied to subsistence. Anecdotally, this can be followed by ensuring stability and safety of kin. As technological practices gain complexity and subsistence delivers higher yield (e.g. through agriculture), institutionalised ways of doing divide labour and are regulated by organisational elites amongst specialists. The by no means universal interplay of socio-ecological and technological systems is one reading of the process by which authority is divided into coalitions of specialists in synch with the increased settlement of communities into villages and cities. Consolidation of a systematised tribal and kin-based 'social order' can be consequences of such a pattern; but to assume this as a universal or consistent law of development is to fall prey to dramatic over-simplification on the nature of social and spatial organisation over time.

Movement, Settlement and Territorial Ownership

It is interesting that the themes of movement and settlement highlighted by Mumford are inherently patterned practices which can be linked differently to naturally occurring cyclical rhythms. One simplistic reading of this analogy is the seasonal migrations of animals often driven by biological requirements (e.g. they go where the food is). Through seasonal weather patterns, access to resources changes and the stability or safety of the environment changes. Survival requires movement as the access to food, forage or herds changes with the cycles of the seasons. This may have been common in the Mesolithic era, but was again not universal, as the evidence of both movement and settlement vary greatly across particular geo-social contexts. It is likely, despite the swirls and eddies of change, that settlement required more complex material technologies if not social patterns, though simple and complex are relative terms when discussing 'progress' (Wright, 1986). Some settlements were successfully resilient and developed, others did not. Southall's discussion of the 'first signs' of urbanism in Jericho (Palestine), Hacilcar and Çatal Höyük (Central Anatolia) and Jarmo (Tigris-Euphrates Valley) shows that each can yield evidence of significant technological advances in basic agriculture, irrigation and animal husbandry, as well as animistic and symbolic religions, and yet all were abandoned (Southall, 1998: 23–24). Interestingly, whilst reports on the timelines of each settlement differ greatly, movement, settlement and then further movement of this kind occurred as early as 9000 BCE and on to as late as 5000 BCE (Blouet, 1972; Flannery, 1972). Through periodic settlement and movement humans began to develop more sophisticated technological interventions and geomorphic means of environmental management. As such, humanity gradually began to become less and less subject to the cyclical rhythms of nature as their ability to impose their needs on the environment began to advance. The rhythms of the seasons contributed to movement, but when a location became untenable it could result from negative resilience of human actions as much as from hostile environmental conditions. The results are as varied as the causes. Shnirel'man notes that the 'scarcity of resources may be either absolute or relative' (1982: 224). The absolute being caused by climate change – seasonal shifts or natural disasters – and the relative by the direct/indirect actions of humanity – the direct exemplified by over-culling local game, over-grazing of cattle and the indirect by an increased draw on resources through population density or migration.

The 'State of Nature' is constructed here not as Rousseau's 'Garden of Eden' or Hobbes' primitive violent place. Nothing so resembling an ideal type can be found in archaeological evidence. The reality is much more likely to be a biologically oriented series of cyclical changes. Cyclical changes in this sense are those conditions imposed upon the human externally by ecological environment but also internally by human biology – early resilience of this type emerges from the ecological conditions for breeding and survival (e.g. favourable climate, sustainable food sources, etc.). This cannot, however, disregard the importance of formative institutionalised knowledge (e.g. forms-of-doing) drawn from socio-cultural attributes (e.g. ties of kinship), tasks (e.g. foraging, hunting) and technologies (e.g. weapons, tools). Nature as ecological conditions, it is supposed, will become less central to decision-making as the conditions that inform the need to move are more easily controlled by more sophisticated tools, agriculture and farming. As more linear, morphological, even perhaps machine-like patterns come to dominate the rhythm of everyday life, the social order drifts from one of movement to one of settlement, subsistence and even domination of the natural world. As positive resilience of the settlement increases more complex social organisations emerge and interactions change.

In a small group, personal relationships are a key driver of the institutions and organisations of a given order. In larger social groups that develop in established settlements the personal relationship is less of an organisational driver. The physical attributes and characteristics of a person become less likely to inform their position in the social hierarchy, i.e. the fastest and strongest hunter may lay claim to the leadership of the tribe, but membership in the elite amongst a more numerous social group may be determined by heritage or wealth (e.g. close relation to the crown) as personal genealogies become more complex and elites more distinct and variegated. Socially ascribed attributes of position, power, duties, rights and responsibilities become more influential in creating elites, and designating who has access to what level or type of authority in a more complex organisation or social order as a result. Organisations that emerge operate within a patterned rhythm of change alongside other variables, institutional values, resource requirements, competition from other groups to shape cognitive and thus behavioural processes. When taken as a whole we can, through our analysis, try to draw out some of the characteristics of a given social order at a given time by charting these changes to the form of particular knowledge, practices, institutions and organisations. These therefore must include the changing geomorphic, technological abilities, socio-cultural customs and values, the method of making, sharing, or taking resources or products and the authority to organise in creating social order or disorder. Change emerges, initially at least, from these changing conditions of possibility for survival with the natural world, but it becomes ever more complex as 'progress' takes hold.

There is no singular model for tracing progress holistically. Some cultures have reverted to nomadic lifestyles, others have increased settlement and cultivation of the environment to increase surplus and trade; or enhanced the community resources and security of the environs to reflect better the needs of the populous as the interplay of forms enhance different levels of effectiveness and efficiency. Characteristics of settlement in the first villages, towns and cities can be perhaps best traced through analysis of the beliefs, rules and norms that allow institutions and organisations to take root in ordering the everyday lives of the wider people. Some of those characteristics include: a shift from intensely personal towards more impersonal relationships, the development of more complex systems of ownership and exchange (such as of patron–client networks), and limited access to the organisational forms that manipulate interests to ensure social order (North et al., 2009a: 32–39). Importantly, spiritual culture appears to have been a significant facet of the institutionalisation of beliefs and norms as rules of conduct. Animist shrines – for example bull-horns found at Çatal Höyük archaeological digs (Hodder, 2008) – have led scholars to suggest that as settlements became tied to specific spiritual locations, the drift towards permanence was enhanced. This in turn allowed for a more productive form of social cooperation based on collaborative customs and beliefs. Architecture also takes on more symbolic importance in such permanent settlements. The importance of particular animal bones and skins in the symbolic decoration of dwellings and worship sites themselves evoke more complex functions and divisions in the use-value of urban locations.

These shifts also highlight the importance of particular roles played by individuals within the community. Some stories and myths imbue 'forms-of-doing' with status or value attributes, as expertise in 'forms-of-acting' might also allow elites to form and create more complex organisations. The city in this sense did not replace the previous ways of being, but rather brought together and increased the efficiency of productive forces and the scope by which social divisions and hierarchies of possession, ownership and exchange were to become more formal (Mumford, 1961: 42). The embodiment of ownership in terms of specific purposive uses of land (i.e. domestication for agriculture, animal husbandry, spiritualism – church or cemetery, housing, etc.), possession takes on a new significance beyond the primitive interpretation of territorialism as a cyclical opportunism dictated by the requirements of survival. The socially ordering force ascribed by rules into formal law, seen as codification of beliefs, traditions and customs, can be seen to come from the relationship between humans and the land itself. Schmitt suggests that this is best seen through the apportionment of space as territory for the purposes of cultivation. This productive relationship required social *and* spatial ordering for the community: 'Then, obviously, families, clans, tribes, estates, forms of ownership and human proximity, also forms of power and domination, become apparent' (Schmitt, 2003: 42). Territory is no longer *occupied* but it is *owned*, from the tribal collective as a group living on the land to a community of individuals who have 'rights of possession' to the space they inhabit. The nature of this ownership also reflects much more of the segregation of distinct hierarchal groups alluded to by Rousseau, who warned of the dangers of this productive possession in his work on the social contract:

> Such was, or should have been, the origin of society and laws, which gave new fetters to the weak and new forces to the rich, irretrievably destroyed natural liberty, established forever the law of property and inequality, changed adroit usurpation into an irrevocable right, and for the profit of a few ambitious men henceforth subjected the entire human race to labour servitude and misery. (Rousseau, 1987: 70)

Aggregations of juridical influence in the positional nexus of social roles would not come to fruition as a system of capital exchange, such as that depicted in Marx's notes on cooperation (Marx, 1974 [1867]: 336–352) for many centuries, but the roots of human servitude to labour, property, ownership and possession can be traced back to these early territorial occupations. Occupation of territory alone is not enough to drive change, nor the growth of surplus resources, nor the rise of labour specialisations. The interplay of forms drives the drift from kinship and convenience associations (perhaps between tribal groups) towards capitalistic modes of productive cooperation (in the early city-states). Interplay between changing conditions and relations (social, cultural, political, economic) informs the complex evolution of elites with the authority – as recognised organisations – to direct or orchestrate the order of everyday life. The interplay creates conditions of possibility for institutions to gain inertial momentum through formalised organisations. These are manifest also in spatial and architectural sites, from shrines and temples to fields and fortifications, further reinforcing the alignment of forms into a coherent ordering of everyday life. This in turn influences the course or direction of development in spurts and flurries of change. To this end, progress is variegated progressive and regressive, evolving into different forms of authority with both positive and negative features of resilience.

Characteristics of Authority

It is important to note that the dynamism of this process is such that it cannot be locked into a specific trajectory that occurs universally. Nor is there a coherent point of view with a consistent language for unpacking the process of change. What Poggi refers to as the three forms of social power for achieving one's goals in the creation of a 'State' could be framed as (a) economic, (b) ideological, (c) political (Poggi, 1990: 4), we might equally see these reflected differently as (a) access to resources, (b) access to knowledge, (c) access to organisations.

Equally, we need to incorporate the mirrors of these forms in cultural rules [nomos], beliefs [mythos] and norms [ethos] that allow institutionalised forms of doing and forms of acting to emerge. Mumford points out that:

> only a culture that is dead and buried ever remains stratified, without undergoing displacements and upheavals; while non-material culture is mainly fibrous in nature; though its long threads may often be broken, they go to every stratum, and even when out of sight they may play an active part. (Mumford, 1961: 31)

Unravelling these cultural 'threads' speaks to the interplay between forms of beliefs, rules and norms, in particular how they adapt, or resist change. Both religion and law are good examples. Religion is deemed important as a characteristic of social order because it enhances the conditions of possibility for cooperation as much as it creates divisions for conflict (Fukuyama, 2011). Law is important because it shows the formalisation of customs, traditions and 'rules' that act to distribute power out of the hands of individuals into the hands of coalitions and elites, allowing order to be franchised across larger social groups. Whoever has access to the institution of religion, of legislative or juridical power, of ideological knowledge or economic resources informs both political institutions and organisations. This interplay informs the creation of coalitions and of elites that then exercise authority to create order – towards whatever ends they are able. What coalitions or elites are in ascendancy informs which rules are most important, and how they are made manifest in the 'art of governing' to produce particular subjects in particular ways. An analysis of the discursive formation of a given mythos, nomos and ethos can help to align the non-material aspects of social order with its material forms of knowing, doing and acting. The discursive formation is thus a mode of production that can be traced to chart the evolution of organisations, institutions and the objects and subjects that emerge. However, too often the non-material processes of quotidian 'living' are treated as separate from, or subordinate to, political and economic forms. The attempt to identify a coherent social order must take into account both material specificities and the non-material idiosyncrasies. As we have all too often seen, political and religious organisations can act together, overlap and oppose each other when elites have competing interests embedded in the respective organisations for diverse and unexpected reasons – a good example being the secession from the Catholic Church by the British Monarchy.

A good lens for tracing some general characteristics of a given time is to better understand customs, traditions, spaces and places *as well as* political and economic influences on how elite coalitions renegotiate the legitimacy of their authority. The conditions, relations, institutions and organisations are perpetually remade across all of these forms and the resilient characteristics of this remaking should be apparent to some extent through the changed forms of authority used to govern, but also through the forms of acting out life by the individual – examples include religious rituals (prayer, confession, fasting), legal traditions (trial, punishment), economic customs (employment, taxation) – as a subject created through the 'art of governing'.

For example, rituals of leadership in a warrior system were based on masculine verity and strength in the time of the Mongolian Khans – for example, Temujin, Jumuka and Ong Khan in the eleventh century. They are tied to symbolic notions of service through the 'shepherd' in Judeo-Christian religions, and these symbolic leadership roles are combined in myths and legends of Lugulbanda (Sumerian king and poetic shepherd-hero), or early Gods such as Dumuzi and Tummuz (Sumerian and Babylonian shepherd gods).[1] Foucault discusses the power of the spiritual for social ordering in terms of pastoral power and the direction of souls in a salvation that is connected to subsistence in the transition from feudal to early-modern models of social ordering (Foucault, 2007 [1978]: 123–137). Equally, such principles of ordering are implicit in the ownership of land and the extraction of wealth from that land (in the form of tithes, rents, etc.) and the inequalities of such institutionalised processes.

In discussion of the manifestation of these roles as authority one might refer to the 'will to power' as discussed by Nietzsche when he refers to the twin roles of the *ascetic* and the *barbarian* as directive influences with polar attributions. The ascetic is linked to admiration, and elevation itself tied to the proliferation of joy. At the other end of the cycle, 'torment, then blows, then terror', where violence and threat of violence satiates the extravagance of the lust for power (Nietzsche, 1977: 218). Striving for distinction and the threat of violence appears through Nietzsche as a required element in the creation of the elite. It is a requisite component a priori for cooperation amongst the elite both in subjugation of others and also in sustaining itself. The cost of engaging in violence by such logic cannot exceed the cost of cooperation or the coalition will collapse, subjugated once again to the whims of individuals. The logic holds true through the 'sticky' or *resilient* qualities of such characteristics in both institutions and organisations over time.

As noted above, the creation of coalitions and elites are formative of organisations, these elite groups embed social order in everyday life by limiting access to the privileges of membership in a dominant coalition, limiting access to institutions (such as worship, martial training, property ownership or trade). Such systems engender cooperation by creating credible incentives for cooperation amongst the members of the group – limiting opportunities for randomised personal violence, limiting membership of access to the organisation, arbitrating the framework for making juridical decisions and controlling access to the privilege of ownership. Ownership in a broad sense here incorporates ownership of land for the extraction of rents, of resources, productive trade and also of knowledge for manipulation or mediation of belief and norms of conduct (i.e. laws). These general characteristics in the operation of authority also presuppose control over

---

1   There is some more interesting work on the nomenclature of power in Sumer and Ebla by Pettinato (2000).

the formalised and specialised roles of violence that take on a martial and military aspect, in what have been termed 'basic natural states' (North et al., 2009a).

The 'Natural' State

It is useful to note how the changing role of authority is tied to certain cultural contexts, particularly when looking at the type of actions authority is allowed to take within a given social formation. One can reflect upon the personal interactions a dominant coalition may be allowed or able to intervene in. In the stage of development where a culture or society is typified by the hunter-gatherer, kinship engenders intensely personal relationships, coalitions with elite status are thus often small and short-lived. In subsistence settlements, survival and basic needs are high priorities – e.g. sustainable food and shelter. Elite coalitions are more likely to emerge to control the surplus of land and resources. The access to institutions of worship and formalised systems of education or trade are more likely to develop as privileges of elite coalitions in such a context (North et al., 2005). Securing survival requires the security of both the physical *and* the spiritual. Where these become formal institutions, the elite coalition are more likely to become formal organisations with authority to control access to such privileges, as surplus sustains. This is a dangerous and unstable alignment linked to the immediacy of demands placed upon the dominant coalition and subject to the whims of the environmental context (e.g. good/poor harvest). These alignments of social order arose as far back as 10000 BCE, but the forms of which limited-access social orders are comprised are residually present today. In earlier formations the role of the religious leader (ascetic) and the warrior (barbarian) are common authority figures. Danger is the common imperative for change and arises most commonly from a combination of the precariousness of the social order and the latitude in the system before a breakdown in order becomes irreparable. Settlement informs a degree of stability but can also enhance the 'stickyness' and rigidity of a given order through increased specialisation and systemic interdependence. Despite the assumption in many anthropological enquiries that early urban centres formed endogenously and in peaceful circumstances, the evidence from Neolithic, Bronze, Copper and Iron Ages does not support this (Southall, 1998: 23–53).[2] Order is a product of the interplay between violence and peace as much as between order and disorder, and both are often mediated by the particular institutionalised and organised forms of authority that seek to protect or limit access to resources, technology or the institutions and organisations themselves. For example, the means by which surplus production of food is protected by particular organisations is interdependent on the conditions, relations and institutions of everyday life.

---

2   The assumption of peaceful development is perhaps illusory in so far as the numbers of combatants are not comparable to modern day open warfare – the scientific equivalent of not adjusting for inflation when comparing the price of bread at intervals of 500 years.

As the interplay becomes more complex we see more developed systems of protection enshrined in technologies – from axes, walls, etc. to military drones and mechanised infantry – but also in political institutions and organisations – from tribal 'Big Man' models of authority to the complex parliamentary government of a nation-state.

North et al. (2009a) distinguish between natural states with systems for limiting access and open-access orders in their genealogy of violence and social order testing the delicate balance required between particular alignments of military, political, economic and religious forms of ordering access (Ibid., 2009a: 41). When an upheaval takes place in an urban location, those most affected in the population or the elite regardless are often caught in the tide of change and have 'little choice but to obey, whether they were openly enslaved or subtly enthralled' (Mumford, 1961: 66). Violence can break out over rights of access, thus the earliest forms of organised conflict between competing groups of humans. The best examples of this conflict are often found in archaeological and anthropological evidence that give locally specific examples, for example the Babylonian empire on what is now modern-day Iraq and Iran. At first, conflict was more centred on the establishment of control over a territory. Conflict between distinct coalitions with the authority to mobilise military force in particular cities or regions began to arise more commonly *as a result* of the centrifugal forces of urbanisation and increased competition between city-states, be that for land yielding strategic or luxury resources or for control over sites of cultural significance. Authority in these early formations would then be typified initially as a *de facto* authority emerging from the requirements of early systems of cooperation amongst elites in a natural state. As such, the political form of a sovereign authority emerges from the relations of exchange by which the symbolic call to come together initially occurs (for example religious site, temples and traditions), the requirements of ensuring safety of the formative citizens (that which makes them dependent on the dominant coalition for protection) and the evolution of rules that enable an organisational coalition as the legitimate directive authority.[3] All of these forces would necessarily be tied to both the productive labour of the formative citizen and the conditions of the socio-spatial environment within which all exchanges between them take place, suggesting that the attractive security, ease of trade and such 'comfort' factors inherent in the linear circadian pattern of existence outweigh that uncertainty of a nomadic cyclical existence, engendering the

---

3   David Grove suggests that: '... towns and villages should be distinguished by function. The historical origin of towns lies surely in the need to concentrate in one place functions related to a wider area than a village, such as markets, administration or defence. Thus we may define towns as settlements offering a given variety or level of certain characteristic services. The precise threshold may vary with the culture and level of development of the country or region' (Grove, 1972: 560). It is posited in the above that this is similar to the variegated evolution of cities.

conditions for the expansion of conurbations into sovereign city-states and the various forms of natural state that have pervaded much of history.

It should be noted that the transition from hunter-gatherer social orders to agricultural cultivation and the natural state is not in any way a superior form of social order, it is simply far more efficient at extracting surplus and sustaining organised coalitions. The natural state limits access to the forms of organisation, and all organisations in natural states limit access to resources (both of knowledge and goods), privileges and activities (North et al., 2009b: 56), for example institutionalised education, worship and trade. However, they must also contend with the possibility that overspecialisation in these areas may create new elites. New elites may contend with the privileged position of the dominant coalition. At its heart, the natural state is always in a state of struggle and of becoming something else. It is an ongoing negotiated system, renegotiated through the interplay of forms through time–space–place. Whilst there are general characteristics to natural states, there have been significant variations in the specific functions and institutions that have arisen from diverse mythic, ethical and nomic traditions. To this end it is important to note that the 'limited-access order is not a specific set of political, economic, or religious institutions; it is a fundamental form of organising society' (North et al., 2009a: 31). North et al. present a typology of the natural state, illustrating general characteristics in the alignment of forms at different stages. These are:

*The **fragile** natural state*   coalitions struggle to remain coherent in the face of both internal and external violence. Personal interests and individual identities undermine the coherence of the coalition with rapidly shifting balances of power that threaten the coherency of the social order. Any significant shock to the system, such as swiftly changing prices or availability of resources, disease or civil disruption, death or killing of a coalition member, can lead to the emergence of a new coalition or significant realignment of personal interests within the dominant coalition. Wielding social power to direct the actions of others and the distribution of resources is critical, but equally 'economic and political systems are closely enmeshed with religious, military, and educational systems' (North et al., 2009a: 72). Formal institutions tend to be more fluid, rules as laws are not likely to be consistent across the whole social body, and both public and private law[4] is simple and malleable to the needs of the patron–client networks it operates as a primary deterrence and as a means of settling disputes. Examples of this coalescence of forms can be seen in the tribal laws of Anglo-Saxon, Gothic and Nordic tribes.

---

4   As defined in the Justinian code: 'The study of law consists of two branches: law public, and law private. The former relates to the welfare of the Roman State; the latter to the advantage of the individual citizen. Of private law then we may say that it is of threefold origin, being collected from the precepts of nature, from those of the law of nations, or from those of the civil law of Rome' (Title I, Book I).

*The **basic** natural state*   coalitions are far more stable, with coherent institutions of public law that stabilise and strengthen the organisational framework of the coalition. As such, the institutionalised forms are far more durable and the coalition less subject to internal fluctuations driven by individual personalities. The rules of operation for the reproduction of the coalition over time are therefore far more likely to be institutionalised themselves. Processes for succession of leadership, transitions between dominant elites, management of economic issues (extraction of rent, tax or tribute) all still create possibilities for conflict to arise. However, the coordination and consistency of stable arrangements reduces the immediate danger of violence as a form of resolving disputes. An early example of a transitional fragile to basic state might be seen in the Babylonian code of Hammurabi, and more developed in the Roman Republic. It is important to note that the balance of elites, there may be more than one operating in a stable basic natural state, is key to the sustainability of the order. It is by no means certain that a basic natural state will develop into a mature natural state; as we see in the case of the Roman empire, the stability of the organisations ebbs and flows, as does the reflection of institutional forms, beliefs, rules and norms that dictate how and why a particular coalition or even individual should have authority to rule. A basic natural state therefore still requires that all of the elite groups that form coalitions are bound within the State itself, and are directly composite elements of the governing authority. A good example of this is the role that religious organisations play in the coalition during the middle ages. There are numerous elites, the royalty and landed aristocracy and the Church, for example. However, the church does not exist separate from the state itself, priests and bishops perform functions of the State within a wider coalition between these elite groups. Furthermore, the organisations are not as durable, therefore making long-term stability in the reproduction of the organisations less likely. When these key figures are drivers of organisation, such as the king for example, replacement of the ruler or dynastic change may require new organisations to emerge (Ibid.: 43–46).

*The **mature** natural state*   There is, between the basic and the mature natural states, a difference of degree rather than in the kind of organisations they engender. The mature natural state is capable of maintaining durable institutions, but also durable organisations that exist outside of the boundary of the State itself. These organisations are perpetually lived in so far as they can survive and reproduce outside of the membership of the coalition, i.e. 'the identity of the organisation is independent from the identity of the individual members' (Ibid.: 46). In such contexts the institutions need to evolve to be more sophisticated and become embodied in practices that can outlast the changes to a dominant coalition; such might be the creation of a formal and independent system of courts, and the recognition of an organisation as a legal person subject to laws, rather than directing reprisals or mediation to the specific members of that organisation. A formal rule of law is required for mature natural states to be able to coherently apply institutions to the mediation between organisations and the dominant coalition, regardless of whether these organisations are internal, such as in municipalities within the state, or external, in the form of cults or associations (such as the Freemasons) and companies (such as the East India Trading Company).

Where the transitions between these forms occur there are fundamental shifts in the balance of forms that constitute the institutions of everyday life and the dynamics of the organisation as a dominant coalition. Initially, the fragile 'cult of personality' may drive authority, but as more mature forms emerge the personal becomes less important than the position. Institutions such as the rule of law become 'perpetually lived' and limit the exercise of absolute power as *de facto* forms of authority; the resilience of the institution becomes a positive influence on the trajectory of change. The links between how beliefs, rules and norms are formalised into institutions of laws, ethics and behavioural standards are threads of the material and non-material forms of interplay creating more resilient institutions and organisations.

From these beginnings the potential for a broader view of interplay emerges. Environmental conditions, technological capabilities, power relations and institutions and organisations interplay to create social order. The appraisal of authority above links space to time, thus a spatial history can be deepened. The emergence of authority from a spatial history teases out the complex interdependencies underlying the creation of formal institutions and dominant coalitions. This is presented as a formative process of ongoing interplay with traceable characteristics. These can be found in archaeological evidence of conflict and peace, in the written or anthropological evidence of institutions or organizations, giving us some of the characteristics of a social order at a given time. This is not a chronological evolution but a cross-scale reading of interplay as complex systemic interdependency.

The example of authority as an organising influence on discursive knowledge frames the process of gaining power as an aspect of social ordering, but this is contingent on the alignment of institutions (e.g. worship, land ownership, education, trade) and organisations (e.g. church, monarchy, bureaucracy, corporation) in which it is made manifest for the resultant form of order emerging. These components in turn operate concurrently with the ebb and flow of ecological conditions and social relations enhanced by surges in morphological interventions through technological innovation (e.g. wheel, iron axe, construction, machinery), often engendering a growth spurt in urbanisation. In many instances the process of change has collapsed, only to re-emerge in another form later. In Mongolia at time of the Khans there was a distinctly different pattern of authority, technology, ecology and economy to that occurring in Mesoamerica during the Inca period or Mesopotamia under the Sumerian or later Persian, Roman and Hellenic orders. Social ordering operates in different patterns across a broader 'cycle of consolidation, stabilisation, stagnation and eventual fragmentation and chaos all over again' (Southall, 1998: 38). These cycles of production and destruction seem to operate as a centrifugal pulling together and casting apart of particular environmental conditions, technological innovations, institutionalised social relations and organisations. The resilience of perpetually lived aspects creates positive resilience. Concurrently, the cycle of production and destruction, settlement and movement may develop its own inertia, and this creates the potential for negative resilience through an inability to adapt or change to the emergence of new conditions from the interplay. The conditions and relations through which urbanisation and organisation occur thus seem to ebb and flow differently in configurations distinct to a specific time and place, but rarely exactly replicated in the same way.

The different configurations of authority seem to create organisational elites with different influences contingent on the types of institutions most dominant. This could emphasise the military, the priesthood, or the trader. It also tends to allow for distinct architectural forms to emerge in the places within which these privileges and activities are acted out, in the military camp, the church or marketplace. Spiritual monuments precede large dwellings as representations of importance, but these feed from each other in symbolic competitions for importance, status and value. Thematic connections can be made through different forms of religion and agglomeration around memorial sites; settlement and trade evolving from surplus; the evolution of social hierarchies into dominant coalitions of interest. These all act in different ways to feed urbanisation as a consequence of enhanced stability as it emerges from the formalisation of institutions and organisations out of the myths, ethics and norms of particular time (e.g. tribute to the religious caste will gain favour of or access to divine wisdom). All of the above seem to evoke diverse and variegated systems of interdependency. Where societies become stable and develop more fruitfully these tend to an alignment that is more linear, with strong nomothetic understandings of time–space–place imposed on everyday life out of mutable, yet resilient, mythical beliefs and ethical norms.

The shift away from externally dependent cycles of movement and settlement towards more internally stable and linear urbanisation is a common 'doorstep condition' for the evolution of a natural state, but one of many variations. Others include the limiting or opening of access to spiritual security and physical security through resources or privileged activities and membership in elite coalitions. Such forms operate centrifugally to reproduce variegated total, relative, equivalent and generalised forms of value in 'everyday life', such as the value of materials, resources or use-values of a location. The forms vary in each alignment. Exchanges *are* systematised and conditions of survival implicit in the movement–settlement–movement cycle, but these are effectively supplanted by the formal stabilising influence of more complex institutions and organisations. Change is not a smooth transition but emerges in progressive and regressive spurts and flurries, coalescing into different social orders. The patterns of change are constantly in flux, as such the moment of change is one of perpetual transition and is effectively creative and productive in what it destroys – it is *poietic*. The complexity of poietic interplay allows us to step away from approaches that might privilege more game-theoretic models of experience. A rhythmanalytic reflection on this spatial history suggests that the relative stability in which many early urban centres emerged can be enunciated through a metaphor of *eurhythmia*, as stable, healthy and productive. Equally important are the periods of conflict, not less productive but typified by *arrhythmic* bifurcations of the social order and the forging of change through periods of conflict. The ideal alignment is one of meta-stable equilibrium between the interdependent components, but this is a metaphor for a *utopia in absentia* and poses the dual dangers of stagnation *in situ* but also in a rose-tinted anthropologism. If the interplay is treated as perpetual this suggests that both stability *and* conflict are required for progress between fragile, basic and mature state formations. Transition is far more common than a static alignment to a particular model:

> A clear if not self-evident implication: once one discerns relations of force in social relations and relations of alliance, one perceives their link with rhythm. Alliance supposes harmony between different rhythms; conflict supposes arrhythmia; a divergence on time, in space, in the use of energies. The relation between forces requires the domination of one force and draws on the relations of alliance as means (and not ends), is accompanied by a disassembly of time and spaces: of rhythms. (Lefebvre, 2004: 68)

In this way, the suggestion can be made that a top-down genealogy of urban development can be drawn alongside the rhythmanalytical analysis of everyday life in time–space–place of everyday life. The stability of systemic interdependency is embedded in the dominant alliance of particular coalitions as organisations that limit access. By limiting access the trajectory of change becomes stabilised in the orderly flow of everyday life through institutionalised ways of knowing, doing and acting through particular social relations in particular locations (spaces and places). Anthropological and archaeological evidence suggests that circadian patterns of activity were affected by the shift from settlement–movement cycles to more permanent urban settlements. This institutionalised less emphasis on *literal* survival and more on the *type* of survival, engendering an interest in praxis that underpins social ordering until the modern era. The focus on management of the increased surplus arising from urbanisation and technological development among other forces acting upon the poietic continuum create a linear directive emphasis, acting upon the inertia of change through beliefs, rules and norms as well as environmental and geographic morphology sets up a framework of knowledge that is focussed on the knowledge of how to live best. No longer is this the driving force of social order (as discussed in Part II) but it is a significant characteristic of early natural states. Access to comfortable living standards, the emergence of more secure conditions of everyday life and more stable perpetually lived institutions and coherent organisations increases exponentially the complexity of systemic interdependency. Most significantly, the complexity of interplay is inexhaustible, and the unlikeliest of intersections can emerge in contradictory ways. This is how *polythetic relativity* emerges as a lens through which particular forms gain influence in the *polyrhythmia* of stable periods, but as has been suggested, change is often more rapid during periods of conflict than stability, so it is towards these dangers that we now turn our attention.

Securing Safe or Dangerous Settlements

Stability and conflict appear as key characteristics in the emergence of settlements; more complex interdependencies and advances, however, seem to stimulate more rather than less conflict between groups. The architecture of defence did not seem to develop until conflict between city-states became less the internecine clashing of tribes and more organised warfare for resources and control over sovereign territory. This has been pointed out again in previous research (Coaffee et al., 2008: 9–13), but refutes both Hobbesian 'war of all against all' as well as the harmonious primitive 'world without walls' implied by Mumford. Rather, the relations and conditions for the development of architectural technologies, such as large-scale fortifications, were not commonly consistent until a certain plateau of formation was reached. Keeley (1996: 58) has also pointed out that smaller, more mobile, 'bands and tribes' did not so much 'neglect' fortification but that 'the social and economic conditions requisite for undertaking such construction' were not common, or even, where the relations and conditions for development of these defensible forms of architecture and territorial occupation were available, the cost was not equal to the benefit to be gained. Economic imperatives (such as control of traders to the population) and fear of the other (keeping us in and them out) were equally likely to have been important purposes of walled enclosure in early towns and cities.

The above discussion has pointed out that the city in its fledgling form was not a simple manifestation of convenience but a complex systemic interdependency across numerous forms. Not every village would grow into a town and not every town would grow into a city; in fact, the surviving and more permanent city-states were exceptions rather than the rule, and many of the largest and most significant urban conurbations have been vulnerable to a wide range of overlapping ecological hazards, security threats and human or technological risks. Many of these ancient or pristine cities ran afoul of warfare, internal struggle and ecological or biological disaster, being razed, rebuilt and destroyed again many times over. In offering a discussion of the vulnerable city in history, it is useful to reflect upon: war and destruction of the city; the natural disaster – importantly including the responses to disaster which allow for resiliency to sustain the urban form. That incorporates in turn responses to environmental and ecological hazards, anthropogenic (man-made) risks from economic, socio-technological, medico-biological or civil disruptions. Further, the importance of spatial ordering – such as boundaries and fortifications – for the institutional and organisational ordering of the city and authorities that sought to sustain it have been developed. Whilst the interplay of these forms gives us a first step into rolling out a spatial history of order in a genealogical method it is necessary also to look at some of the challenges in ancient, feudal and capitalist systems. Thus we can move forwards with a better understanding of the rhythms of social order in the city.

Chapter 4
The Struggle for the City:
Disaster, War and Disorder Over Time

All cities are mad: but the madness is gallant. All cities are beautiful: but the beauty is grim.

Christopher Morley

Danger, Order and Disorder

Following on from the discussion of ordering through authority, institutions, organisations and urban settlement, this chapter takes a different approach to the evolution of order, and particularly *disorder*. This chapter emphasises the tensions and challenges to order authority can engender, as the institutions underpinning it or the organisations exercising it are faced with disorder arising from the unexpected. Here, more attention is drawn to the physical form of the city, its buildings which can be destroyed, its walls that may protect, and the citizenry who may suffer from unexpected, and often disastrous, events of many kinds. In some circumstances one might even argue that citizens have in fact been the source, and potentially the cause, of a disastrous event through poorly maintained urban environment, a lack of hygiene, civil unrest, uprising or riot. By taking a more thematic approach it isn't possible to include every possible event or conflict in history chronologically. Neither is it my intention to imply that there has been a continual line in the way disaster has been dealt with or the type of authority used to deal with danger. There is no straight line of change that can be charted from an origin to the present. It has been suggested, however, that one can better trace changes that have occurred in the resilience of different forms of authority or urban forms which, as they interplay, coalesce into particular alignments of complex interdependency at different times. These are traceable as manifestations of social change in both order and *disorder*. Values, beliefs or scientific knowledge, the organisations involved in political and theological systems, as well as the technologies used to build great monuments and humble dwellings, all are forms that can be drawn into this analysis. The Bronze Age city-states eventually expired, as did the Athenian democracy and the city-state system of Ancient Europe, as did the Empires of Mesoamerica and of Rome, or the dynastic empires of China, and all for different reasons as the rhythms and patterns of interdependency drifted and changed. The previous chapter has outlined some insights into order and authority, as emerging from this interplay. Now a broad schematic emphasis is placed on disaster, war, (dis)order and the city. This is intended to apply interplay through a different lens, rather than looking at how the institutions and organisations are shaped through human agency this suggests that external influences clearly influence the conditions of possibility for change, affecting what is carried forward by whom in the realignment of order that emerges from the disorderly. It also will round out the historical aspect of the book with some critical pointers to trends of change in the modern day alignment of order and disorder in urban life (Part II) using a comparable framework.

Chapter 2 set out the conceptual tools; Chapter 3 began to apply these to order and authority; this chapter will apply these tools to disaster, war and disorder. Put simply, the trajectory of change is interrogated by applying the more abstract theory discussed previously to concrete empirical evidence. This allows the analyst to trace key stimulating influences on change in the urban social order, in action identifying the incremental shift towards a 'tipping point' where a different way of being, a different way of doing things, a different form of ordering our experiences may emerge from the ongoing interplay. It is not straightforward to unpack the role that disasters have played in change over time. It is perhaps slightly simplified by a focus on urban disasters, but only slightly. What follows will piece together information from a number of sources across a range of disciplines. The reward is tantalising glimpses into the intuitive nature of an archaeological turn in the spatial history of change, order and disorder.

Urban Hazard and Environmental Crisis

There is often a relationship that verges on a symbiosis between the stability and continuance of a social order and the patterns of the natural environment. These relationships can be far more complex than simple desires for the fulfilment of basic needs or the manipulation of passive resources subject to human harvest. Beliefs, rules and norms are connected through institutions to the natural world. This may take the form of cultural and religious practices, the trace evidence of which can be teased from the practical design of a home, temple, street, farm, village or town. Such archaeological evidence begins to give insight into why settlement may have occurred in that particular location.

Changes to the environmental equilibrium can stimulate the movement and settlement of whole civilisations. So in understanding the order and disorder of early settlements it is necessary to engage with environmental crisis. One may think of this in terms of the particular hazard agent (e.g. cyclone, earthquake, volcanic eruption), but systemic climate change[1] brings to light the interdependency of ecological factors in the access to resources (for hunting, farming, building, trade, worship, etc.). This interdependency can cause unpredictable shifts in the logic for staying or going when faced with environmental crisis. Perhaps most significant in our thinking is often the disaster or catastrophe, and never more

---

1   It should be noted that in this context it is not the politicised debate over the natural or human *cause* of climate changing that I am referring to rather the recognised ecological processes underpinned by scientific evidence.

than when so dramatic is the event that it leaves legends of destruction – such as Sodom and Gomorrah or Pompeii. When the environmental calamity strikes the repercussions can affect not just cities, but whole civilisations. A major climate event can irrevocably alter an economy, culture and whole way of life. A more detailed taxonomy of disaster types is offered later (Chapter 7), but environmental considerations must form part of the discussion in the struggle for the city in history; important not only because of the disaster event but the creative ways in which the potential for danger was differently managed, organised for and designed out in innovative ways, rendering different communities, cities and civilisations resilient in different ways. A prime example of such organised environmental management is the dependence of some early Indus and Nile Delta settlements on seasonal flooding for irrigation, enriching cultivation and harvest from local flood plains. Without seasonal flooding the mineral-rich earth that stimulated subsistence agriculture would have yielded poor harvest, created a vulnerable dependency on the annual cycle.[2] Drought and flooding can also play a decisive role in the destruction of settlements as well as their survival. In one case, the shifting sediment and stable mud-flats that supported agriculture led to land erosion. The resulting subsidence had a catastrophic impact, eventually altering the flow of the Nile at its North-Eastern Delta so much as to completely submerge the Eastern Canopus and Herakleion, dated around 750 AD (Stanley et al., 2001).

Riverine flooding is also a danger, but one that has often been manageable by the construction of levees and dams, for example on the Yellow River, the Rhine, the Danube and Po rivers. Evidence suggests that much flood management was highly organised during several early Chinese Dynasties. In Ancient China water was also seen as a tool of warfare, and the flooding out of armies was used as a legitimate tactic (Cheng, 2009: 13–14). Flooding and fire, also, are significant features of the ecological landscape in China. Some of the earliest organised farming (as much as 7,700 years ago) harnessed both fire clearance and flooding for cultivating rice (Zong et al., 2007). Further, arguably the first typological approach to disaster management was developed in China as long ago as 2,500 years, citing Guanzi, *On Land Appraisement*:

> A man who is adept at running a state should eliminate Five Hazards. One is flood; one is drought; one is harmful weather including storm, fog, hail and frost; one is pestilence, and one is fire. These are called the Five Hazards. Flood is the most severe one among the Five Hazards. (Cheng, 2009: 108)

As an early typology of hazards, this has much in common with more modern risk registers (see Chapter 7) and shows that systematic approaches to ecological dangers have long been a feature of social ordering.

---

2   The UNESCO project on water diversity has highlighted the importance of such a resource for the identity of some contemporary tribal societies (UNESCO, 2008).

Another example of the danger posed by ecological hazards is evident in the destructive force of volcanic eruption. The Bronze Age eruption of the island of Thera, part of the Santorini archipelago in the Aegean Sea, may have been the downfall of the palatial Minoan city of Akrotiri. The city and surrounds have shown signs of habitation and settlement from as early as the fourth century BCE, and Akrotiri appears to have been a major centre of the Minoan civilisation. The eruption of the Thera volcano had widespread repercussions for the development of the area, the nature of production across Minoan civilisation, and had a knock-on effect on the urban environment, the economy and the political stability of the civilisation. The disaster was central to destabilising Minoan influence over the region, laying the conditions of possibility for an expansion of Mycenaean culture from the mainland, leading to Mycenaean domination of the area for some years (Driessen and Macdonald, 2000). Some evidence also suggests that the tsunami linked to this eruption could have affected the restructure of civilised power throughout the region and the long-term transition of power in the area towards Greece and Rome (Antonopoulos, 1992). The eventual decline of the Mycenae Empire, from roughly 1200 BCE, may also have been triggered by a combination of ecological and economic crises, themselves stimulated by an inability to absorb the roving populations displaced by other climactic events into institutions and organisations of the day (Castleden, 2005).

If Akrotiri was the equal of Pompeii in architecture, civilisation and population in its most celebrated time, Pompeii gives us another example of the impact a natural disaster can have (De Boer and Sanders, 2001). The eruption of Mount Vesuvius in 79 AD was in fact so powerful as to engulf the cities of Pompeii, Herculaneum, Oplonti and Stabiae (Giacomelli et al., 2003). An interesting ecological feature of the disaster was that each of these settlements was affected differently. Archaeological evidence shows the destruction from the eruption to be widespread from a combination of air-fall pumice ejected by the eruption (leading to widespread asphyxiations and building collapses in Pompeii), 'ground-surge' in the form of a cloud of volcanic ash and hot gases sweeping at ground level (affecting Stabiae, Oplonti and Herculaneum), compounded throughout the region by the better-known pyroclastic flow or 'pyroclastic density currents' (PDCs) of molten rock (Sigurdsson et al., 1982; Luongo et al., 2003). Even one ecological disaster can have widespread effects; despite the comparatively advanced architectural technologies of the time, no single urban defence strategy could possibly have encompassed all of these hazards. Whilst the pyroclastic flow is relatively easy to avoid for people but causes massive destruction of land and property, the 'ground surge' is deadly to human life but leaves the infrastructure largely intact. There are also socio-political ramifications to be considered. Pompeii had been involved heavily in the 'Social War', and was in a state of rebellion or civil war with the capital in 90 BCE; the conflict was not long, lasting around a year, and the victory of the Roman army was convincing. Nonetheless, Roman hegemony over the Samnite region of Italy had been threatened. The eruption effectively ended any potential future threat to the authority of Rome from Pompeii or any of the settlements in the province, effectively allowing a re-concerted control over the region by the established Roman authority for years to come.

Another common disaster in history is the earthquake. Earthquakes have affected many settlements, with myths of cities damaged or destroyed completely by a combination of volcanic or tectonic activity – often the 'cascade effect' (when one problem triggers another problem elsewhere)[3] of related tsunami or flooding, resource shortages and generalised disorder from the destruction of infrastructure heighten the impact of earthquakes considerably, a common problem of many earthquakes even today. Earthquakes are depicted many times in the Old Testament of the Christian bible, invoking the wrathful God:

> He stood, and measured the earth: he beheld, and drove asunder the nations; and the everlasting mountains were shattered, the perpetual hills did bow: his ways are everlasting. (Habakkuk 3: 6)

Such references are perhaps unsurprising given that Palestine and Jordan lie on tectonic fault lines throughout the region, and there are many other references to earthquakes in the Bible (De Boer and Sanders, 2004: 22–45). Another well-known example from the Ancient world is Constantinople (Byzantium), which was shaken as early in recorded history as 342 BCE, and frequently thereafter (Downey, 1955). Many vulnerable islands and developed coastal areas in history, as well as recent times, have not been exempt from this risk, as seen in Thailand [2007], Samoa [2009] and Haiti [2010]. One earthquake in particular, the Lisbon earthquake in 1755, has been reinterpreted as perhaps the first 'truly modern disaster' (Dynes, 1997), in so far as:

> The earthquake occurred when there were many strains between tradition and new ideas about progress. It was a time when traditional ideas and institutions were being challenged, when nation states were being created, and when rivalries among states led to tensions and conflict. Further, it was a time when the bonds of traditional religious authority were being challenged by a growing enthusiasm for intellectual freedom and for reason. These major political and institutional shifts were reflected in the meanings that were assigned to the Lisbon earthquake. (Dynes, 1999: 2)

Any of the above ecological/environmental hazards can act as a trigger for disorder potentially undermining the stability of established authority. It can expose the negative resilience of a population and/or coalition to disorder from refugees, or even to military attack from those neighbouring coalitions that were less affected. The processes of economic production, consumption, exchange and subsistence can be disrupted, creating further disasters in the form of disease or civil unrest.

---

3   This is returned to in Chapters 7 and 8, but a good introduction to cascade effect literature is Kinzig et al. (2006).

Equally, different forms of knowledge can give different reasons for the physical or spiritual agent of disaster, challenging established forms of thinking with new interpretations of the factors that create such cataclysms. Such shifts in knowledge can inform the resultant actions one should take to deal with the impact and disorder, from prayer to the building of dykes and dams or even the abandonment of the site entirely. These diverse layers of interplaying forms and factors can be drawn out as the doorstep 'conditions of possibility' for 'regime shifts' and cascading change, through which actors create or influence the trajectory by potentially challenging the meta-stable equilibrium of the dominant order at multiple levels. In the case of Pompeii, the threat of civil unrest and opposition to the Roman elite was removed through the destruction of the underlying problem, i.e. the rival coalition/elite lost its power base as represented by the city. The same could be said of the fall of Akrotiri for the Minoan civilization, and subsequently for Mycenae. In the case of Lisbon one might argue that the reflections of Voltaire and Rousseau, amongst others, represented a shift towards the wider scientific and philosophical Enlightenment, which undermined – and replaced in some cases – the power of religious or theological knowledge and religious elites. This can be seen as indicative of the regime shift towards scientists and intellectuals as the dominant moral authority, exhibiting the wider realignment in the beliefs, rules and norms of urban ordering as it becomes something else. As Aradau and van Munster (2011) surmise, the 'catastrophic event was both entwined with the existing politics of knowledge and was among the conditions of possibility for the emergence of new modes of knowledge' (Ibid.: 125).

To summarise, environmental hazards should be seen as key forms that can actively influence the meta-stable equilibrium of a civilisation in both positive and negative forms of resilience. Such events have also clearly had an influence on the interplay of anthropological, technological and evolutionary resilience over time. On the one hand, anthropomorphic cultural traditions can establish 'forms-of-doing' that are often formative of *nomic* order – in the worship of natural sites such as volcanoes, sacrifice to a vengeful deity or even the representation of disaster as the will of a deity requiring appeasement – and inform beliefs, rules and norms. Disaster events can perpetuate an anthropomorphic myth or legend; as noted previously, God's destruction of Sodom and Gomorrah follows this pattern. From another perspective the loss of the luxury resort and fertile farming resources could have upset the balance of Roman authority in the region, but equally could be seen as removing a potentially antagonistic power base by eliminating much of the Pompeian elite. In the case of Lisbon poet and philosopher Voltaire, in his 'poem on the Lisbon Earthquake', as well as in *Candide*, and Rousseau, in discussion and letters to Voltaire, both weighed in on the philosophical import of the disaster, contesting the theological and scientific explanations (Dynes, 1999). The planning and reconstruction of the city also embodied this realignment through the bureaucratic governance of the Marquês de Pombal reflecting the rise of civil bureaucracy over pastoral religious authority forms. The challenge to the power of the aristocracy, the Inquisition and the Jesuit elite in Portugal, were manifest in the inspiration for government reform undertaken by the Marquis de Pombal following the earthquake. His effort, as the Minister of State for Portugal, to use a scientific rationale and bureaucratic power was a direct challenge to established ways of thinking, doing and acting. It both explained and reacted to the *cause* and the *impact* of the disaster using a non-religious logic, and was perceived as a direct threat to social order. He undermined the knowledge base of existing religious organisations, banished members of established elites, replacing them with his own family members, and undertook structural reform equating to a third of the positions in government being replaced (Dynes, 1997: 10–13). This reorganisation of power allowed for a direct and collective response to the effects of disaster by state organisations. Importantly, this still limited access to organisations to the elite, the organisations were unsustainable beyond the lifecycle of the individuals. However, the new elite challenged the established social order through a policy mobilisation of natural philosophical methods and civil bureaucratic governance. A regime shift may have been primed by thinkers such as Voltaire and Rousseau, but in Lisbon it was triggered by exposure to the earthquake and the actions of Pombal. Subsequent writings on Lisbon by Immanuel Kant have even been attributed as the birth of the modern science of seismology (Fuchs, 2008: 47–49) and utilising scientifically based evidence for the consequences of such disasters (de Almeida, 2008: 160). In any of the above examples it is clear that resilience to environmental and ecological hazards has had a significance influence on patterns of change in history.

Disease and Disaster

Another disruption to order with potentially disastrous impact is disease. This might be the disease itself, but equally the interplay of medical knowledge or technology with other forms of knowledge is just as important to understanding the relationship between disease and disaster. Institutional values, organisations, environment and so on can all act as influential forms in this interplay, encouraging the conditions of possibility for a disease to take root or, equally, preventing or eradicating such conditions.

An interesting approach to the study of disease in this context can be found in the identification of pathological conditions in human remains championed by Ortner and Putschar (1981), and the sub-fields of paleoepidemiology, paleopathology and bioarchaeology.[4] Such approaches draw primary evidence from skeletons and biological remains, and secondary evidence from iconography or documentary evidence of the period. There are, of course, problems and limitations in both sources of this type. For example, on the one hand, placing documentary evidence in a socio-cultural and historical context with any degree

---

4 For a more comprehensive review of the development of paleoepidemiology and bioarchaeological analysis of human remains, see Waldron (2007) or Buikstra and Beck (2006) respectively.

of accuracy, and on the other hand, tracing diseases of the soft tissue in relation to skeletal remains which cannot yield data on such topics can make ascertaining fact quite tricky (Roberts and Manchester, 2007). However, verifiable evidence can help to give weight to an argument when these sources are brought together in giving us a better idea of what is likely to have happened in the life of a given individual. This might not allow us to make broad-brush statements of truth but it can perhaps help to underpin ideas about the trajectory of a disease over longer periods of time – factoring in the interplay of socio-economic, cultural, technological and environmental factors when we widen our gaze.

Paleopathology and the archaeological anthropology of disease in the city have shown that the biological is another form inherently connected to the technological, the political, the economic, psychological, cultural and the spatial ordering of different periods. The most commonly acknowledged diseases in history are the plagues and epidemics (e.g. small pox, bubonic plague). These often begin with a high infection rate across a local population but with potential for widespread infection and a high mortality rate. The spread or origin of a disease may not necessarily be connected to human actions; pools of water which can become stagnant can occur in the natural world (e.g. from rainfall) or through human intervention in the environment (poorly located wells) for example. The spread of a disease through contaminated food or water or by parasites which thrive in crowded living conditions have shown that the process of urbanisation was central to the spread of disease in the industrial world. Predating modern medicine or sanitation, the knowledge that cats were familiars of the devil led to widespread killing of the animal, which only allowed the fleas and vermin hosts to spread the disease faster. Equally, ignorance of stagnant water supplies and pollution from urban industries caused widespread public health problems in the cities of the time. Quarantine and environmental sanitation (e.g. airing of homes and burning corpses and their possessions) were seen as the most effective countermeasures to stop the spread of diseases (Rosen, 1993: 209). Changing cultural or social practices can inhibit or enable the spread of disease as well as environmental conditions, both of which remain central to the mediation of AIDs on the African continent today.

The role of urban form, the organisations and institutions that dominate an urban social order, have as such been inextricably bound to the influence of disease on social change throughout history. There are, however, many problems in such an undertaking. Problems emerge in analysing the visible and invisible aspects of disease. How can the symptom and the language used to embed that which is seen in a patient be drawn together into a comprehensive view of the disease in history? It is often the case that the knowledge through which disease is understood, or absence thereof, plays a significant role. The links we might make in the modern world between hygiene, public health, disease and death are noticeable by their absence in many of the discussions surrounding disasters of this type in the knowledge of the time. The discursive formation of knowledge can emerge from the interplay of these institutional values (e.g. religious fervour or devotion), the influence of particular organisations (such as the church) presenting particular representations of disease, bio-political interventions in the separation and/or isolation of the afflicted can have impacts on spatial organisation. The interplay here is a drift in the alignment of thinking, doing and acting for the representation and management of illness.

One useful example is the generic representation of disease as a curse of the Gods in the classical writings of Herodotus, Homer (and even frequently in the Christian Bible). A more analytical presentation of 'facts' was undertaken by Thucydides, who described symptoms and specific conditions of affliction in an epidemic during the siege of Athens at the hands of Sparta during the Peloponnesian War. Whilst the specific disease in question in the Athenian case is widely disputed (Longrigg, 1980), two points can be made. First, the knowledge through which medical facts were presented (i.e. as a discursive formation of a given truth) were situated in the event, in this case a siege. The institutionalised myths and cultural traditions contrasted with scientific and medical knowledge (e.g. hygiene, sanitation, etc.). The balance of such discursive formations in presenting a given truth changes depending on the interplay of dominant institutions, as well as the forms and status of scientific knowledge or technological interventions available. Second, if the evidence provided by Thucydides (in the Athenian case) is to be given any weight, there were noticeable changes in the balance of institutionalised values as a result of the outbreak: a discursive transformation occurred. Specifically, reference is made to the willingness (or the decline of this in the face of almost certain death) of Athenians to accept suffering for the wider public good. This is a value at the heart of the logical democratic social order of the time. Traditional burial rites were abandoned and widespread despair has been recorded in this account as leading many citizens to engage in rapacious self-satisfaction or hedonism. In the face of a doubly grim fate of either death by disease or at the hands of the Spartan host outside the city – which was unaffected by the outbreak – such pressures on the social order caused widespread upheaval and even abandonment of the accepted standards of behaviour underwriting everyday life. Similar stories of a breakdown in coping capacity can be found in other historical records, perhaps not often of debauchery, but certainly civil unrest. More recently, the bubonic plague outbreak in Early Modern Russia saw attempts to enforce quarantine over affected urban areas. In 1654 this led to widespread civil unrest in Moscow, and in 1770–1771 to bloody and violent riots (Alexander, 2002).

As noted above, the forms of knowledge at play can have significant impacts on the conditions of possibility within the lifespan of an illness, as can wider environmental conditions (urban and rural), institutionalised relations and organisations with the authority to direct actions. The interplay of these forms can result in a range of outcomes, none of which are certain, but which can all be reflected upon in retrospect to learn valuable lessons. There can be a precarious balance between the environmental and/or biological conditions, knowledge of the causes and likely path of a disease, the ability of civil government to act, the potential fear and panic of the population, institutionalised values from religious as well as scientific versions of 'truth'; all can play a role. In some circumstances – typically when there is a high mortality rate attached to the outbreak – one may see the emergence of particular strategies of denial and containment intended to integrate death itself into the everyday, thus rendering the ever-present macabre spectacle of death acceptable to the requirements of maintaining social order. The reorientation of conditions, relations and institutions or organisations that comprise and constitute order are clearly of note in understanding the pattern of interplay and the trajectory of change. This pattern is perhaps different from the disaster or catastrophe of a volcanic eruption, tsunami or earthquake, but certainly within the same spectrum of influence as recognisable perturbations of the social order. Again, this can be unpredictable. In the case of the Latin American expansion, the Conquistadors were able to dominate not simply by technological superiority but by the impact of smallpox, which they introduced to the continental population with devastating impact, on the city of Tenochtitlan in particular (Pohl and Hook, 2001). In the case of European colonial expansion onto the African continent, the particular infections affecting both colonisers and colonized; the ability to reduce and/or cure diseases played a different role in the supplanting of local social ordering. The predetermined (however erroneous) sense of superiority underpinning colonial expansion allowed an assumed moral justification for the manipulation of local cultural and ethnic differences. One part of this process was the mobilisation of medical knowledge on related issues such as sanitation, but in others through the Christianisation of indigenous medical practices which were dismissed as at best superstitious hokum and at worst witchcraft or magic (Korieh and Njoku, 2007).

The impact of disease on all social order is as a mediated form of knowledge within particular conditions of possibility. It also engenders technical and technological interventions in time–space–place in a different way from ecological or environmental danger. Foucault (2003 [1963]) connects to these topics in *The Birth of the Clinic* to the languages and spatial ordering of medical knowledge at the roots of modern medical science. Through the approach to life and death as a discursive formation, the knowledge that gives us an understanding of the causes of life and death become more legible as another form of note. Cascade effects in medical knowledge are often seen as immanent to the patient, through the internal risks to the patient of a treatment when diagnosis may be imperfect or incomplete. However, the resilience of institutions and organisations can also be sorely tested by biological dangers, as can other interdependent systems. Whilst the biological framing here suggests disease is influential in both the ecological and the biological, in both cases the human agent is also a factor of uncertainty. As such, perhaps the most influential dangers are those that emerge from within the human condition – from conflict, war and civil unrest.

Conflict, War and the Urban

Conflict can be ambiguous and takes on many forms, be it the conflict between individuals, between coalitions or even within particular elites. Warfare is at first glance easier to define. Our contemporary assumption is that warfare is an organised conflict governed by formal rules of engagement between the armies of two sovereign nation-states. However, this is a very limited view of warfare. Unpacking the conditions and relations of war as a form of conflict is a point of departure, but treating war as a perturbation to a social order helps to better interrogate particular (re)alignments in the resilience of institutions and organisations. The discussion of forms allows us to draw on strategies, tactics, technologies, architecture, politics, economics and ideology as forms within the interplay. This is linked later (Chapter 6) to the order of the post-industrial city and entrepreneurial capitalism, using the same method with a more intense focus. Here, by building on the previous discussion of authority and urban order, the importance of the human in creating, destroying and manipulating (even unintentionally) the conditions of possibility for conflict are expanded in more depth. Many of the classic texts that discuss war have tended to be somewhat dismissive of conflict in aboriginal, tribal and indigenous cultures, preferring instead to focus on the features of conflict contemporary to their time of writing. This can lead to a somewhat generic treatment of the myth of the peaceful savage, for whom violence is inherent to the human condition. It can also lead to an equally generic treatment of primitive and ritualised low-intensity conflict that does not really address the nuances of what actually happened. Any analysis is thus limited, and any typology or genealogy placed on a shaky foundation. The tendency is, as a result, to give a presumptive view of modern tactics, strategies and techniques of conflict as somehow superior to those of the 'noble savage', and the only understanding of conflict that is relevant is one which takes the Peace of Westphalia in 1648 as the point of departure for analysis. Debunking this myth gives some insight into the importance of war, but also its complexity, opening up other aspects and types of conflict for analysis as key forms, features and stimuli of change.

Myths and Concepts of Ancient Conflict

Quincy Wright (1942) and Holbert Turney-High (1949) are potentially two of the most influential writers of the twentieth century on the subject of early forms of conflict. Quincy Wright identifies in his text *The Study of War* that context is vital to the act of definition:

> It [war] began with animals in the psychological sense. It began with primitive people, untouched by civilised neighbours in the sociological sense. It began with civilisation in the legal sense. Only since the advent of continuous

world-cultural contacts in the fifteenth century has war existed in the modern
technological sense. (Wright, 1964 [1942]: 25)

War is here treated as amorphous, with multiple sensical framings. By contrast,
Turney-High may have titled his book *Primitive Warfare* (1949 [1979]), but
only insofar as the term was oxymoronic. The advent of that which could truly
be considered warfare was defined through the technologies, strategies and
tactics of the modern era. Both Turney-High and Wright acknowledge a certain
animalistic and psychological need underpinning 'primitive' war, in stark contrast
to the economic, political or material gain associated with 'civilised warfare'.
A counterpoint to these works is provided by Keeley (1996) in his attempt to
debunk the myths of peaceful savages engaged in largely ineffective low-intensity
conflicts. Analysis of archaeological evidence of conflict between primitive tribes
notes that the predetermined concepts of scale, technology and conduct do not
hold water under scrutiny. Keeley suggests that warfare in the pre-historic world
was equally as serious and devastating as its modern counterpart. Rather than
being inferior, 'primitive' warfare was rather war reduced down to the essentials
– i.e. killing, incapacitating or terrorising an adversary whilst staying alive by any
means necessary. War in both the 'primitive' and the 'modern' sense is the use of
power through relations of force to dominate, repress or eliminate opposition. This
stripping of war down to its essentials suggests that it is, in fact, modern warfare
that is often the more ritualised, stylised and beholden to abstract legal rules and
cultural *mores*. Such rules are often so complex they can only be applied when
the conflict is between similar groups (i.e. nation states), leading to Clausewitz's
aphorism that 'war is the continuation of politics by other means'. Politics is
used here in its broadest sense as the interplay of institutional forms of doing
manifest in the authority of particular organisations at a given time. Foucault
suggests inverting this aphorism to '*politics* is the continuation of *war* by other
means' (Foucault, 1997 [1975]: 15, emphasis added) as a means to rebalance these
assumptions; in this sense, 'war' was first, 'politics' came later.

This returns us to an earlier suggestion that at the root of all organisational
ordering is the (often not so) silent threat of force, and the perception of the
legitimate right of an organisation to use that force in opposition to an 'other'.
Such is evidenced by the form and conduct of warfare in the colonial expansions
into Africa and the Americas. In both of these cases, when the 'civilised' rules of
engagement are suspended, the advantage goes to the most resilient forces. The
superiority of the civilised in the face of less technologically advanced cultures
was less a strategic or technological superiority but more often than not superior
resilience to the diseases that were either brought with the colonising forces or
intentionally spread by them, such as smallpox, measles and the like. Another
potential myth is that as the size of a population increases, the likelihood of
conflict with others also increases. Statistical evidence suggests that population
density is less a cause of war than economic exchange and inter-marriage, as
such frequency of contact between groups is more likely to be an indicator of

potential conflict than size. Though where population density is connected to the exchange of resources (including those required for breeding) there may be some links, but these are hard to verify (Keeley, 1996: 117–120). Perhaps the most significant difference Keeley identifies is one of logistics (Ibid.: 175). The very institutions and organisations that are the foundation of tribal societies and settlements (discussed in the previous chapter) allow for systems of authority to emerge, but they often require multiple specialisms from members of the society, e.g. the hunter-warrior. The scale and circadian patterns of such orders often prohibit the use of, for example, siege tactics or prolonged military campaigns. Rather, they tend to emphasise the highly successful guerrilla tactics of small, temporary, flexible and mobile forces in which all members of the group have the potential to become citizen-combatants of a sort. Committing a large, professional military force with sustained supply lines is inimical to the pattern of the small-settlement tribal bands, as is the professionalisation of the duty to fight if required. Perhaps it is ironic, but certainly not amusing, that a return to guerrilla tactics in the modern world by smaller, technologically inferior forces has been proven to cause problems for the 'civilised' armies of the West in any number of more recent conflicts. Relations of authoritative force are embedded into the institutions, organisations and operations of everyday life. This is significant in understanding the conditions of possibility for change, and the trajectory that change may take, in the interplay of conflict and order. Further, in many cases the inability to distinguish between friends and enemies, such as the lawful bearer of arms and the citizen-combatant, are forms dependent on other systems (such as the rule of law or rules of engagement).

Typology, War and Analysis

What we know about war changes with the historical context. It is not a static or scientific process. Nonetheless, war does often refer to a martial or military 'science', thus conflict is another process subject to scientific scrutiny (Vasquez, 2000). Each type of conflict has distinct repercussions for how we understand the role and nature of danger, but also of the institutions, organisations and wider forms of influence affecting such conflict over time. However, as we have seen, we can also look further back and include examples of conflict from ancient orders to widen our view. As such, it is useful to visit a typology of conflict to apply the topic to a wider set of examples. Such examples give us a sense of how patterns of change that I am trying to draw out in this analysis can come together differently at different times, or reflect similar trends, even centuries apart. One broad typology has been offered by Chaliand as follows:

1. Ritualised wars – Archaic, traditional or tribal. Localised and often not to the death.
2. Wars with limited objectives – Potentially the modern version of a ritualised warfare moderated through laws in the modern age. Codified conduct for behaviour through

institutions or a social framework which are widely agreed upon by protagonists. Historically this could be represented by dynastic disputes. Evokes the medieval formal and ritualised conflict, e.g. battle of Agincourt.

3. Conventional wars of conquest – More predatory in objective seeking to coerce opponent into conformance with defined goal, lack of compromise as an outcome. May involve the annihilation of an enemy, or potentially satisfied with establishing military dominion such as in the case of the Conquistadors dominion of the South American empires, or US military dominion of the Native American Nations.

4. Mass wars – Absolute war, identified by Clausewitz. French Revolution, World War I and World War II. Annihilation of armed forces of the enemy through direct confrontation and potentially including collapse of civilian infrastructure and institutions as a result of widespread terror tactics (not limited to but including summary or mass executions, deportations or bombardment).

5. Wars without quarter – Typified by civil or religious warfare in which no quarter is possible for either protagonist. Examples are spread throughout history, including: The thirty years war, French wars of religion, civil war in the US (1861–65) and Russia (1918–20), religious conflict in India (1936–39), the Hindu–Muslim conflict in India (1947–48) and potentially including the recent evolution of non-state vs. state-coalition combatants in the war on terror. (Chaliand, 1994: 7–8)

Chaliand does attempt to exclude the conflicts of 'primitive societies' from his presentation of ritualised warfare in this typology. As such, it could be argued that this typology falls afoul of many of the assumptions in the study of 'primitive war' critiqued by Keeley (1996). All too often, the causes of war at different periods of history, if not the goals, methods and outcomes, are all too similar – often, but not always being (a) economic (access to resources or territory are included in this broad bracket), (b) religious and ideological (between competing 'faith-based' orthodoxy), or (c) retaliatory in response to a previous action (like-for-like cumulative vengeance). Causes of conflict, if not always war, can equally emerge from unexpected quarters, such as alliances or treaties placing obligations of mutual defence on the coalition member organisations, World War I being the obvious modern example. A typology of this type is a useful barometer for the wide range of conflict types, but is not a conclusive categorisation.

A further point of interest is in Chaliand's use of documentary analysis from key historical texts to show how ideological differences are embedded in religious, military, civil and historical texts. Such ideas are a key form for analysis to get at the concepts underpinning the form of war, be it a specific battle, a campaign or a broader trend in the historical period. Of course, some of these are born from ancient times, such as the hit and run guerrilla tactics of tribal groups. Others may be specific to thinkers who flourished due to technical or strategic innovations in their time, as seen in the innovative strategic interplay of the Napoleonic era. Perhaps related, the emergence of Clausewitz's concepts of 'trinitarian' warfare or Van der Golt's, and later Ludendorf's, understanding of 'Total War' each give us different perspectives on by whom a just war can be fought, what the purpose of war is and different ways to understand not just the rules of engagement but the terms and conditions of victory and defeat in different types of conflict (Van Creveld, 1991). Whilst authority may have been born from the shepherd and the hunter, the rules of conduct that became laws were forged in conflict, rules that are now widely recognised to have been formalised as conflict between sovereign nation-states since the 'Peace of Westphalia', a *nomic* international ordering that is supported or, at times, supplanted by the technological abilities of antagonists (we will return to this last point later).

What is offered in review of Chaliand's typology is by no means an exhaustive or comprehensive list of the varieties of conflict. The effort to create a typology can only ever produce a broad schema for understanding some prevailing characteristics as they emerge from the interplay of forms. Each type of war listed above evokes characteristics of particular social and spatial formations from which the causes of conflict are hard to place. The causes, methods and goals tend to cross over, giving an oscillatory effect to change within the ongoing interplay.

Rasler and Thompson's (1989) discussion of *War and State Making* draws on a similar logic where they clearly distinguish between global war and inter-state warfare in the attempt to show 'how specific types of war influenced specific types of state in a specific historical era', yet accepting that any discussion of the oscillations by which war emerges needs to include 'whatever evidence seems pertinent' (Rasler and Thompson, 1989: xvi). It is unclear from such an approach if all typologies must emphasise the tactics or logistical characteristics as separate from the causes or goals of a conflict, or if logistics and methods are simply the arena within which differences are most readily apparent. All the conditions of possibility within which conflict emerges appear to be influenced, in whole or in part, by these contextual variables, and each takes on different weight in the context of the specific conflict. Why the Crusades? Why the First World War? Why the Peloponnesian War? Why Vietnam? All come forth from different alignments in the oscillation of forces at play, all emerge from different coalescing forms at the given time and place. The nature of aggression, the defensive requirements of resources or locations, the generalised threat a population must face within a defined territory, all are certainly significant and must be considered alongside wider issues such as institutional beliefs or values, events that may engender retaliation, doctrinal or ideological differences in religion or government, economic tensions, resource demands and so on. Such tensions may be fleeting or transitory but can also last over very long cycles of conflict. Perhaps the most relevant example for later chapters is that of the Christian and Islamic social orders which have been in constant flux between conflict and peace since at least the seventh century AD, but the nature, form and conduct of that conflict is very different at each conflagration.

In offering his typology of war, Chaliand highlights the need for a wider lens in thinking about conflict, suggesting that the aging of the population, birth rates, immigration and achieving relative political and social peace can be seen as more, or at the least equally, significant than the purely military aspects of defence (Chaliand, 1994: 46). More often than not it appears as though the interplay between the technology of warfare, the tactics and strategy of the enemy and the strategic thinking ingrained in a given culture coalesce into a system of practical necessity, engendering a series of logical responses to the risks faced particular to that specific conflict. Such a process is historically contingent upon changes to ecological and social pressures, but also to technological opportunities for a range of engagements.[5] Conflict becomes the connection of distinct engagements that, when aggregated, amount through the resilience or fragility of systemic interdependencies in the survival or destruction of a way of life.

Conflict is thus another crucible by which a social order may be tempered, transformed or even broken, thus becoming something else. Only broad trends can be drawn from each example of conflict, and most often this is in strategic or tactical thinking by learning from what went wrong, rather than what went right. As we can see, using 'war without quarter' as our example in the typology offered by Chaliand above, the examples of conflict given to illustrate war without quarter as a 'type' occur across a span of several hundred years. The conditions of possibility from which these conflicts emerged cannot be the same in each instance, nor can the strategies and tactics or technologies used to fight them. What has been traced here are some rough examples of how these conflicts promoted a change in institutional beliefs and values, in theories of the nature of conflict, in the organisations such as the military, the governing body or even the order of tribe, city-state, nation-state.

Such transformative processes at work in the everyday lives of citizens within the body politic have a lasting impact on features of a social order, leaving traces of trends of social change that might be drawn together into a trajectory over time. Some of these dominant trends have to be acknowledged. In terms of warfare this might include the treatment of warfare between sovereign, representative nation-states since the Peace of Westphalia, for example (Schmitt, 2003 [1950]: 145). It is this wider trajectory that we return to in the final analysis of this discussion of social order and social change. Having discussed some of the ways in which conflict can be developed as a key form in the perturbation or transformation of social order, it is useful to return again to the theme of urban form itself, alongside this wider focus on conflict, to show how these complexities can be drawn out further.

---

5   Nomadic armies, for example, are often dependent on resources and technology but can have long-lasting impact, despite the emphasis earlier here on settlement as a part of the urbanisation process. Settlers and sedentary social orders have not always been the most stable in the face of military threats; for example, the Huns, Avars, Mongols and Vikings have all played significant roles in perturbation of settlement-based social orders.

Conflict and Fortification

Conflict was something that has been proven to be far more commonplace than has previously been thought but, as the links between authority, order and disorder have been tied to settlement, technological advancement and the increased complexity and interdependency of a wide range of systemic forms, we need to revisit this feature of the urban form before moving on. Perhaps most regularly discussed in the history of urban conflict is the role of fortification. Fortification is tied to the concept of defending a location from hostile attack. Natural formations provide the most basic fortifications, but fortification of the settlement and of the city throughout history have not been undertaken only for military defence. Whilst fortified settlements or encampments have often acted as retreats or refuges during periods of heightened conflict, they have also often been located at a site of economic exchange or where there is a resource of strategic importance, such as the arable land and water in the Rhine-rift valley of Alsace (Ashworth, 1991: 16). Fortifications, in the common form of walls, take on multiple meanings beyond the immediately obvious military defence. Walls can form the boundary of an elite residence, or a symbolic boundary around the site of burial for particular social castes (Chang, 1991: 157). They may house the military in fortresses, enclaves and training grounds separate from non-military specialists (Parker, 1988). Such separation can be enacted to distinguish status, ownership or security, and walls can be used to separate demographics within the population or to separate insiders from outsiders by placing boundaries around whole settlements.

Fortifications are also often found along the territorial frontier. They are far less common amongst nomadic peoples due to the labour and resource-intensive nature of such endeavours. Rarely could early semi-permanent fortifications be thought of as cities, but as evidence from the early city-states of the Indus valley shows, fortifications are a regular feature of larger settlements; the same is true of dynastic China. Each fortification needs to be placed into the historical context of interplay between socio-cultural, juridical, political, economic, technological, environmental, architectural and artistic forms. From farms to walled castles to market places and more this remains the case.

Amongst the earliest fortified cities that can be verified by documentary evidence is the city of Jericho in 8000 BCE, the city of Çatal Höyük in 6500–5500 BCE, and the Sumerian city-state Uruk around 2900 BCE (Tracy, 2000). Evidence suggests the building of the brick walls of Uruk can be attributed to the legendary Gilgamesh. This cannot be verified conclusively as the evidence comes from an inscription heralding tribute to the war leader, dated to repair work on the walls conducted around the eighteenth century BCE (George, 2003: 90). Regardless, this would suggest that this early city was fortified by a significant brick wall of some size, which was later rebuilt and improved upon. The meaning and purpose of the walls changed over time, though it is difficult to confirm if the walls of Uruk were initially built for a ceremonial purpose or out of a defensive need: the symbolic value of their connection to Gilgamesh was a feature of the repair, but tells us little else. Walls of this type can be important for military defence, but equally their symbolic value is not the only peacetime role of fortification. Having an effective boundary in place around a conurbation allows the ruling elite, through guards and access points, to control entry and egress. This allows tighter control over the regulation of commodities within the city itself, the extraction of rents from trade, and thus limiting access of those inside the walls to products or ideas from outside. In some cases, fortifications also limited access to education institutions or to religious sites within the urban boundary (Lepage, 2002: 257). While it might not be unreasonable at a glance to suppose that frontier settlements were more likely to have some form of fortification for a military purpose, it is equally likely that formal fortifications or walls of stone were in place for other regulatory limitations of access to institutions and organisations. To assume a military defence was the only, or even primary, purpose of fortification is simply not supported by the evidence.

When reflecting on the scale of fortifications another point can be made about the nature, form and function of ordering. The size and permanence of the wall as an architectural form reflects the relative conditions of possibility for an organised authority to direct such construction work. A poorly organised group with an unstable internal structure is not as likely, perhaps, to be able to undertake a large-scale architectural project. A wall is more than a functional project, it is a brand of ownership on the landscape, an act of intent that symbolically states that ownership of this site by this group is permanent. The more stable the institutions of the group (cultural, economic, political beliefs, values or traditions) the more likely sustained work can be directed into mobilising the resources required. Though clearly some mysteries still abound and our best guess is all we can offer (e.g. Stonehenge on Salisbury Plain in England). In the case of city-states of roughly classified Ancient, Classical and Medieval periods (Hansen, 2000), fortifications were significant undertakings, but were not required for the stability or survival of settlements. The need to control access to markets during peacetime noted above draws us into an interesting link between the need for stable ordering in the formal military sense and the need for a civic ordering during peacetime, for which walls are one of a number of architectural forms that support social and cultural ordering practices. We will return to the issue of warfare in current times in later chapters, but for now it is to the issue of population control and the role that the public can play as a potential disruption within the interplay of urban everyday life.

Civil Unrest and Urban (Dis)Order

In the discussion of war it is too easy to forget that conflict is not always defined by the nation-state. Where institutions are shared through values and beliefs, coalitions can emerge from the powerless as well as the powerful. Some of the bloodiest examples of urban disorder have emerged from the populous as civil unrest. Often such conflagrations burst into being when the differences between individuals and inequalities between groups are forced into the open. It should be noted here that I am not referring to civil war – as the struggle for ascendancy of rule amongst elite coalitions of the powerful – nor explicitly of revolution and the overthrow of government – for example in the French Revolution. The particular point of contact for the discussion of disorder is where the policies of the ruling elite cause disruption in the everyday life of civilians – those not necessarily involved directly in coalitions with authority as used to rule, but subject members of the body politic, thus citizens. Examples of urban disorder and civil unrest direct use away from top-down appreciations of structural forms to the experience of the city in history. It highlights where a given order may be challenged by a competing set of interests, and where competition over access or unequal access can stimulate internal perturbations to the social order. Disorder is the counter-pole to order, and is equally important as a force of change. The struggle for the everyday life of the city can be used to open up fault lines between individuals, coalitions and powerful elites, at times triggering dramatic periods of positive and negative change. The disorder created by urban unrest, and even riot, can in some cases be seen as symptomatic of wider social problems and inequalities, perhaps emerging from abuses of power in a limited-access social order. It can also be seen as wanton opportunism by criminals and hooligans or as rational, selfish action to contravene the normal orderly flow of commerce for personal gain by alternative means. It may also be seen as the hysteria of 'the mob' destroying for the sheer joy of destruction. Regardless of the cause, purpose or intent of civil unrest it is a form of disorder – the breaking of rules through disorderly conduct – and is important in understanding the interplay of order and disorder.

Often, disorder can emerge when there are strict limitations of access focussed on resources tied to basic needs (e.g. housing, food), on organisations (e.g. government, guilds) or on institutions of betterment (e.g. education, vocations). This can cause unrest to the point of open opposition to the dominant elite. At such a point, a failure to address the inequalities by a dominant elite or coalition can result in civil unrest. One trigger point in circumstances of heightened tension can result in conflict. Failure to address institutional or organisational reform can trigger conflict. The fragility of social systems and high levels of interdependency is such that social problems can contribute to a lot of forms of civil unrest. Historically, violent repression is the first and last line of defence – especially if there are no strict limits placed on the legitimate use of violence by coalitions of rule. The particular circumstances and resultant resolution of civil unrest has obvious implications for the trajectory of change and the resultant reconstitution of beliefs, rules and norms.

Rome is a good case study of this process. Examples of urban disorder and civil unrest were arguably more dramatic in the city of Rome, but civil conflict was a regular feature of the Roman social order, and in fact a tool of politics throughout the whole Empire, not just in the capital. Civil violence was a legitimate tool that could be used to disrupt order – as a tactic to circumvent a Senate vote (*intercessio*). It was also a feature of market dynamics, for example in 'grain riots'. There is evidence to suggest that corn dealers, millers, bakers and large landowners were commended by local magistrates for undertaking violent uprising in protest against pricing controls (Nippel, 1995). Milder resource shortages are more likely to be absorbed by the institutional resilience of the populous, lacking the capacity to inflict more than temporary or mild unrest. The 'mob' was a Roman institution, to be respected and, at times, feared. Recorded conflict in the city in the sixth century can be attributed to regional, ethnic and family rivalries between the 'Seven Hills of Rome' or between circus and theatre partisans (Brown, 1998). Papal elections could also be a source of civil unrest and violence (Walsh, 2003). Demonstrations were frequent features of public gatherings, festivals and popular assemblies. *Mobile vulgus* could quite easily trigger conflict between communities and lead to the destruction of property in the city.[6]

Unrest among the population has not always turned violent as it frequently, but again not always, did in Rome. Throughout history, where there have been channels of legitimate protest built into constitutional or consumption frameworks – of the State and everyday life respectively – there is much less frequently adequate evidence of a riot taking place. Where access to organisations is institutionalised in more open processes, correspondingly the social order is more resilient to perturbations such as resource shortages (e.g. food). This can be said to be true of the Athenian model of assembly consultation and in the late-Republican Rome, where entertainment in theatres and hippodrome simulated contact with the people as a means of disseminating, even explaining in some limited sense, the economic or social policy as propaganda, a more publicly accessible format for information (Garnsey, 1989). These forms of interplay between the ruler and ruled are also often tied to specific architectural forms that are vital to the lived experience of the particular historical context, in the agora, the coliseum and theatre. Equally, the festival and peaceful protest are linked to the public spaces and public streets of the city, which to all intents and purposes are governed in public trust on behalf of the people by the ruling elite and the respective organisations of social order, but frequently are reclaimed in protest, be it violent or peaceful, in the enactment, undertaking, performance of civil unrest. The control of urban space is a significant feature of civil unrest and the landscape of struggle for control – as social ordering and the creation of disorder with equal measure.

It is important to link civil unrest with 'policing' organisations of social order and control, but not to call all these groups 'police'. Policing is a relatively modern concept, with distant etymological roots in the *polis* of Ancient Greece. At its most crude the policeman is a 'man of the city'. As an organisation they are tasked with maintaining social order and as an institution with building consensual processes for negotiating the form of that order between policemen and the community

---

6   *Mobile vulgus* refers to the Latin expression 'the fickle crowd'. Democracy may be 'the rule of the people' but during civil unrest this is all too easily capable of descending into a fragile ochlocracy or 'rule of the mob'.

'sometimes oiled by corruption, but more often sealed by favours and friendships' (Ignatieff, 1979). The result is a complex balance between an institutionalised and organisational function of the unenviable role, whereby the police stand between the rulers and ruled to maintain order and reduce or eliminate disorder. Further, it is usually a thankless task. Mladek (2007) makes this point well, reminding us:

> As the revolutions in France and America have shown, it is a crucial difference as to whether citizens perceive themselves as objects of administrative control or as subjects of the law. The recovery of early concepts of the police reveals that law and the police belong to completely different traditions and set out different goals and ideas about the role of government and the state. (Mladek, 2007: 2)

Policing is not the enforcement of law as directed by the ruler; it is often rather the enforcement of law in spite of the ruler. Should the police act upon the specific direction of the state they are no more than a branch of the military enforcing control of the populous, rather than negotiating the protection of the body politic. The role the police take is thus very different in different contexts. The historical context reflects the alignment of beliefs, rules and norms; the type of city and spaces; and the remits and legitimate actions available to those organisations involved in carrying out the enforcement of authority. The control of particular types of information and processes affects the ordering of individuals and locations. Policing as social 'ordering' functions so as to 'keep the peace', even ordering the rules of exchange between individuals and amongst communities. Such organisations have had a long history of negotiating and enforcing control – not just of the public forum but of the institutional rule of the elite – in forms of knowledge that are allowed to be distributed throughout the wider civilisation at a given time.

Throughout history there have been a range of organisations for enforcing social order, in ways similar to what we might now think of as the police but with distinctly different purposes from modern public policing. Organisations of what can, in a simplified sense, be called social control in many pre-industrial social orders were infrequently tied directly to government, rather to limited-access elite coalitions or special interest groups. One might argue that the formal policing of social order in its modern sense begins with the democratic nation-state, as prior to this there is far more evidence for (a) informal social and cultural controls – of the family, clan and community or established traditions for interaction – and (b) of the formal threat of reprisal embedded in authority mechanisms of theocratic or martial force held by a small elite or a sub-group of that elite – such as 'Knights-errant' in medieval aristocracy or the 'Inquisition' in Carolingian theocracy. In Saxon England the 'fyrd' was a military force used to maintain order, but it was one drawn upon as needed from amongst able-bodied men of age, a method echoed in the Cromwellian 'guards and garrisons' and local militia used for similar purposes until the establishment of the 'thief-taking' 'Bow Street Runners' – founded in 1749 by Lord Fielding in the face of a particularly violent outbreak of organised burglary – and later the 'Peelers' – established in London by the Police Act in 1829 – who were arguably the first modern non-military police force tasked with maintaining social order in the city.

An interesting example of the 'interplay between forms' that we have used to thread through the discussion thus far is the relationship between civil unrest and the development of organisations of social ordering, specifically distinct from military or direct forms of rule. England at the turn of the nineteenth century is a good case study of how the process of change can roll out. England, and Britain as a whole, had for a hundred years, from near 1760, been a land of increasing contestation over the alignment of institutions and the structure and power as used by elites in the Royal Court and in Parliament. By 1810 the economic fallout of stagnating trade to the Americas precipitated a collapse of several English banks. Whilst agriculture was still the major industry, combined spatial changes such as enclosure, expansion of canals and roads, and rapid industrial urbanisation placed the pressure for change firmly at the forefront of widespread public dissatisfaction with the state of government. The Napoleonic war had also caused problems in the process and price of importing grain, leading to the Corn Laws, which artificially inflated the price of grain to protect cereal producers in the UK – but contributed to growing poverty in many previously agrarian and subsistence farming communities. Pressure on the Poor Laws were increased, workhouses and failure to raise wages – in contemporary currency many families in 1811 would be earning 7–15 shillings[7] a week (Darvall, 1934: 20–21). This enhanced the social unrest amongst the emerging industrial working classes and resentment of the emerging industrial middle class of factory and mill owners. Following Waterloo in the June of 1815 soldiers returned home to a depleted England under strain; as soldiers were often conscripts of dissolute background this created further social and economic tensions. The mandatory billeting of soldiers was unpopular, with local families or tavern owners expected to bear the cost of housing and upkeep under already difficult conditions. Cavalry in the form of mounted Dragoons or Yeomanry were frequently used to keep down highwaymen in the period, but also as a means to disperse unruly crowds before they could turn into violent mobs.

Such was the concern over the use of violence against the people that it was a requirement that 'The Riot Act' of 1715 be read aloud to the crowd by a local magistrate before the military were able to use weapons to disperse a mob (hence 'reading the riot act'). This was far from easy, or consistently applied, when the mob may be throwing projectiles and wielding clubs or tools as weapons. So common was civil unrest and urban disorder that 'the mob' has been referred to as the 'fourth estate' of the British realm (Babington, 1990: 11–20). Babington further proceeds to use the Gordon Riots in London [1780] as a case in point (Ibid.: 20–31), where in calling for a repeal of the Catholic Relief Act, a march of some estimated 40,000–60,000 of the Protestant Association led by Lord

---

7   12–25 pounds in adjusted GBP (2012).

George Gordon. Subsequent arrests and rescue of arrested men by protesters led to outbreaks of violence – even where the Riot Act was read the mob turned on the Magistrates, burning several homes. During the three days of rioting that followed, the military were powerless to act, for the local magistrates were fearful that the mob may turn on them again, many thus refusing to read the Riot Act. The eventual intercession by the Monarchy and Parliament authorising military action was required to begin dispersing the crowd. As a result, the riot raged for several days and the subsequent debate over the appropriate use of military force under the Common Law raged for some time. The 'cherished irregularity' and 'licensed anarchy' of 'old England' (White, 1957: 33), dominated by the 'Whigs' and landed gentry of the country, was increasingly challenged by both widespread civil unrest and a new wave of radical reformers and rational industrialists.[8] The realignment of political, economic and religious orthodoxy during this period was to inform the balance of beliefs, rules and norms for much of the next 200 years (Royle and Walvin, 1982; Sack, 1993), but not without some further significant flashpoints.

Whilst being an exception rather than the rule of urban order, the events in Manchester at St Peter's Field [1819], later dubbed 'Peterloo', give another striking example of the problems of dealing with urban disorder and the importance of bringing into focus the forms that feed into the ongoing reconstitution of social order. The local watch or town constables were no better organised than during the Gordon riots, and both local and national government was often perceived as corrupt and ineffective. The highly organised cavalry were trained for war not policing (though had often never seen a battle), and other ordering institutions, such as public charity, did not go much further than the public soup kitchens and squalid workhouses. The Police Commission in Manchester was responsible for street cleaning, street lighting and oversight of the local constabulary and fire service, but the dispensation of justice remained with the local magistrates, who were largely former industrialists or Anglican ministers with little sympathy for the Non-Conformist reformers and radicals – the likes of Henry Hunt (chief speaker at Peterloo) and other radicals from the working classes (Read, 1958). Hunt and other agitators were seen as 'desperate demagogues' who 'harangued' the 'labouring classes' to such an extent that the magistrates felt 'we anticipate, at no distant period a general rising, and possessing no power to prevent the weekly meetings … we, as magistrates are at a loss how to stem the influence of dangerous and seditious doctrines which are continually disseminated'.[9] The conflicting perception of the magistrates (in this case the coalition of elite) with the local constabulary was supported by the local Salford and Manchester Yeomanry and the 15th Hussars, however the military force of the latter was only to be used in the advent of violence. In this case this was not strictly followed, the

---

8   A seminal text on these tensions remains E.P. Thompson's (1963) *The Making of the English Working Class*.

9   State Trials, A B, p.1372, cited in Walmsley (1969).

magistrates having deciding that the size of the gathering and its general temper were beyond the range of civil authorities to control, and having issued arrest warrants for Hunt and the ringleaders, called upon the military to aid them. The inexperienced Yeomanry were first to the field, and by the evidence did not intend to disperse the crowd but to aid in the arrest of the ringleaders. This is where historical records diverge most significantly over who struck first, but the end result was armed Yeomanry and a violent mob clashing. The Hussars eventually arrived, and after reading the Riot Act quickly cleared the field. The exact figures of those hurt cannot be established but the Manchester Relief Committee noted 'eleven dead, including both civilians and one constable, and injuries of between four to five hundred ranging from sabre and shot wounds in the crowd from the Yeomanry and Hussars, civilians rundown by horse or crushed in the crowd and stones thrown, battered by clubs and rails amongst all concerned' (Marlow, 1969: 150–151).

Of course this is an exceptional case; whilst there were similar problems throughout England at the time there is also evidence to show that Chartist reform and the highly unpopular 1834 Poor Law reform had relatively little impact in the ordering of other cities, such as the nearby Liverpool, throughout much of the same period (Power, 1992: 38–67). This is not to say that there was not political protest that resulted in violence, and where these resulted there is evidence that violence was the result of over-reaction by magistrates and agents of order, as at Peterloo. In Liverpool the forms of violence were linked to sectarian conflict (e.g. Protestants and Catholics), trade disputes (e.g. from striking workers and trade unions), the wholly legitimate violent conduct at elections (from festival atmosphere and drunken disorder), also including some small scale spontaneous brawling and direct actions against authority (e.g. trashing of a doctors during cholera epidemic, anti-police rioting) (see Bryson, 1992: 104–113). The interplay and conditions of possibility for such flashpoints clearly trigger different cascading effects depending on the local as well as regional and international contexts.

As noted above, riots form a part of the political life in many alignments of social order. They represent not a function of order, but of disorder through contestation as 'a *constituent* element in the local physiology of power and conflict' (Bohstedt, 1983: 5, original emphasis). Bohstedt also notes an important feature of a purely historical approach to the subject of rioting, insofar that one cannot assume that rioting is a rational response to a real or imagined grievance; such an approach assumes or 'suggests that the rioters' "rationality" was a function of innate human nature rather than the product of historical factors' (Ibid.: 11). Where civil unrest occurs, and coalesces into conflict (e.g. riot) they can emerge from a confluence of shared beliefs – be they religious, social or cultural – and can be tied to something as simple as the need for food (Bohstedt, 2010).

Institutional networks of kinship, community, camaraderie, political or labour association often pre-exist and can be mobilised 'horizontally' to gather individuals' shared interests into collective action. In fact, gathering to discuss what to do is often as threatening to dominant elites as direct action. Such networks can also be mobilised 'vertically' where some grievance *may* exist to challenge the authority of those who are seen either as a threat or as competition against local interests. They can also be spontaneous, resulting from a particular incident acting as a flashpoint for opportunism amongst the mob, in almost all cases of peaceable gathering turned violent there is at least some anecdotal evidence that 'trouble-makers' have insinuated themselves in the ranks of those who are attempting to make a point of protest. Equally, inadequate tactics for crowd control, insufficient resources or slow and poorly organised response mechanisms have stimulated disaster from otherwise harmless civil unrest. That said, some riots have cascade effects leading to the death of a ruler, a change of power or even civil war. In such cases the interdependency and complexity of the process makes a comprehensive reading difficult.

Towards the Struggle for the Contemporary City

This book has built a review, albeit in brief, of how we conceive and construct the trajectory of change and the discursive formation of social order and disorder over time. Drawing on philosophical frameworks of knowledge and time–space–place, the problems of social order and disorder in the urban have been highlighted as complex systemic interdependencies across ways of thinking, doing and acting in different locations in different times. Spatial history and genealogy are important conceptual tools, used here to apply the more abstract theory to some empirical evidence of change, drawing out the interdependency and complexity of interplay as the lens through which change can be better understood. When analysing the characteristics of a time period, and offering commentary on the potential positive and negative tendencies of resilience in that particular alignment of forms, the problems of using spatial history alone are evident in the interpretive anthropologism in archaeological evidence, but this evidence has helped to debunk some of the assumptions underpinning some of the previous approaches to the city in history. The previous two chapters have drawn on paleoepidemiology, paleopathology, bioarchaeology and some innovative approaches to palaeoanthropology that can help to situate change in a genealogical reappraisal of historical conditions, but it can never tell us truly how people actually lived. That is something we can only infer. However, in applying this logic to the city of today we have first-hand evidence of lived experiences. We can attack these empirically with the tools of genealogy from the top down, but also with rhythmanalytical logic from the bottom up.

The struggle for theory has been tied to the struggle for the city in history, and the focus now moves on to linking this method of analysis to the present. Whilst this is a wide-ranging project, the goal of it has always been to try and find a fresh angle from which to bring more depth to our analysis of the contemporary ordering of the democratic city today. Some of these tensions will be addressed in the following chapters, looking first at the logic of democratic order, the authority that permeates that ordering and the form of the city itself, teasing out tensions in the experience of the city and the dangers that might yet need facing.

PART II
The History of the Present

History ... is, indeed, little more than the register of the 'crimes, follies, and misfortunes' of mankind. But what experience and history teach is this – that peoples and governments have never learned anything from history, or acted on principles deduced from it.

Georg Wilhelm Friedrich Hegel

We have to know the historical conditions which motivate our conceptualization. We need a historical awareness of our present circumstance.

Michel Foucault

Chapter 5

The Struggle for the City:
Democracy, Regeneration and Urban Order

[W]hen we look back historically and geographically about the way in which New York was built, Toronto was built, Birmingham was built, Moscow was built, Shanghai was built, it isn't as if those places were built with the very distinct idea about what kind of people we wanted to be.

But the result of that urbanization has been the creation of a certain kind of human society, and we have to pay attention to what kind of human society this is.

David Harvey

Theory, the City and the Present

The first part of this book has defined and applied a rough socio-spatial genealogy to the patterns and rhythms of ordering and disordering the city in history. This has drawn on examples of both order *and* disorder to first, define the tools and method of analysis, and second, apply the theory of change over time to historical evidence. Excavating tools and theories has highlighted how wide the net can, and must, be cast. There is no singular theory that can encapsulate everything, whilst political economy may not sit at the centre of this discussion such elements are regardless important. The theoretically informed, empirically grounded genealogic method traces the oscillation of interplay as change, outlining the permeable interconnections in the realignment of form to give insight into how particular features and characteristics are carried forward into the new realigned urban social order. Tracing change over time in Part I offers only a very wide focus, setting up the framework for Part II, which now narrows that focus to the democratic, post-industrial and global city.[1] The question becomes, how can these concepts and methods be used to better understand the change around us in the city, here and now? This chapter will discuss the general characteristics of a democratic urban order; these forms of spatial governance and governmentality identify the entrepreneurial turn in the management of the city. The implications of this turn as an institutionalised form of thinking and organisational form of doing have

---

1 The trajectory of contemporary change must be tied to the dominant social order of the present, and this does refer strongly on Western experiences of democracy and urban forms, but the tools remain the same in comparative analysis across other cultures. The focus in this chapter is thus narrowed to Western democratic cities (UK, Australia and the US); however, some broader global commonalities are left open for further discussion.

repercussions for the legitimacy of some forms of acting for the users of urban locations, framing the form of resilience we have or may aspire to more clearly. The subsequent chapters will discuss the real and imagined perturbations of the entrepreneurial order facing the democratic city – returning to hazards, risks and threats once more – refining what it is that is being protected and the role of the contemporary concept of resilience.

The Democratic Urban Order

There are two key parts to this discussion. The first looks at the broader general characteristics of the global democratic urbanism that frame the concept of the city, the second at the micro-relations of power in the experience of the city. Combined, this contextually embeds the interplay of these forms in how urban democracy is governed and what that means for how we are intended, and are able, to use (or better *experience*) the city. There are clearly periods when certain forms of thinking, of doing and acting gain prominence, even dominance, in the (re)constitution of order. For example, when public flogging was an accepted norm for the punishment of criminals, when ethnicity commonly defined access to services or locations, or when to work in the service of the public was seen as an altruistic duty rather than a personal means to an end. The process of interplay between beliefs, rules and norms informs the alignment of everyday life by granting or limiting access to a series of institutions and/or organisations, but also locations. The rules of the game are played out by actors in diverse coalition in specific locations, thus the everyday life of democracy is inherently contested as it becomes something else [*in statu na'scendi*]. This chapter suggests that the alignment between 'mythos–nomos–ethos' and 'thought–knowledge–action' in the context of a specific 'time–space–place' of the democratic city shows the emergence of a more entrepreneurial alignment of democracy, with repercussions for the urban ordering of everyday life. In this chapter, the top-down analysis of general features and characteristics of authority and ordering meets an analysis from the bottom up to draw out the quotidian everydayness of living and identifying the micro-processes of interplay *in statu na'scendi*.

General Features, Characteristics and the Opening of Access

The following section identifies typical features of democracy in the post-industrial city. Importantly, building on the reflections on North, Wallis and Weingast's (2009a) typology of natural states (see Chapter 3), the opening and closing of access to spaces of government and to spaces of the city helps to set up analysis of contemporary organisations and institutions in a broad context. The context can then be applied to current trends in the alignment of beliefs, rules and norms systemically embedded in the city through the production of urban space. Though broad characteristics are spatial and platial at this point of departure, the analysis should not be seen as privileging space and place. Rather, this situates the characteristics of urban democracy within a framework that acknowledges the multidimensional *characteristics* of time–space–place. Beliefs, rules and norms provide a foundation to democratic ordering; the analysis of order requires both top-down and bottom-up review to unpack how the time–space–place of the democratic city is experienced. Analysing the institutions and organisations of democratic authority shows how the (re)production and (re)generation of the city emerges from particular conditions of possibility, we effectively trace the trajectory of change between tipping points. This is not a linear critique of the mechanisms and techniques of ordering, but an integrated critique of how that processual order (re)constitutes experiential options for those living within the city; put more simply how choices and decisions are shaped by the interplay of forms. The underlying logic of the quotidian at play in the democratic city can be exposed to give a glimpse of cyclical and linear repetitions that occur in everyday experience. It begins to address what order emerges and how it is secured, for and by whom and for what purpose. But to access this critique one must first address the general features, characteristics of the modern order and the potential for opening and closing access in the current alignment of the State.

As discussed in Chapter 3, access is important. Most natural states are not democratic, so choice is shaped by access to institutions and organsiations. Though some natural state formations have had characteristics of democracy access is often limited to small homogenous coalitions and in particular symbolic, ritualised sites and practices. For example, for the assembly democracy of Athens, the *agora* was a place in which beliefs, rules and norms underpinning the functions of democracy were embodied and enacted. The institutionalised ethos was performed here as the right to self-government (*demos*). Yet access was limited to a group of men recognised by formal assembly. *Demos* was effectively institutionalised through the principles of equal speech [*isēgoria*], equality under the law [*isonomia*], the equality of voting (inclusive of the opportunity to take on a political office) [*isopoliteia*] and in debate upon the *Pnyx*. These institutionalised principles allowed the organisation of the assembly [*ekklesia*] to exist beyond individual members, even if powerful personalities and mythical superstitions could sway the decisions that were made by the ruling coalition of slave-owning men (Keane, 2009: 33–41). Despite these principles, limited access to the *agora* itself was an organisational limitation to access that reinforced oligarchic decision-making, locally (e.g. by excluding women and embracing slavery) and geo-politically (through competition between city-states).[2] Today, as then, regulating

---

2   The processes of local democracy amongst the Acadian League were, for example, different to those of Athenian order; the Athenians even refused to help the league limit the power of Sparta, to their eventual detriment. It is, as such, worthy of note that in these fledgling democracies there is no singular set of laws that could be franchised universally, but that each variation of democracy reflected subtle variations on the wider rules, belief and norms that were implicit in the time–space–place of that specific group or coalition.

the political, economic and military pressures on a territory brings coalitions into competition, even when the internal alignment is similar. Open or limited access can be operationalised at the macro level – e.g. economic sovereignty (UK refusal to join the European single currency zone) – or the micro level – e.g. socio-cultural conformance (state regulation of religious paraphernalia in public schools). The alignment of these forms in defining the transition between types of order is useful in charting what the general features of an order are, and what alignment is dominant at a given time.

For North et al. (2009a), there are many distinctions between fragile, basic and mature natural states and more *open-access* orders. Fragile natural states limit access to organisations, to the right to form organisations, and the use of force is open to anyone strong enough to intimidate, threaten or kill to achieve obedience. The doorstep conditions for short- and long-term stability set the trajectory for transition between fragile, basic and mature alignments. Transformation or transition into a more stable form leads to more complex social ordering. For example, after the battle of Hastings (1066 AD) Norman rule in England was consolidated by aligning the interests of the political, religious, military and economic elites into formal coalition. This was achieved through the institution of the 'divine right' of Kings to rule, absolute authority was used to grant title and hereditary land ownership, inclusive of feudal tithes. By limiting access to resources and institutions, a *basic* natural state was formed. Six hundred years of slow change that followed culminated in the Peace of Westphalia in 1648. After 1648, sovereign nations had different diplomatic status, altering the alignment of absolute authority as an institution of ordering. Various elites within the coalition jockeyed for position and power, leading to both internal and external conflicts. The emergence of impersonal legal systems through a 'common law' during this time (from the twelfth century) mobilised coalitions outside of the authority of monarch and aristocracy, leading to increased power for economic organisations, such as merchant groups, guilds and early forms of corporation through banking trusts. This opening of access to formal organisation through institutionalising financial rights realigned the economic as equal or superior to hereditary rights. The personal relationships of the aristocracy formalised through blood ties were undermined by impersonal financial relations. A more *mature* state structure is thus formed with organisations not directly answerable to the sovereign and capable of sustaining themselves beyond the lives of individual members through impersonal wealth rather than personality, kinship or heredity (North et al., 2009a: 104–106).

As these shifts emerge, limitations may be built into the formation of organisations to curtail absolute forms of authority and redistribute social power across a broader base. This is a way of opening access allowing competing coalitions to influence institutional reform through the recognition of their organisational validity. In open-access orders, the entire population can be involved directly

---

A good example of the alternatives and variation in democracy during this time can be seen in Brock and Hodkinson (2003).

in organisations, rather than limiting access to smaller elite coalitions. As such there are relatively few completely open-access social orders, or rather none at all. Formal democratic coalitions became organisations within modern Government (e.g. parliament, trade union, etc.) and multiple parties (e.g. Liberal Democrats [UK], Sinn Fein [NI], Democratic Unionist Party [Egypt]). Access may be opened through an institutionalised 'right to vote' (i.e. universal suffrage) and the freedom to register for membership in a political party; yet access to elites are limited by 'representative' electoral systems, lobbying rules and political corruption. Safeguards are built into the government by institutions, such as the 'separation of powers' dividing the power of government, aiming to limit any one coalition from gaining coercive influence over the people. By creating a balance between comparably independent organisations – to which membership was open to everyone – the internal stability and external sustainability of democratic social orders should, in principle, be secure. At the same time, this security intends to protect the people from government and increase orderly freedom in everyday life through the stable institutions of formal economic and political exchange. The end goal of more open-access orders is to create a balance (often imperfect) in the interplay between rulers and ruled. While this frames an optimistic view of a global rationale for democracy, the alignment of this logic, and its success, differs greatly in different nation states.[3]

The Global Democracy and Capitalism

Due in no small part to post-Westphalian 'statehood', the outcomes of wider democratic reform throughout the last 400 years have often been tied to nationalism, racial demography, state-building and the rise and fall of colonial or imperial interests. This makes it very difficult to excavate a global theory of ordering in the short term using local examples. Longer-term and larger-scale reflections are easier. For example, the Western and Eastern European experiments of social ordering through state-building ended in very different ways (see the Cold War in the next chapter). Throughout history, the attempt to force a particular version of rule onto a civilisation, culture or social order where the institutions cannot sustain the required organisations has largely been unsuccessful, and resulted often in a regression to a more fragile alignment of the state (as seen in Vietnam, Somalia and Afghanistan in the last 50 years). The current political and cultural backlash in the Middle East suggests that the tendencies of neo-liberal capitalist democracies towards military and economic intervention may eventually follow a similar trajectory, though the resilience of democratic ideals sees new institutionalised (re)alignments carried forward in new localised (and often fragile) forms, as seen in the Libyan and Egyptian examples in 2011 and 2012. Whenever a foreign agent

---

3   There is much to be learned here, especially in embracing the counter-intuitive nature of this complexity, from Isaiah Berlins readings of liberalism and pluralism and the positive and negative forms of liberty embedded in this complexity (1990).

has attempted to install a limited form of democracy on systems of beliefs, rules and norms that do not support Western neo-liberal democratic institutions, the organisations arising frequently succumb to fragility and instability, resulting in recidivist autocracy and military dictatorship. What is most unsettling is how often such results have been deemed acceptable as the lesser evil in the face of geo-political and economic globalisation and how often the results lead to new unpredictable realignments in the form of democracy writ large.

The challenges faced in the creation of a stable social order suggest that: 'no compelling logic moves (a) state in either direction. As governments become more sophisticated and institutionalised across natural state progression, they also become more resilient to shocks' (North et al., 2009a: 73). There is no guarantee that democracy will emerge from the interplay of forms through the maturation of a natural state. In fact, following the framework presented by North et al. (2009a), the natural state is still very much the dominant formation of nation-states in the modern world. The challenge to the growth of democracy in recent years shows that progress towards a global democracy is by no means an exponential growth. Throughout the twentieth and into the twenty-first century there has been a ground-swell in democratic capitalism that led to optimistic claims that the 'end of history' had arrived and democracy was now the only system that could be seen as a valid form of social ordering following the conclusion of the Cold War (Fukuyama, 1993). A sweeping optimism was understandable given the raft of first the 'Velvet', then the 'colour' revolutions across many Eastern European and former communist nation-states. The 'doorstep conditions' for the opening of access in these social orders are in several cases aligned with wider changes in the beliefs, rules and norms that were becoming formally institutionalised in the organisations, but also in the behaviour of individuals who had come to the fore or were in rapid ascendance within the hierarchy of given elites and emergent coalitions. One might ask how many people it takes to develop from doorstep conditions into a meaningful step-change to sustainable democratic social ordering.

The fragility at the heart of sustaining these fledgling democracies, and the idiosyncratic characteristics of the social orders that have emerged, tell that tale. Many emergent democracies fail within the first few years as the key figures who led the change fall from grace during the chaotic reform that follows, are assassinated or fall out of favour in a ground-swell of recidivist nationalism, are stymied by the instability and uncertainty of emergent political institutions as capitalism surges into the power vacuum or are beset by the unpredictability of change. It can be argued, but is difficult to substantiate, that where democratic organisational forms prove most sustainable is where the beliefs, rules and norms underpinning these organisations are already embedded deeply in the institutional culture, beyond the dominant coalition. The problems are thus of implementation and alignment of change in complex systems with unpredictable interdependencies. Meaningful change thus occurs when the doorstep conditions are aligned to the tipping point of sustainable reform.[4]

A first feature of sustainable reform is establishing the rule of law as a foundation for public expectations and a balance for authority; organisations must act with a comparatively balanced sense of social justice, as well as utilising the organised criminal justice system to ensure order. This does not necessarily require a formal written constitution, though many of these emergent democracies chose to create a formal charter of rights. The most resilient sense of a rule of law is one rooted in beliefs, rules and norms already present within the body politic. A second feature is organisations capable of living on beyond the life of the members within them, not beholden to the personality of a revolutionary figurehead. Where there is uncertainty the organisation must be stronger, and better reflect the beliefs, rules and norms of the body-politic. If a figurehead is the sole driver of change, this is a powerful character of stability and can create a power vacuum that will drag the organisation back toward autocratic and dictatorial alignment in the longer term. The obvious example is Russia in the last twenty years, but this is also a significant feature of failed or fragile nation-states in the developing world. The third feature is consolidating military force under a central civil authority which remains impersonal and objective. The consolidation of organisational authority requires a monopoly on the legitimate use of violence, yet consolidation of force under a central authority in a limited-access framework creates abuses. As it often does when the alignment of beliefs, rules and norms creates distinctions of 'otherness' within the civil framework – engendering conflict between population demographics or elite coalitions. Most often the opening of access through such turns, as partial and then universal suffrage is aligned with a rise in institutionalised nationalism within some area of the population. This can become a powerful influence on the global ordering of populations, the apportionment of territory and geo-political networks. Elected representatives acting as elites with checks and balances on the internal monopoly over sanctioned violence, though fewer concrete regulations determine the monopoly on appropriate use of inter-state violence. Such ambiguities have been tested in the World Wars of the early to mid-twentieth century, and often underpin the interplay of interests in international relations.

Internationally, mixed outcomes have resulted from efforts to enforce democracy through militarily enacted regime change and through the resultant franchise of limited-access democracy (it is still difficult to determine the outcomes in terms of success and failure). Where these have struggled is most often not through a lack of military effort, rather through failure to articulate the institutional foundations into sustainable organisations; often military coups and recidivism

---

4   North et al. discuss their approach to the doorstep conditions as rule of law for elites, perpetually lived organisations in the public and private spheres and consolidated control of the military (2009a: 151). These bud on each other and as each takes on a sustainable form the transition to open-access order is made more likely, but is not in any way certain.

result and as many fledgling democracies have failed in the last 10 years as were installed through military force. Attempts to consolidate a world order of global democratic capitalism have become realigned within a discursive transformation of the democratic project dominated by neo-liberal political-economic forms of thinking and doing. One might argue that organisational governance of a liberal democratic rule of law is not sustainable unless those organisational coalitions have contextually embedded within the beliefs, values and rules they enact an institutionalised *sense* of the rule of law. To balance the inherent potential for abuse of this institutionalised sense there are internal organisational regulations, monitored by competing organisational coalitions through the civil society and through citizenship. A further, though somewhat melodramatic suggestion could follow; that the biggest threat to successful democratic transformation is not the unchecked power of government or of markets, but the disengagement of citizen ability and responsibility to participate in the daily life of rule.

Inevitably, over time the interplay of forms realigns to an inherent balance reflecting the institutionalised beliefs, rules and norms of the voting majority, which anecdotal evidence suggests is too often an increasingly narrow demographic. Data from the Institute for Democracy and Electoral Assistance (Pintor and Gratschew, 2002) shows that between the mid-1980s and the year 2001 electoral participation has consistently dropped in all global regions. Further, the Economist Intelligence Unit annual report on 'the democracy index' (EIU, 2011) has shown a decline in 2010 of the number of countries that would qualify as democracies, and of the wider metric for freedom in most well established monitory democratic countries. This evidence suggests that we may be entering into a period of ebb following the high tide of 'third wave' optimism on the global democratic project.

The Neo-Liberal Ordering of Access

The global democratic project is one tied to neo-liberal capitalism. Open access in this context is intended to be a mutually reinforcing system whereby (a) shared beliefs are institutionalised, for example in safeguards against the dangers of market participation (social welfare and healthcare), (b) competitive elections give opportunities for non-violent contestation of authority, also fostering market competition and civil society that disperses authority widely to prevent abuses of power, and (c) ensure that systemic attempts to consolidate authority in a more limited-access natural state system is highly expensive for those who may attempt it, thus discouraging any attempt to undermine open access (North et al., 2009a: 111). This is not to say that once a nation-state reaches a degree of complexity the systemic alignment of beliefs, rules and norms will auto-poietically produce open access. Nor does it guarantee that access will stay open. The process as presented by North et al. (2009a) does present a wide assumption that meritocratic wealth creation systems are essentially egalitarian, when we know this is not the case. It also assumes that widely held beliefs are more universal in their institution within organisational systems than they are in informing personal interactions.

The impersonal nature of relations between organisations as opposed to individuals within them is not resolved, as it is suggested that all open access orders are, largely, impersonal. This assertion is made on the basis of the universal delivery of services 'without reference to the social standing of the citizens or the identity and political connections of an organization's principles' (North et al., 2009a: 113).

Evidence shows that whilst such notions are virtuous by our beliefs, rules and norms, they are far from evidence in the practical operation of systems such as the law, rather this is an ideal to which individuals within organisations aspire but rarely reach in the day-to-day delivery of social order. Beyond the legal system itself, we see when we apply such lofty notions to the functioning of the city today that there are common and frequent imbalances in the open access to decision-making and to the impact of strategic decisions about the appropriate rules and norms for appropriate conduct in the time–space–place of the city. The beliefs that underpin decision-making are indeed widely held; lofty notions such as freedom of expression, freedom of association are enshrined as legal 'rights', but these take on mythical aspects more akin to fairy tales than to day-to-day realities of the rules for moderating how we live in and the authorities manage urban locations. Far more common to see and easier to know are the rules and norms which form the focus of day-to-day regulation, and indeed, increasingly, the intent to modify by design the ability for actions outside of those predetermined by those rules and norms as appropriate. The dominant characteristics and features of an open access order are as such:

1. A widely held set of beliefs about the inclusion of and equality for all citizens
2. Entry into economic, political, religious, and educational activities without restraint
3. Support for organisational forms in each activity that is open to all (for example, contract enforcement)
4. Rule of law enforced impartially for all citizens
5. Impersonal exchange (North et al., 2009a: 114)

These are difficult to deny when taking a wide-lens view of social order. The extension of citizenship to all groups, for example through universal suffrage, creates significant shifts in the opening of access and the safeguards against any one dominant coalition gaining too much social power. A Civil Society composed of a broad range of organisations that can be mobilised to limit the attempt of any one coalition to gain too much power, and enshrinement of institutionalised beliefs in formal laws supported by both the inclusive citizenry and the civil society, are intended to create the conditions for a sustainable consensus. However, the consensus view is now one that sees markets as preferable to democracies and measures the success of social ordering on economic principles. In such a system:

> ... economic liberty produces the legitimacy for a form of sovereignty limited to
> guaranteeing economic activity ... Economic prosperity revealed the legitimacy
> of the state for all to see – a state that refused to adopt any transcendent
> perspective and solely guaranteed the rules of economic exchange. (Lemke,
> 2001: 196)

Such logic furthers the impersonal alignment of beliefs, rules and norms to divorce the control of the social from the economic through political institutions. Organisations of government cede control to the market creating a dominating authority across the social order, unregulated by ideology and susceptible to manipulation by corporate elites across scales. Political or politicising organisations can include recognised civil government (such as local authorities) but also social societies (from football supporters' clubs to the brotherhood of masons) or political parties that touch upon minority interests or major parties. Corporations are far more influential than civil or social coalitions in negotiating the trajectory of order, particularly in the juridical and economic spheres (through political party contributions and highly effective lobbying techniques). The complexity of the interplay reduces the separation of powers to an implication rather than an institution when one reflects upon the interplay of profit-making entities, such as corporations, concurrent with political coalitions of rule, in national and international government.

The economic coalition of personal interests undertaken by an impersonal corporation reflects a troubling moral ambiguity. Impersonal action implies that self-serving actions are to be expected by the corporation and that governing or regulating this is impossible due to the very impersonality of relationships created by neo-liberal economic and governing policy. This is the same as the rules governing the use of violence, but violence here is abstract as an amorphous sense of social harm caused by economic deprivation or disadvantage, making it morally non-specific and, as such, impersonal. In an open-access order the rules for the use of violence are also impersonal, but the abuses of authority that are thus created are enshrined in a disseminated accountability of the body politic for the violent actions of the governing authority. If the people do not like what the governing bodies do they exercise their power to oust that authority through an electoral system of checks and balances, intended to monitor and mitigate the social harm caused by specific policy approaches to rule. When this is framed through fiscal incentives rather than social harm the electorate become stakeholders, and the harm becomes framed as the best interests of the market rather than the well-being of the body politic. This coalescence in the interplay of forms might be seen as suffering a risk of economic determinism in the alignment of institutions with economic growth prioritised over social harm. When economic security is the organising principle underpinning citizenship and social justice then the freedom of the market ensures the opening of access as the freedom to pursue impersonal economic goals. This becomes the primary incentive for creating social order and informs the focus of actions taken to create and sustain such an order.

This reflects perhaps a monitory view of 'shareholder democracy', but not a formal representative liberal tradition (Rodrigues, 2006). This reconstitution of democracy creates a distinct ambiguity. On the one hand there is the neo-liberal model representing *individuals* as rational *share*holders in an unequal meritocracy of the institutionalised market; on the other, a paradoxical view of *citizens* as participatory *stake*holders in a collaborative engagement with an organised – and organising – government. Either poses problems when developing a coherent approach to social order. As the earlier discussion has clearly shown, individuals think and act differently depending on their contextual needs. They may coalesce as coalitions of self-interest, yet collaborate in unexpectedly altruistic ways – depending on the dominant beliefs, rules and norms of the time. It also brings into sharp focus the importance of time–space–place, the spaces within which people interact, the understanding of appropriate actions in particular places, the resilience of such sites of action to perturbation and disorder, are all features of making change happen, for it is here that realignment of the beliefs, rules and norms is experienced moment to moment. If we extend Foucault's (1997 [1975]) analysis of the discursive formation of 'discipline and punishment' – through the re-reading of theory in Part I to analyse social order and disorder – then we can suggest that the order is acted out, is lived, is experienced in time–space–place. This time–space–place can then be analysed as the (re)ordering of the democratic city moment by moment. When the gaze is narrowed to the specific sites and locations in which open access is lived, a rather different view of the democratic city emerges; the order imposed on the city thus sets new challenges for understanding the paradox of an entrepreneurial democratic logic.

Characterising the Entrepreneurial Time–Space–Place of the Democratic City

How do the broad characteristics of democratic ordering translate into the analysis of the democratic city? Focussing on what might be called micro-relations of power as they interplay allows us to tease out examples of tension in the everyday life of those specific locations. As such, the mechanisms that produce democratic subjects in time–space–place are particularly useful in aligning the everyday with the broader systemic significance and meaning of 'access' when applied to decision-making *in situ*.

The city in the twentieth century has had a turbulent time. Much urban decline in the post-war period saw the need for a renaissance of the urban landscape and critical infrastructure, targeting areas or specific locations of decay created during the social and economic upheavals of the twentieth century (Amin and Thrift, 2002). Urban decline is seen to have emerged from a number of contributing factors, including: the threat of total devastation during the cold war and its impact on urban planning and design practices (Coaffee, Murakami-Wood and Rogers, 2008); the defensive spatial development of the 1970s and 1980s

(Oc and Tiesdell, 1997a: 2); spiralling inner-city crime rates and the obsession with security amongst urban inhabitants (Sorkin, 1992); the ongoing twentieth-century suburbanisation of housing and the resultant mass migration of the middle classes out of the crowded defensive tenements of the city centre (Oc and Tiesdell, 1997b; Hall, 1998: 965–966); the chain reaction of haemorrhaging financial investment (Oc and Tiesdell, 1997b: 12) and the often media-led birth of an 'ecology' (Davis, 1998), 'culture' (Furedi, 2006) and 'politics' of fear (Furedi, 2007a) in urban life. This contributed to the widening of the metaphor of war to aggressively target the problems of the urban (e.g. poverty, crime, drugs and terror). The neighbourhoods and employment hubs were increasingly disconnected and in disrepair in both image and infrastructure, a state of affairs now addressed by the neo-liberal turn. By adopting global attitudes to the cultural and technological economies of scale now encouraged by economic deregulation, territorial boundaries were redefined, enabling 'foot-loose' capital flows to invest in the emergent network of global creative cities (Brenner and Theodore, 2002; Tallon, 2009: 112). By transforming management to an entrepreneurial model the city could be deconstructed as assets, and organisations of government could take on the characteristics of resilient and impersonal organisations. The political economy (re)constituted the city at the heart of capital and knowledge flows moving between and across scales of territory, place and networks (Jessop et al., 2008). Under pressure to become globally competitive economic and knowledge hubs, the effect of 'splintering urbanism' (Graham and Marvin, 2001) in the post-industrial city created new tensions:

> So universal is this capitalist condition that the conception of the urban and or 'the city' is likewise rendered unstable ... because the concept has itself had to reflect changing relations between form and process, between activity and thing, between subjects and objects. When we speak therefore of a transition from urban managerialism towards urban entrepreneurialism these last two decades we have to take cognisance of the reflexive effects of such a shift, through the impacts on urban institutions as well as built environments. (Harvey, 1989: 6)

This can be expanded to gain more clarity between the organisation of entrepreneurial government, the institutionalised model of governmentality and the characteristics of space and place over time to see how the interplay of the entrepreneurial city is best unpacked. The city as a coalition of localised interests operates as an organisation only insofar as it can be represented as a coalition of impersonal interests, initially driven through a managerial governance strategy of restructuring. This 'entrepreneurial turn' realigns the role and responsibilities of governance agencies towards demonstrating growth through economic performance indicators – used to show that the city and government are successfully managing their assets, alongside fulfilling the statutory obligations of basic services such as welfare, education, critical infrastructure regulation and protection, etc. Neo-liberal ways of thinking and doing have thus become embedded in 'restructuring projects insofar as they have been produced within national, regional, and local contexts defined by the legacies of inherited institutional frameworks, policy regimes, regulatory practices, and political struggles' (Brenner and Theodore, 2002: 310). Entrepreneurial governance reform takes place through the generation of spatial management strategies that can 'fix' the broken city. Concern of the urban public as 'colonised or dominated by particular group[s] or interest[s], thereby losing its inclusive status' (Worpole and Greenhalgh, 1996: 15) is always an issue in maintaining the 'publicness' of specific locations – public streets, public parks, plazas or other open spaces where access is either unmonitored or at least free of charge.

Many such locations were seen to have been colonised by the dangerous criminal, the poverty-stricken young black male and the poor, young single mother (significantly an a-racial stereotype) (Hall, 1998: 983–988). The fall from grace of the city affected the public spaces, culture and view of the city, foretelling the potential collapse of urban social order through a wave of dystopian 'hypochondriac geographies of the city' (Baeten, 2002a; 2002b). Within a broader framework of neo-liberal governance reform, the reaction of governing authorities was to address urban regeneration, not only of the public spaces, streets and architectural forms of the physical city, but also to reimage the city and manage the public and corporate perceptions of the city in a post-industrial global marketplace. The challenges of 'revisioning' and 're-imaging localities' (Jessop, 1997) required a new form of urban management that reflected the shift in the balance of beliefs, rules and norms amongst a tired and fearful urban electorate. The resulting raft of deregulated 'creative entrepreneurialism' in strategies, policies and tactics slowly emerged across both global and local scales (Harvey, 1989: 6), and has been traced by the progress of urban renaissance (Imrie and Raco, 2001), the new urbanism (Katz, 1994), the postmodern (Harvey, 1991) and post-industrial (Miles and Miles, 2000; Miles, 2010) city with a new focus on knowledge economies and service industries (Musterd and Murie, 2010); as such, the entrepreneurial turn in governance is also being linked to attempts to reconstitute the 'citizen sector' (Drayton, 2002) with 'public entrepreneurs' (Hjorth and Bjerke, 2006).

It can be argued that market competition has increasingly become an institutionalised norm in the practical working of organisations governing social order, enshrined in the late twentieth-century urban government practices through pressure to establish cities as products on the splintered global urban network of footloose capital. Diverse strategies of place branding have emerged within monitory democratic structures for securing corporate investment in industrial production and, where possible, positioning cities as emergent hubs in the knowledge economy or as cultural and service industries often tied to tourism and leisure markets. The rise and rise of the entrepreneurial city and the urban renaissance as 'entrepreneurial' strategic policy[5] has created or emphasised

---

5   Good case studies of this in Glasgow and Newcastle can be found in MacCleod (2002) and Rogers and Coaffee (2005).

the tensions in this approach by suggesting that the strategies and tactics of governance may not place the local population on the same priority as economic sustainability in the pursuit of these outcomes. Both the practical governance and the research of such endeavours suggest an implicit reordering of local time–space–place is significant to unpacking the logical order of the everyday city as a result of the 'entrepreneurial turn' (Hall and Hubbard, 1996, 1998). The discursive formation of the post-industrial commercial city emerges from the interplay of forms in new ways that challenge many of the preconceptions of a democratic urban order, previously assumed to underpin the time–space–place of the city of today.

Production and Regulation of Commercial Democratic Spaces

Thus far, the general characteristics of a democratic entrepreneurialism have been discussed and this has been connected to the emergence of an urban entrepreneurialism, but this has not interrogated the patterns of everyday life that emerged through this interplay. This will be addressed using the example of the UK 'urban renaissance'. In 1997, the Labour government appointed the architect Lord (Richard) Rogers to lead an Urban Task Force to investigate the state of British urban policy. Their final report *Towards an Urban Renaissance* was an attempt to bring the UK into line with the high standards of European urban environments (DETR, 2000). Some key aspects of the plan were the emphasis on design-led regeneration targeting brown-field sites and open spaces in declining areas; the demand for local authorities to create comprehensive strategies detailing tactics of regeneration for specific areas (in economy, planning and culture); the redesign of streets, parks and open spaces in order to stimulate more viable uses (for the integration of communities); and the widespread regeneration of the urban environment and the importance of increased partnerships with the private sector (Lees, 2000).

Holden and Iverson (2003) have argued that 'contemporary urbanism is particularly sensitive to how cities are being re-valued between moments of renaissance and revanchism' and that 'revanchist tendencies' appear to underpin the urban renaissance agenda (Ibid.: 58). If indeed we look to wider issues of reform in the nomothetic regulation, to be discussed in more depth below, there are indications in research that the management of militarised spaces, zero tolerance policing and new forms of urban terror (Atkinson, 2000; Belinda and Helms, 2003; Raco, 2003; Coaffee, 2010) and debates on rising fear of strangers and 'the Other' in public life (Ruggiero, 2003) are connected. If this is so, then the reorientation of interplay appears to coalesce around *nomothetic* and *ethical* regulations, having subsumed the prominence of pastoral authority inherent in mythological beliefs. The economic orientation of ordering then favours an implicit revanchism through the perceived need to enhance the flow of capital and the entrepreneurial alignment of governance in practice over altruistic and philanthropic 'publicness'. In contemporary representations of the urban, the design-led strategy and partnership-driven tactics create an 'entrepreneurial stance' underpinning the ongoing change:

> The future of the city resides, so it seems, in embracing an entrepreneurial stance in which state, architect, urbanist and entrepreneur join forces to construct urban 'growth machines' that permit successful development and a vigorous competitive stance in the spiralling inter-urban competition that governs urban dynamics today. Within this market-led urban development, attention to issues of distribution and socio-economic power shrink and pervasive mechanisms of exclusion, social polarisation and diminishing citizenship come to the fore. (Swyngedouw and Kaika, 2003: 6–7)

This new coalition thus combines the influence of key impersonal interests to create new representations of the time–space–place of the city that implicitly privilege the impersonal aspects of social change in terms of urban economic growth. The redefinition of beliefs, rules and norms through the institutionalisation of this in the strategies and practices of the ruling coalitions and elites in government operates at the expense of those to whom macro-economic concerns are not a part of their daily experience, but it does so without undermining the rights and freedoms of meritocratic open access to institutions and organisations. A study by MacLeod (2002) highlighted such in Glasgow, where he argued that relationships between 'entrepreneurial governance, downtown renaissance and the active systems of surveillance ... are intertwined with the advance of the revanchist city' (Ibid.: 603). This, he noted, led to a situation where 'new civic spaces appear to be concealing more active geographies of displacement and marginality' (Ibid.: 613).

As research on the problems of design-led spatial privatisation has expanded, the emphasis on consumer-led activity and private sector management style has also increased as a form of 'ground control' in the city (Minton, 2010). This revanchist agenda can thus be seen to adversely affect the management and uses of public locations in many cities (Reeve, 1996; Jackson, 1998; Flusty, 2000, 2001), with repercussions for the balance of beliefs, rules and norms of conduct across the institutions and organisations of governance. Holden and Iveson (2003) have gone so far as to make explicit the claim that the renaissance of New Labour in the UK may in fact be a form of revenge upon the less powerful urban citizens, linked above to urban decline:

> If the renaissance of these tenderly managed landscapes ... has done much to recover the exchange and sign-value of many city centres, questions remain

about the legitimate use-value of these spaces for a wider citizenry. (MacLeod, 2002: 605, cited in Holden and Iveson, 2003: 59)[6]

If the new city *is* being redeveloped to attract wealthier inhabitants and more profitable consumers back into the city centre, this appears to reflect an urban social order that explicitly privileges commercially oriented rules and norms of conduct. These further are increasingly institutionalised in impersonal economic relations and conditions that subsequently underpin a framework of governance that implements urban regeneration of a more impersonal urban landscape of consumption. It is an approach that institutionalises impersonality beyond the operations of organisations and seeks to embed it into the urban fabric, and thus the beliefs, rules and norms that underpin personal interactions at the level of quotidian interplay in everyday life. In effect, a coalescence of forms across scales has evolved whereby, in providing for some more influential informal and impersonal coalitions within the social diaspora (e.g. the middle-class consumer family),[7] those not in a position to engage with the beliefs, rules and norms of this group are increasingly limited in their access to decision-making, and thus participation in steering the orientation of the interplay of forms in everyday life. This amounts to effective institutionalisation of social exclusion in the governance of the urban (Cooper, 1998: 469; Lees, 2000: 74).

Despite this risk, many cities have begun to harness entrepreneurialism positively to remake their image in a global urban marketplace. Success and stability of the resultant entrepreneurial order is defined by the ability of the local councils or local authorities, as sub-organisations within the wider coalition, to offer a more appealing 'sense of place'. The repackaging of the space–place dynamic goes beyond an impersonal economic package for the investor, but is also an experiential package represented to the tourist, leisure seeker and consumer, thus increasing the potential for economic growth. Town and city centres are isolated as a management priority (DETR, 2000: 120), and linked to evidence-based metrics of economic growth in major cities as case study models of successful regeneration. It is clear at the local level in contemporary urban management, and urban studies, that for many it is the urban and economic imperatives that remain the strongest influences on the direction of urban renaissance:

---

6   The redefinitions of citizenship in policies used for the control of space by the failing Conservative and fledgling New Right policies of law and order can be linked as a starting point of this shift in the managerial perception of urban citizenship, paving the way for urban revanchism and commercial domination of managerial strategies and tactics (Fyfe, 1995).

7   Though the term 'middle class' is used here it is a general abridgement used in order to link into the references of previous research. The notion of class is not developed in this research in any depth, save reference to wealth-graded class distinctions in the lifestyles of young people. Such notions of class as defined by the general registrars scale are limited and outdated. More work on this theme is forthcoming.

> These transformations are strongly connected to the changes that occur in cities, since cities were and still are regarded to be the engines of economic growth, and centres of production, consumption, innovation and accumulation of wealth. Therefore economic transformation implies urban transformation. (Musterd, 2003: 71)

The transformations that we see emerging take root in the institutionalised governance practices, as 'day-to-day' forms-of-doing or technical processes, for example: compulsory land acquisitions, tendered planning/design contracts, private financing of regeneration initiatives and construction projects, increasing subsidy of added value to public space from Business Improvement District companies, as well as fully or partly privatised surveillance networks utilising wardens and guards as pseudo-police to enforce the privately defined use-value of semi-public locations in the commercially oriented urban landscape. The material specificities of such transformations impact upon the kind of trace evidence that we can pick up from empirical research. The analysis cuts across scales of social order and disorder (the neo-liberal capitalist democracy) to include territory, place and networks (the nation, city-region, knowledge-hub, suburb, street), but also incorporate design, strategy and tactics of governmentality (surveillance, environmental design, bye-laws) to embrace the experiences of everyday life for those living in the city (actions, perceptions, reactions, choices). Tracing this interplay between complex systems moves closer to an appreciation of the quotidian interstices of lived experiences. We can start to really get into the fine-grained empirical evidence for the realignment of beliefs, rules and norms underpinning the trajectory of change.

Blurring Public and Private Time–Space–Place

The distinctions between public and private underpinning the conceptual representations of urban locations are blurred (Cuthbert, 1995; Defilippis, 1997; Clarke and Bradford, 1998; Madanipour, 2003). As such, the principles of acceptability generated in strategic entrepreneurialism – linking to the shifts in wider social and moral consciousness – reflect how the wider public – as participating citizens – perceive public activity reflexively. Where there is a culturally significant fear of difference, this implicitly serves the entrepreneurial redefinition of acceptability. Processes of 'gentrification'[8] become explicit through the perceived legitimacy of economic growth as a higher goal, even as evidence of improvement irrespective of the impact on those not included in the prescribed model of use-values attributed to locations. This displaces marginal groups, but is perceived as legitimate exclusion as these were not the consumers

---

8   For more on gentrification research, see Atkinson (2000), Hackworth and Smith (2000), Lees (2000), Phillips (2002), Slater (2002), Smith (2002), Visser (2002), Cameron (2003).

targeted in the demographic proposals for redevelopment. The social problems beneath inequality are dispersed rather than solved, and specific problems at the roots of social exclusion lose their importance as central drivers of governance. Simultaneously, attempts to reinvigorate the culture of the locality attempt to inspire local inhabitants to take pride in the city itself (see Evans, 2005; Miles, 2005) but do not target the specific needs of the local populous, rather emphasising economic outcomes as solutions in and of themselves.

The use of the city is realigned towards commercially viable recreation as a cultural, knowledge and economic 'renaissance' (Holden and Iveson, 2003), but it is not democratic. The urban environment implicitly pushes distinct minorities out of an area or location and, on the basis of moralising arguments that marginal groups pose a criminal or security risk to consumers, these spaces are subjected to tighter spatial regulation. This implicit hegemonic exclusion does not solve the problem of urban disorder, it simply displaces the tensions into another area; one where the presence of a problematic group in the flow of capital does not interfere with the reimagined entrepreneurial landscape. In principle this process follows a simple logic, that displacement and dispersal is legitimated by urban regeneration strategy. Such strategy is aligned with the belief that cities should be 'clean and safe'. Rules of conduct can be imposed on those spaces by semi-private management corporations to ensure that they stay so, and the realigned norms are thus conceptually transposed into such locations. A similar logic underpins Crime Prevention Through Environmental Design (CPTED) and urban surveillance tactics and technologies, neither of which effectively address the causes of problems but rather seek to minimise the conditions of possibility for action and thus reduce the exposure of the potential victim. Explicit legislative actions are also incorporated into the management of fringe acceptability in civil orders such as Anti-Social Behaviour Orders (ASBOs), as well as the broadening use of security and terrorist-related legislation for the policing of public protest, showing how these can easily have unintended knock-on effects for the pre-emptive and proactive management of disorder, as shall be discussed in more depth in the next chapter.

The renegotiation of the public city has some significant repercussions for the roles balance of beliefs, rules and norms, aligned with wider democratic sensibilities in time–space–place. It has been proven, in the European Court of Human Rights in 2002, that owners and managers of private spaces have the rights to dictate the rules of conduct, and even dress, within the boundaries of locations owned in public–private partnership and/or managed by a private company. A case in the satellite town of Washington in the North East of England – near the regional capital Newcastle upon Tyne – illustrates this point. In this town, a shopping mall named The Galleries dominated the town centre, with little or no open public space of comparable size to the open areas inside the mall, specifically in terms of footfall and pedestrian traffic. The Court found that the private owners were within their rights to constrain activities that they felt were a negative influence on the flow of commercial activity through their commercial space (Anon, 2002), specifically in this case relating to political canvassing and protesting against the expansion of the mall onto a public playing field nearby. As the owning interest (Postel) were not considered a public organisation within the European Human Rights Act, and the space was 'quasi-public' after the sale to a private company, the Human Rights Act (specifically Articles 10 and 11 which secure the right to protest on public land) no longer apply (Russell, 2009). Such 'quasi-public' privatisation is often linked to private malls and commercial spaces and transit hubs, but has been rolled out in some cases into the city streets and public parks during periods of exceptional circumstances or perceived high risk. The emphasis on policing social order and protection rather than social control and exclusion is palpable in the rhetoric, but not clear at all in practice. This is far more often due to a lack of clarity in the governance and legislative framing of practices rather than the operational remit and responsibilities of key agencies, though disagreement over such intent rages on amongst commentators. In a case study of redevelopment in Newcastle upon Tyne, several police officers remarked that the council and local traders had previously suggested the police 'should do more' to remove the 'perceived threat' of disorderly youths, but the police preferred to deal with 'the reality of crime rather than over-reactions' to what individual traders perceived to be disorderly conduct by young people.[9]

Regulation and Reaction

Research has shown that tactics and technologies of observation, such as CCTV, do not have much, if any, effect upon the use of the space or on the reduction of crime, despite the widespread investment in the infrastructure. CCTV is increasingly cited as a central reason behind the increased feeling of safety amongst the public, but also for the increased feelings of safety amongst marginal groups who may gather under the camera as they are aware of the protection the camera purports to instil. A critical case in the national press in the summer of 2005 was the public furore over the ban on hooded apparel in Bluewater Shopping Centre in Kent. The need to identify young 'thugs' who hide from cameras in such clothing has been cited as a reason for the ban, supported by the Prime Minister under the rhetoric of anti-social behaviour. It is tempting, of course, to lay the blame for these changes at the door of authoritarian neo-liberals in government, or the equivalent neo-conservative demagoguery that rails against ill-defined multi-culturalism and welfare appeasement in favour of the meritocratic values of patriots that bind us and reinforce our social solidarity in uncertain and dangerous times. These may well be contributing factors to the underlying decay of the idealistic dreams of representative democracy. However, at the core of more liberal democratic state structures, the truth is that such shifts

---

9   Interview with beat commander in Newcastle upon Tyne city centre, January 2003 (for more, see Rogers and Coaffee, 2005; Rogers, 2009).

could not occur if they did not reflect, in whole or in part, the beliefs, rules and norms underlying the everyday lives of citizens:

> People are rightly fed up with street-corner and shopping-centre thugs; yobbish behaviour, sometimes from children as young as ten or 11 whose parents should be looking after them; Friday and Saturday night binge-drinking which makes our town centres no-go areas for respectable citizens; of the low-level graffiti, vandalism and disorder that is the work of a very small minority that makes the law-abiding majority afraid and angry. (Blair, 2000)

Alongside the *Anti-Social Behaviour Act* (HMSO, 2003), and the widespread mix of responses to the new morally driven New Labour rhetoric on community (Imrie and Raco, 2001; Ferguson, 2002; Cochrane, 2003; Holden and Iveson, 2003; Raco, 2003), challenges to these new anti-social behaviour laws are in process. Among the most significant of attempts to challenge the blurring of distinctions between public and private space in the UK to date – and the apparent support of this in urban renaissance policy – came from human rights activist group Liberty, who are challenging an ASBO in the Richmond area; their leader stated:

> The Prime Minister has prioritised creating a culture of respect in Britain. He should remember that respect is a two-way street. These powers fail to distinguish between the innocent and the guilty. No one objects to reasonable sanctions for bad behaviour. He should attack that behaviour and not all children. (Anon, 2005a)

Recently, this view has been ratified by the European Court of Human Rights, specifically regarding curfews affecting young people under 16, as stated by Liberty: '79% of police forces in England and Wales have imposed 9pm curfews on the under-16s in their area, regardless of whether they have done anything wrong' (Anon, 2005b). The legality of these curfews are now under review following the overturning of one such case in the Richmond area, and the long-term effect this could have on anti-social behaviour legislation is as yet unknown, though the Home Office are appealing the decision (Andalo, 2005). The interplay of distinctions of identity and performative activity in public space with the rhetoric of anti-social behaviour create a direct opposition between representations of space – driven by entrepreneurial strategy from managers and stakeholders – and representational spaces – street-level experiences driven by spatial practices. Draconian exclusion measures are, in this example, made implicit within the operational tactics of behavioural legislation underpinning the management of citizenship and access to both the organisations of rule through variegated consultation practices and management of public spaces.

Two key issues emerge from these examples. First, it is apparent that increasing the efficiency of the democratic city is driven by economic rather than socially inclusive imperatives. Managerial reflections of success are not socially inclusive to minorities, privileging the needs and wants of stakeholders through the conceptual orientation of strategic planning towards cultural economic imperatives. These economic imperatives become synergic with the perception of social benefits through: the embracing of social-order-driven environmental improvements (such as CCTV cameras) – further problematic due to the broadly ambiguous best practice underpinning crime control tactics (McCahill, 2000, 2003; Coleman, 2004a, 2004b; Klauser, 2004) – where conflation occurs between the anti-social and the 'nuisance'; the development of improvements to city-centre architecture through the commercially driven understandings of competition and success – represented by the co-option of private sector managers into civic roles and exacerbated by the increased emphasis on economic success indicators as opposed to difficult social problems; and the lack of regulation in ensuring consultation and participatory democratic process. Secondly, acceptability in public space is increasingly defined through the prescriptive morality implicit in these renaissance-driven conceptual designs rather than by the underpinning logic of a rule of law and participatory regulation. These overly rational spatial representations are another facet of the privileging of commerce over civic imperative in management, but have wider implications in the perception and definition of appropriateness through aesthetic considerations. The highly blurred distinction of public and commercial space leads to a confused public perception of appropriateness and a reaction against public activity on the part of young people as the liminal and disorderly spaces of youth are subsumed and redeveloped into pseudo-public commercial spaces. This engenders an altering of the spatial practices of those engaged in use of specific areas through the methods of perception and reaction to the perceived appropriateness, or lack thereof. Unpacking these tensions is central to understanding the imbalance between beliefs, rules and norms in restructuring the city. One can argue that in the current formulation of urban social order there is a strong tendency towards an emphasis on rules as regulatory enforcement of norms, which in and of itself will create conflict between various belief systems across the urban population which do not map into this system of rule. Rather, the intention of creating a balanced system of reflection through appreciation of the interplay between beliefs, rules and norms emphasises a more inclusive renaissance in both policy and space, reducing the emphasis on economic growth and homogenised urban aesthetics, and requiring 'alternative spaces of citizenship' to be explored:

> Any attempt to understand struggles over citizenship must therefore not restrict the account of power relations to those made visible and tangible in the city itself. Rather it must consider the on-going creation, recreation, and closure of a range of political spaces and spatialities. (Holden and Iveson, 2003: 60)

As the membership or occupancy of public space changes then the dominant consensus within that space will also fluctuate from moment to moment according to the balance of individuals. This can be mitigated by the relative social hierarchical position of those actors (e.g. in terms of their relative authority). For example, in the contemporary city a large group of youths can be moved on by a pair of police officers, for example. However, the societal or civilisation orientation of regulations or laws (as *nomos*) does not change as quickly as the interplay of immediate ethical norms or the mythical beliefs informing the sense of place for different users of locations *in situ*. This is especially evident when using the example of public space. When a public space becomes habitually dominated by a particular group it can become over time laden with symbolic meaning for that group in the sense of place, and the space itself can take on a different pattern of values, or a distinct ethical framework dominated by that demographic, coalition or perhaps 'subculture'. This frequently creates tensions in the management of locations, in their maintenance for a specific purpose not reflected in the actions of users. Here, questions arise on the nature of validity, territory and citizenship in the real lived experience of public space as a result of these normatively driven moral judgements of appropriateness:

> [I]t is not simply the disparity between the normative and the real that lies at the heart of some of the problems, but that we also need to rethink the relationship between civil society and the state, the public and the private, and the mechanisms of exclusion and inclusion that regulate membership of socio-cultural and political communities. (Kofman, 1999)

The dynamic process of differentiation between acceptable and inappropriate is based on the perception and interpretation of each individual or 'user' in a public space of all other users, groups, symbols or boundary markers. This of course includes the economic, socio-cultural and political identities of each individual, perceived, interpreted and reacted to moment to moment by each individual, and indeed each group as a coalition representing a common identity as they are encountered through time–space–place. Application of this contrast between collectively distinct notions of acceptability becomes particularly significant to the 'production of meaning' in public space. This is applied to the perception of young people as a group, often on the fringes of acceptability but not entirely criminal, in many cases. By developing the 'normative moral landscape' as a form of perceived knowledge underpinning the interplay between different groups (with different perceptions of appropriate public behaviour/activity), the mediation of responses through social relations can be applied to the strategies and tactics of management and linked with the reactions of local businesses and wider public communities to large youth gatherings in public space.[10] This process in itself is a large part of the hegemonic connection between elements of a Lefebvrian approach to the

---

10   This relates to both self knowledge (personal identity) and the perceived knowledge of others (appraisal of others' identity based upon symbolic indicators and expressive activities occurring through time). This is clearly recognisable in the public reaction to large youth groups in public space of a distinct subcultural identity. Punks,

production of space and the governmentality of a 'conduct of conduct' embedded in the ways of doing governance (discussed in Chapter 2). Conflict results between the concepts of space imposed upon a location, the perception and reaction of people to each other in a particular location at a given time and the uses of the location as they occur in each location.

The way in which users of public space reflect upon each other and pass through a location as time passes and as users enter and leave the boundaries of a specific location reflexively informs the meaning of that site. Equally, this informs the normative balance of the moral landscape embodied within it, for each individual and all users or participants, in a constant oscillatory process of becoming. This informs a singular moment of perception and reaction within spatial practices constitutive of experience, but one mediated in interplay with the imposition of a conceptual order on that location. By assessing this 'pathway of perceptive moments', spatial practices appear as a filtration system by which meaning can be produced and tied to the architectural boundaries of specific spaces through the lens of the individual's experience of the time–space–place. Each of these spaces has specific yet ambiguous interpretations from the perspective of each individual (as a user), all of whom generally act within the tenets of acceptability in line with their individual morality moment to moment as they experience a location. However, this experience is mediated concurrently by the concept of the location transposed through its design, management and conceptual ordering. This might be seen as the imposition of an entrepreneurial order embedded in the construction, management and regulation of the site.

Towards New Security Challenges and Ordering Regulation

The entrepreneurial urban order of a democratic city represented here is one that is, at its core, a well-intentioned reflection of mythic ideals and beliefs dominated increasingly by rules and norms of conduct that pull open the gaps in those ideals for exploitation by economic coalitions of interest. It is difficult to suggest that these are truly impersonal, rather that the personal economic interests of those at higher levels of the coalition are less apparent in the impersonal interplay of organisations within this framework of governance and governmentality. The open access logic underpinning the creation of an ordered commercial urban landscape is one that is driven by lofty ideals of economic inclusion but also subjective practices of implicit spatial and processual exclusion. It is inherently unbalanced in the engagement with the less powerful when they are not formally organised. The technical ways of doing are framed to enable economic forms of engagement as democratic functions of social order. The balance of access in a democratic urban order is one embedded in myths and beliefs of democracy, but the rules

---

for example, were famous for inciting 'fear' or 'moral panic' from the wider ranging conservative demographic in 1970s and 1980s England (Hebdige, 1979).

Resilience & the City

and laws that seek to balance these beliefs require a regulation of ethical conduct by location that does not map with the experience of the entire body-politic. The time–space–place of the city is, as such, mediated through an imbalanced spatial production. The meritocratic sense of what participation means is institutionalised through economic alignment in forms of thinking and doing, and as such operates in a limited way for those not engaged in economic activity. The next chapter will look at some of these variations by applying the challenges of maintaining an open-access social order in context and going deeper into an understanding of how regulation of the democratic city is emerging in line with the dangers now at the forefront of concern. The focus returns, therefore, to the role of disaster, violence and conflict as risks, threats and hazards to the urban social order. Alongside this is insight into the connection of wider practices of crime control and social ordering at a different level, as suggestions on the connections between these will begin to be made. It is quite clear that the challenges to creating a balance between the urban renaissance of the commercially refined democratic city with the challenges posed by the need to manage risks, hazards and threats in the democratic city are far from simple.

Chapter 6
The Struggle for Security: Ordering the Resilient City

I have an affection for a great city. I feel safe in the neighbourhood of man, and enjoy the sweet security of the streets.

Henry Wadsworth Longfellow

A Genealogy of Contemporary Danger

The previous chapter brings together the genealogical appraisal of interplaying forms in a troubling and potentially pessimistic view of an entrepreneurial urban social order. The discursive formation of this social order is presented as embedded in a neo-liberal democracy, one highly concerned with economic considerations. One should also note that this is not economic to the exclusion of human, social and cultural concerns, but rather a conception of the economic-oriented order as liberating the individual from inequalities and the imperialistic rule of political organisations, coalitions and elites – seen to be dominant features of Government and of the urban social order in the first half of the twentieth century. Perhaps such centralised Government-centric control was necessary during the World Wars, but in a globalising democratic project it is the 'market' that orders freedom. This is an approach that privileges economic coalitions, entrepreneurial freedoms and 'consumer' or 'shareholder' citizens over ideological elites. The beliefs, rules and norms in policy and governance are easily aligned with 'governmentality' – as a form of ordering that seeks to free individuals from tyrannical authority through free-market forces, thus producing new subjects better aligned with the market. However, translation of Friedman's (1962; 1980) and Hayek's (1973; 1976; 1979) economic neo-liberalism into social policy has resulted in a narrow reconstitution of beliefs, rules and norms with more limited than open general features and characteristics in the resulting alignment of social order. The citizen subject thus produced is a rational and selfish individual, seeking betterment in their own ability to consume; this is now implicit and endemic within many social policies and undermines the rational logic of economic ordering that it purports to create.

One might look at this discussion and say 'so the institutions are imbalanced, the organisations are imperfect. What else is new?' and one would be right to do so. There is not a perfect inclusive system of rule on earth that can include everyone when we operate at the global scale of contemporary civilisation. A pragmatist might look at the system as imperfect but perhaps the best we have managed to create so far; but as the increasing frequency, scale and scope of crisis and disaster suggest, there are new challenges facing the continuance of this order coming to the fore. Social order can ill afford to become entrenched in sticky political institutions if it is to grow on a positive and stable trajectory, if it is to be resilient to the challenges now faced. The current alignment of complex systems is changing not just the process of governing but the spaces of everyday life in ways that are potentially not resilient to these diverse dangers. The wider interplay of forms of thinking, doing and acting is central to understanding the struggle to maintain a fragile social order, and to transform into a more adaptive alignment at the heart of this discussion. The struggle for security discussed in this chapter reflects the cross-scale changes to institutions and organizations, and highlights the trajectory of change through a different lens, that of danger. The discussion of danger through the ongoing creative-destruction of global neo-liberal capitalist democracies in the face of old, new and evolving risks, hazards and threats is where we now turn.

Re-Contextualising Risk, Hazards and Threats

Risks, hazards and threats are amongst the repeating topics throughout this discussion of urban order and disorder, and it is important to note that despite all being constituted as dangers these are all treated as having different causes, but are often constituted in similar terms. This implies that when treated as potential disasters, all of these dangers represent 'the interdependent cascade of failure triggered by an extreme event that is exacerbated by inadequate planning and ill-informed individual or organisational actions' (Comfort, 2005: 338). This is equally true of wars that are promulgated by seemingly legitimate nation-state governments as of accidents or attacks by extremist groups, depending on your point of view. These themes cut across all of the major aspects of what we are, in fact, securing in every interpretation. In terms of risks we see a tendency towards the specification of man-made dangers, socio-technical risks of industrial capitalism. A simplified view is to suggest that risks emerge from the negative consequences of human agency, or from cycles or systems established by human action. Hazards pre-exist and are not dependent on human agency. Hazards 'derive from the natural processes of events' (Hewitt, 1983: 10); they are physical agents of the natural world embodied by ecological or environmental cycles. Threats are human also, but these are not the same as risks; threats emerge from formal military conflict between recognised nation-states, socio-political or religious coalitions and networks. For example, there may be a risk of disorder in the form of civil unrest amongst the populous – during an economic upheaval such as the Great Depression or the Global Financial Crisis – but this is different from the disorder engendered by a declared threat – made by a formal coalition, be it state-based (e.g. Irish Republican Army) or a cellular non-state organisation (e.g. Al Qaeda). There are potential interdependencies in the interplay between dangers, what can be called 'cascades' or causality chains. The different forms have been described as (a) Cascading Failure – a disruption in one infrastructure causes a disruption in another, which then causes sequential failures in other infrastructures; (b) Escalating Failure – when a disruption in one infrastructure causes a worsening of the failure already occurring independently; (c) Common Cause Failure – when multiple infrastructures are affected simultaneously by the same source of disruption (Little, 2002; 2010). These are far from comprehensive, however. For example, when hurricane Katrina caused a levee failure there was severe flooding in New Orleans, the power supply was subsequently interrupted, but also, later on, the sewage and clean water supply were also interrupted. This represents all of the above categories in different ways. Equally, human, ecological and technological systems have interdependencies that are vulnerable to generalised cascade effects. A threat (e.g. bomb) or a hazard (e.g. flood, fire, earthquake) can trigger both human failures (e.g. looting of food stores) or technological failures (e.g. damage to power cables). Human agency is not a system directly connected in the way infrastructure is hard-wired together, yet organisations and institutions of order also exhibit similar systemic frailty despite having different characteristics or components. A rough taxonomy cannot encapsulate every characteristic or component of every potential danger, nor of every potential consequence, but it can help direct how we deal with it, helping to focus priorities for where action may be required. Thus, broad typological approaches to these distinctions can be extended into more formal knowledge and applied in various contexts as required by different organisations.

For much of the last hundred and fifty years threat is prominent in the struggle for security, due on the one hand to the constant warfare – from the Boer war to the Iraq and Afghan conflicts of the early twenty-first century – and more recently the transformation of terrorism from state agencies to non-state cellular extremist networks. Concurrently, the social and environmental sciences have benefitted from institutional and technological advances, leading to both hazard and disaster studies gaining profile and influence. The study of hazards, vulnerabilities and risks use different approaches, but all address elements of environmental and anthropogenic risks. These areas of interest cut across the rough typology offered above, and when viewed alongside the previous discussion of democratic and entrepreneurial urbanism there are numerous ways in which hazards, threat and risks can be added to our analysis of the struggle for security. The new security and all hazards approaches can also give insight into the ongoing realignment of beliefs, rules and norms in the conduct of everyday life in the democratic city. The interdependencies are not always immediately apparent, so hazards, threat and civil unrest in the contemporary city will be discussed independently below, then brought together as 'all hazards' in the discussion of resilience in the next chapter.

Ecological and Environmental Danger: Hazards, Disasters, Vulnerabilities

Significant attention has been paid earlier to the role of natural disaster, the environment and ecological concerns as an influence of social order and change. One can read this as having given emphasis to the external factors relating explicitly to the disaster event as an agent of change, but this would be only a limited view of what has been presented. Attention has also been paid to the interplay of rules, beliefs, norms through which the disaster is thought of, understood and 'dealt with' differently – in the institutionalised forms of thinking and organisational forms of doing that allow the affected to manage or mitigate impact, and the resulting disorder. Disasters read thus have external causal features but are still formed discursively and socially constructed. How a civilization learns from exposure and adapts brings to light the (re)constitution of forms of thinking and doing to create 'resilience' in the interplay of complex social systems (see the next chapter). One must look at the interplay through particular definitions of disaster and crisis (and, to a lesser extent for us here, catastrophe) to understand the danger posed to the democratic city by ecological and environmental danger.

Defining the Contemporary 'Disaster'

The concept of disaster is highly contested, with perspectives from a range of academic disciplines and professional front-line expertise. Disaster and crisis may be seen as different forms of similar or related events in a complex taxonomy (Shaluf et al., 2003; Quarantelli and Dynes, 1977), but it is acknowledged that there is no single definition that can fit the purposes of such a diverse group of interests and stakeholders (Quarantelli, 1987; Cutter, 2005). The approach taken here considers the interplay between these forms of thinking. Gilbert (1998) argues that the understanding of disaster in social science research has been divided into three broad stages: (1) a duplication of war, insofar as this is attributable to an external agent which draws a reaction from the human community; (2) an expression of social vulnerability as an inward-looking social process; and (3) the entrance into a state of uncertainty tightly linked with the impossibility of knowing if danger is real or imagined. The 'classical' definition of disaster echoes this first paradigm, presenting disaster as the negative impact of an external 'physical agent' (Killian, 1954). This can be seen as the geophysical agent itself, the consequences of that agent and the way in which the agent is understood (Moore, 1958; Fritz, 1961).

A number of more socially oriented definitions throughout the 1970s and 1980s present disaster as a socially constructed form of 'consensus crisis' with risk of 'social fracture' (Gilbert, 1998). Such approaches build on the impact of the geophysical agent but go further in addressing the disorderly nature of human conflict in relation to disaster. A socially constructed disaster might prevent normal social functions from taking place beyond the critical infrastructure damage created by a geophysical agent in the form of an ecological or environmental hazard. A disaster as such is linked to institutionalised knowledge, as well as to the actions of individuals, organisations and communities before, during and after it occurs, but can have very different causes, characteristics and results. Over the last 50 years there has been a continual refinement of the core concepts and typologies underpinning disaster research (Quarantelli, 1998). As particular trends emerge and ebb away, the shifting emphases have included: a priority on either psychology, organisations or systems; debating the unit of analysis (individual or group); merging and bifurcation of focus on the complexity of individual, collective or organisational behaviours under stress; the need to understand pre-impact or post-impact stages and change; the need to build complex or generic models; debate over the priority of short- or long-term consequences, and the need to better embed the academically institutionalised disaster research into public policy for agencies on the front line (Quarantelli and Dynes, 1977).[1] More recently, cross-disciplinary approaches build on these debates to define 'disaster' as more than an ecological crisis event with an impact on people and physical 'things' in order to integrate the best of prior approaches; thus presenting disasters as a cycle of 'stability-disruption-adjustment' (Perry, 2006).

The 'hazards' approach is somewhat different from the 'disaster' literature but has arrived at a similar point. In 'hazards' research a very clear link is made between ecological and human systems highlighting the joint vulnerabilities of both forms and potential 'hazard adjustments' (ecological, biological, cultural) to mitigate these dangers (Tierney et al., 2001). This arguably incorporates a sense of the hazard agent as emerging from the natural world, i.e. as an ecological hazard which can affect human agency (e.g. flood, fire, etc.) and vice versa in the case of socio-technical dangers (e.g. pollution, etc.). The work of Gilbert White has been central to the development of this research:

> [In] Gilbert White's work neither the concepts of human mastery over nature nor a vulnerable dependency are accepted; neither human beings nor nature are fixed or finite. White shows how nature and human society interact to produce both resources and hazards. (Kates and Burton, 1986b: xv)

In this approach the complexity of choice and constraint are used as variables to inform the study of 'human ecology' (Kates and Burton, 1986a: 325). Importantly, it is the links between geophysical agents and human systems that are at the core of this approach. Much of the work inspired by this approach has moved away from the unity and transformation that underpins the socio-ecological logic of White. Instead, 'hazards' research has tended to focus on improved command and control in organisational structures and technological fixes to ecological problems (Hewitt, 1998). As such, it is often outcome-oriented linking improvements to

---

1   Much of this research can be linked to the influential Disaster Research Centre (DRC) in the United States.

critical infrastructure that can be designed and implemented to mitigate the impact of physical agents on human systems (individuals, organisations and communities).

A potential third approach is underscored by concepts of 'development' and 'vulnerability', looking at scale and the interplay between local, regional and global levels. Interdisciplinary development studies can be seen as 'anchored' in political economy and searching for social, political and economic structures that lead to poor quality development (Fordham, 2006). Poor development can thus itself open the conditions of possibility for disaster to occur, an issue at the heart of global risk society theories and central to debates over the social cost of uneven economic development, and the creation of global cities with very high vulnerabilities amongst the poorest embers of society. All too often, case study research highlights the staggering vulnerabilities in 'cities of slums' juxtaposed with the glass and steel development of global financial exchanges (Davis, 2006). The focus of research here is often divided between the participation by the community in securing the city for themselves and on highlighting the vulnerability of particular areas and demographics to push for disaster risk reduction policy and increased focus on human security in the face of danger (Pelling, 2003; Pelling and Wisner, 2009).

Typology, Taxonomy and the Disaster Cycle

There are two common themes in all of these approaches. On the one hand is the categorisation of disaster agents (from any and all sources), on the other is the cycle of activities to deal with the dangers they pose (by any and all individuals, coalitions or organisations). The OECD (Dayton-Johnson, 2004) developed ecological and environmental disaster agents into a typology that included both environmental and biological events from 1900–2002 (see Table 6.1). The most frequent events were wind storms (28.91%) and floods (27.11%), followed by earthquakes (10.21%), epidemic (9.89%) and drought (8.87%). This excludes from the definition man-made industrial events such as pollution, oil or chemical spill which have an impact on the social and ecological system. It also omits dangers to the food supply chain posed by potential biological crises to non-humans, such as 'foot and mouth' or 'blue tongue disease'.

Such dangers are biological, but emerge from issues of sustainable supply chains. Contamination of food and water are causally linked to severe loss of life for the population of many developing nations, and as such are worthy of inclusion (Koc et al., 1999). The way natural hazards are categorised is important for understanding the treatment of specific dangers and prioritising work amongst specialist and expert organisations. Different government agencies or private organisations have different concerns, but also different capabilities to bring to the table, and different uses for typologies (like this one) when produced by researchers. The natural disaster is primarily *ecological*, emerging from the natural processes of the environment, or *biological*, in terms of human, animal and plant diseases.

Table 6.1   A typology of disasters

Disaster type	Frequency	%	Disaster type	Frequency	%
Drought	782	8.87	Flood	2,390	27.11
Earthquake	900	10.21	Insect infestation	72	0.82
Epidemic	854	9.69	Slide	449	5.09
Anthrax	4	-	Avalanche	76	
Arbovirus	132	-	Land Slide	373	
Diarroeal/enteric	349	-			
Diphtheria	4	-			
Intestinal protozoal	6	-			
Leptosporosis	10	-			
Malaria	36	-	Volcano	169	1.92
Measles	36	-			
Meningitis	149	-			
Plague	16	-	Wave/surge	42	0.42
Rabies	7	-	Tidal Wave	19	
Respiratory	25	-	Tsunami	23	
Rickettsial	6	-			
Small pox	11	-			
Viral hepatitis	7	-			
Unknown	56	-			
			Wild Fire	270	3.06
			Forest	183	
			Scrub	87	
			Wind Storm	2,547	28.91
			Cyclone	411	
Extreme temperatures	263	2.98	Hurricane	335	
Cold wave	160	-	Storm	793	
Heat wave	103	-	Tornado	174	
			Tropical Storm	83	
			Typhoon	510	
			Winter	241	
Famine	77	0.87			
Crop Failure	11	-			
Drought	14	-			
Food Shortage	51	-			
Other	1	-			
			TOTAL	**8,815**	**100.00**

Source: EM-DAT (2004).

These might be framed as what Ulrich Beck referred to as 'pre-industrial risks' emerging unpredictably from the bio-ecological systems of the natural world. Environmental or ecological hazards thus need to be conceived in broader terms, as inclusive of the risks posed from developed industrial capitalism, the anthropogenic and technological risks posed by globalised production and consumption, the vulnerability of interdependent supply chains for the delivery of basic needs, goods and resources. The potential cascade effects across systems under stress can give a picture of the links between cause (shoddy design of flood defence), incident (Category 4 Hurricane), event (major levee breach), phenomena (flooding, loss of life, damage to property) (Little, 2010), but this is only a broad picture. The detail of the events is in the interplay between the institutions, organisations, the infrastructures and the individuals, etc. through and over time. Rather than a static and singular definition, a flexible set of definitions is more useful. This can then be applied to particular organisational requirements in distinct settings where disaster may have an impact.

Dangerous Threats: War and Military Urbanism

One way of drawing together the key issues of war, security and terrorism is what Graham (2010: xiii) highlights as fundamental qualities of the 'new military urbanism', in so far as the public (communal) and private spaces of the city, the infrastructure and the population can all be reconceived as simultaneously 'a source of targets and threats'.

The prevalent metaphor of war is one that has come to signify more than the literal conflict between organised armed forces, though that meaning is as relevant now as it ever has been. The war on poverty, the war on crime, the war on drugs, the war on graffiti, even the 'war on everything' by Australian satirist collective The Chaser, war is a powerful metaphor for the commitment to change, unto the destruction and eradication of the object. The global war on terror is oxymoronic, given the military emphasis of methods used to execute the often seemingly unplanned pathway to an elusive and ill-defined victory. Yet war remains at the heart of the requirement for increased security and the planning and redevelopment of urban locations underpinning urban transformations now underway.

The formation of the city and the realignment of urban form through war and security have a long history of relationships in democratic orders. Following from the World Wars of the early to mid twentieth century there was widespread change in the conduct of warfare and significant impact on the urban environment, leading to massive investment in infrastructure and property throughout reconstruction years which followed. This significantly stimulated the economy and freer markets for the movement of finance and greater financial incentives for cooperation. During this period massive cross-border movements were not limited to communication and resources, but also included massive movements of peoples. Migrant cultural minorities were quick to formalise membership in the civil society through creation of ethnic or religious societies and clubs, as well as participation in the culture of working-class organisations and trade unions as civilian, non-corporate and non-government or 'third sector' organisations. Scientific management of the workplace as well as the industry allowed for a consolidation of capitalist organisations, whilst the government and civil society undertakings in social programs ameliorated the institutional consolidation of a moderate form of open access for these third sector organisations. The changing social, economic and political conditions saw key shifts in the balance of other institutions in the interplay of beliefs, rules and norms in flux. The widening of state provisions in education and welfare created unprecedented levels of inclusion; universal suffrage also contributed to wider social change, as did the rise of new models of social insurance to reduce the risks of market participation across social divisions, for example unemployment, health and accident insurance programmes. This uneasy alignment of interests has informed social, political and economic tensions ever since in the attempt to balance the strong sense of nationalism emerging from the wars with the open-access multiculturalism at the moral heart of liberal democratic traditions, and the need for minimal standards of social security alongside economic and geo-political security.

Equally, there have been substantial shifts in the role of the nation-sate in the conduct of warfare. The terminology of a revolution in military affairs (RMA – see Table 6.2) in its modern usage can be linked back to the Soviet Armed Forces in the 1970s and 1980s, and was adopted by the American military soon after, however the framework of revolution as a metaphor for transformations in the conduct of war can be compared to the shifting interplay of wider forms beyond the technological and organisational emphasis given to the contemporary variation, as evoked in the discussion of Chaliand's typology (discussed in Chapter 4).

Technology has been a significant feature of warfare in the twentieth century, with blitzkrieg tactics, the use of aircraft carriers to extend the range of bombing missions and the development and deployment of submarines to counter the growth of combined naval and aerial threats, up to and including the nuclear arms race and the subsequent attempts to rebalance through disarmament. The revolutions thus presented may appear primarily technological and tactical, but have much wider antecedents in the institutional culture of key organisations to overcome before being successfully implemented as directed actions or operational tactics. In many cases, the use of the term revolution itself is somewhat misleading.Military organisations and the conduct of warfare have, throughout history, been shown to have an institutional inertia. This makes the trajectory easy to trace but also has made many of these organisations resistant to change, as shown by the British military operations in World War I and II and the American military operations in Vietnam (Murray, 1997: 76). For our discussion here it is a useful segue into from the conduct of war to its potential impact on the urban, as a destructive influence; as the form of warfare relates to the construction of the city, to its destruction and to its subsequent rebuilding.

Table 6.2   Potential revolutions in military affairs

Time Period	Innovation	Form of Revolution
14th century	Longbow	Cultural
15th century	Gunpowder	Technological, financial
16th century	Fortifications	Architectural, financial
17th century	Dutch-Swedish tactical reforms	Tactical, organisational, cultural
	French military reforms	Tactical, organisational, administrative
17th–18th centuries	Naval warfare	Administrative, social, financial, technological
18th century	British financial revolution	Financial, organisational, conceptual
	French Revolution	Ideological, social
18th–19th centuries	Industrial revolution	Financial, technological, organisational, cultural
19th century	American Civil War	Ideological, technological, administrative, operational
Late 19th century	Naval war	Technological, administrative, cultural
19th–20th centuries	Medical	Technological, organisational
20th century	World War I	Combined arms, tactical, conceptual, technological, scientific
	Blitzkrieg	Tactical, operational, conceptual, organisational
	Carrier war	Conceptual, technological, operational
	Strategic air war	Technological, conceptual, tactical, scientific
	Submarine war	Technological, scientific, tactical
	Amphibious war	Conceptual, tactical, operational
	Intelligence	Conceptual, political, ideological
	Nuclear weapons	Technological
	People's war	Ideological, political, conceptual

Source: Adapted from Murray (1997: 70).

The revolution of military affairs is in this light also a social-spatial and organisational influence in the ongoing transformation of time–space–place.

It is important to link the institutional values underpinning potential change back to the organisational inertia. What was happening to stimulate the realignment of workplace culture in the organisation, what wider socio-political, cultural and experiential moments can be incorporated into the complexity of change over time? For the analysis of the interplay of forms to hold water it must therefore be broadened to include socio-anthropological considerations.

In the UK during the First World War, for example, the mass mechanisation of production through the adoption of the production line model of munitions manufacture allowed for the swift mobilisation and replenishment of arms; this further reinforced the widening of the franchise to women. It also contributed to the creation of wider conditions of possibility for social change in the mid twentieth century by incorporating younger people into the workforce. This new market of consumers with disposable income fuelled by the subsequent post-war baby boom would eventually become recognised as 'teenagers'. The beliefs and norms of teenagers raised a challenge to established beliefs, rules and norms throughout the 1960s and 1970s, in turn contributing to wider social reforms, both positive and negative. On the one hand concerns of a potential communist uprising in many circles of American government emerging from the Cold War cross over Murray's revolutions in 'intelligence' (conceptual, political, ideological) and 'nuclear weapons' (technological), stimulating legal reform, and explicit rules (in policing strategies) for the control of beliefs to reinforce a capitalist and democratic norm across the social order of the day. Equally, the commercialisation of youth subculture has also contributed to subsequent widening of beliefs around equality and freedom of choice through the expansion of consumerism in everyday life.

It could be argued that such social change in the beliefs and norms reflexively inform and are informed by the adoption of free-market neo-liberal approaches to government in the 1980s through to the present day. These changes have all influenced the underpinning logic of social ordering in different ways and, taken in relative isolation, are interesting case studies. Bringing them together, albeit even in a cursory fashion as has been done above, shows that the interplay between forms can be viewed through a wider lens. When this is attempted we can see the patterns in this ebb and flow over time. It can be argued that no period in history has seen as much dramatic, or perhaps rapid, change as the twentieth century. Of key interest to us in terms of charting the links of war and conflict through the social ordering of the entrepreneurially aligned democratic city are 'nuclear war', for its effect on the planning of the urban landscape, and the concept of 'people's war', which as an ideological, political and conceptual form of warfare links strongly to the framework of authority and ordering of beliefs, rules and norms. Furthermore, it repositions the importance of understanding the distinctions between the criminality of terrorist actions and the fringe acceptability of the challenges to social order posed by political protest and direct action in contrast to urban disorder from criminal activity or rioting and civil unrest.

Danger From Anthropogenic Risks: Terrorism and Civil Unrest

In connecting the concerns of warfare and conflict to the individual citizen and the city, there are two final forms to address in the struggle for the city. The first is the threat of foreign or domestic terrorism, and the second is civil unrest resulting from either civil disorder or public protest. Both of these are dynamic processes that are increasingly at the heart of attempts to redesign the city and plan out the potential for disruptions to the orderly flow of commerce in the entrepreneurial realignment of time–space–place. Equally, both of these are intimately linked to both the reconstitution of our concepts of war or warfare and to those of disaster previously discussed in this chapter.

Terrorism is a problem. Not just in the obvious sense of danger posed by a terrorist attack, but in terms of bringing to bear an objective analytical focus on a concept that is changed by the perspective from which one views it. The adage 'One man's terrorist is another man's freedom fighter' is now a cliché and not a particularly useful one; however, as to what can be called terrorism, this is defined by international laws that surround the legitimate conduct of war. Context and perspective thus are as important as the legitimacy of the beliefs, rules and norms by which conflict is conducted. In this sense terrorism is war conducted by any means necessary, usually outside the legal constraint of any 'rules of engagement' sanctioned by a nation-state, international regulatory agency (such as the ICC), or NGO (such as the UN). Using this approach one can reflect upon terrorism as the failure by the antagonists to distinguish between soldiers and military-related critical infrastructure as 'legitimate combatants' or 'targets' and civilians or public spaces where civilians gather as 'innocent bystanders'. International conventions such as the Geneva and Hague Conventions 'thus differentiate between soldiers who attack a military adversary, and war criminals who deliberately attack civilians' (Ganor, 2002: 288). The situation becomes more complex, however, when incorporating non-state actors and coalitions not thus bound by the rules of traditional warfare, as previously classified. Also, complexity is added when a coalition may see the citizen as complicit in the actions of governments or as a heretic by religious doctrine, and therefore a legitimate target. Modern thinking in the context of the 'war on terror' campaign has been forced to draw on different conceptions of non-state cellular coalitions, as well as theological reasoning for conflict not seen since the crusades. Whilst such cellular networks may share institutionalised beliefs and norms, they do not often subscribe to traditional organisational structures nor to the Western logic of legitimate warfare. The post-Westphalian traditions of 'just war' that centre on the identification of a legitimate enmity have a tendency to somewhat exalt the legitimacy of violence undertaken on the moral and political authority of the state in unwholesome ways that do not reflect or incorporate the collateral damage and potential for this to be seen as state-sanctioned terrorism, or for the implications of terrorism within a state where coercion is used to enforce social order (Asthana and Nirmal, 2009).[2]

A rough framework of terrorism in recent history would see many different forms of political, criminal and pathological terrorism. A dominant alignment is 'political terrorism'; arguably the most studied of these forms, the field draws on notions of social revolutionary, nationalist or separatist and political theology (Hudson, 2002). A second interesting alignment is 'criminal terrorism'. Whilst an act of terror is certainly criminal, this refers at once to the cross-border crime (e.g. people trafficking) often tied to the financial web supporting extremist groups, but in a more prosaic alignment it can also be linked to debates over civil disobedience and anti-social behaviour – an anecdotal link made perhaps most concrete in the UK during the Queen's speech to the nation in 2006. This political rhetoric can be used to notionally bridge the gap between anti-social criminality (discussed in the previous chapter as a direct threat to the entrepreneurial city) and the logic of visible security that emerged from the 'war on terror' and the London bombings in 2005. Echoes of this rhetoric have appeared clearly in the USA (Molina, 1993), the UK (Garret, 2007) and Germany (Boyne, 2004). A third is 'pathological terrorism', which suggests the individual decision-making can be unpacked through a psycho-social framework. This is problematic insofar as the approach risks divesting terrorism of its political nature entirely, as well as raising issues over choice and agency of the individual (Branyar and Skjølberg, 2000). Where this might be more useful is in understanding the seemingly random act of a disturbed individual, but of course these are exceptional and unusual examples, and thus limited in their use to specific case studies. The redefined meaning of war tied to global cellular terrorism is one that has significant repercussions for the regulation of violence by sovereign nations, but also for the forms of violence undertaken by other non-state political groups – tensions over issue-based direct action protest (e.g. Greenpeace) and the declaration of 'war', in some cases 'holy war' (jihad) which is significantly different from a 'just war' in the Western judicial tradition. The redefinition of war has also had an impact on other forms of dissent short of violent attack against the body politic (this is returned to in the discussion of protest below). As seen by the site and target of attacks, in the 1980s the focus of terrorism has been affected by the nature of conflict, but also by the interplay of actions taken to reduce vulnerability to attack. As government officials and state buildings are 'hardened', the attention of attackers moves to 'soft' locations such as vulnerable critical infrastructure networks and public locations (Gilbert et al., 2003; Coaffee, 2010). The city is a key site of importance for unpacking the interplay of war, terrorism, security and safety for those moving through and living in the city, especially as in such a

---

2   Such 'humanitarian' logics have, however, been used at times as a partial justification for war, for example in military interventions in Bosnia, Iraq, Afghanistan, Somalia and Libya.

war both the city and the citizen can be interpreted as both targets at risk and the source of potential disorder through civil unrest.

The Danger of Civil Unrest: Disorder, Disobedience, Protest and Crime

In Chapter 4 the issue of civil unrest was linked to examples from Republican Rome and industrial Manchester. Now the same framework is applied to public protest, riot and policing of the contested space of protest in the city of today. Arguably, since Baron Haussmann's plan for Paris the design of urban space has been an essential consideration for how the urban population experience the urban, with conflict at its heart. It has been established that different types of unrest occur for different reasons at different times – war and the destruction of the city by conflict is ever possible, as is civil unrest leading to destruction, disruption and disorder. Urban space is often conceived in terms of conflict and disorder, and such conflict often emerges from civil protest against inequalities, exclusions or abuse of power by the dominant coalition. A genealogical appraisal of beliefs, rules and norms can be aligned with the production of contested spaces reflecting the rhythmanalytical contestation of time–space–place to interrogate these conditions. More simply, we can use the toolbox developed in this discussion to uncover (a) what is being contested by whom, (b) what the contested location means to all parties, (c) particularly, how it *should be* or *is being* used aligns with particular attempts to order or disorder everyday life, which gives insight into how contestation of order is experienced by all involved. The answer to each of these points adds another lens through which we can focus a sense of meaning and thus better understand the reality of what occurred and why. When considering civil unrest there are many informing variables, including ethnic divisions, theological differences, economic inequality, urban design and socio-cultural malaise. Other forms that have a bearing on the contemporary treatment of civil unrest include security and terrorism, political protest, criminality and anti-sociability, which have been addressed to some extent above. It is useful here to draw on some examples to show how these forms interplay in different contexts.[3]

Urban Decline, Race Riots and Regeneration

Urban decline (as discussed in the previous chapter) was a feature of the post-World War II city in many countries, and some of the most striking examples of civil unrest of the twentieth century were perhaps the American 'ghetto revolts' during the 1960s. Organisations of government and institutionalised inequality

---

3   This is not intended to be read as philosophical 'contextualism'; rather, using context as an orientation for the application of genealogy and rhythmanalytical logics in a phronetic social scientific enquiry. For more on phronetic social sciences, see Flyvbjerg (2001).

alienated the African-American community, failing to meaningfully include the demographic in the democratic process, economic exchange or in the spatial management of the city. Forms of access to institutions and organisations were limited in this context through institutionalised racism against African-Americans, political malpractice in local and national government, economic deprivation and consumer exploitation, and residential segregation often in urban tenement communities (Fogelson, 1971). This complex interplay was addressed in the National Advisory Commission on Civil Disorders (NACDC), or the Kerner Commission, which in summary of the racial divisions at the heart of the violence stated:

> Violence cannot build a better society. Disruption and disorder nourish repression, not justice. They strike at the freedom of every citizen. The community cannot–it will not–tolerate coercion and mob rule. Violence and destruction must be ended–in the streets of the ghetto and in the lives of people. Segregation and poverty have created in the racial ghetto a destructive environment totally unknown to most white Americans. What white Americans have never fully understood but what the Negro can never forget–is that white society is deeply implicated in the ghetto. White institutions created it, white institutions maintain it, and white society condones it. (NACDC, 1968)

This was in response to two riots in New York, three in New Jersey, one each in Philadelphia and Chicago (1964), the Watts Riot in Los Angeles (1965), civil rights and race rioting in Cleveland, San Francisco, Chicago (1966) and the Newark and Plainsfield riots in New Jersey, as well as unrest in Detroit, and Minneapolis (1967) continuing into 1968 following the shooting and death of Martin Luther King. Such widespread civil unrest could not be attributed to a cultural malaise in the inner city community, it had to be deeper and linked back to social, economic and spatial deprivation. There was also contestation over the Equal Rights Act (1964), the reaction of peaceful protesters to police tactics and the wider changes the end of segregation created for ways of doing and acting in the broader urban civilisation. Civil unrest was also thus not seen as entirely criminal, designed to destroy and loot or even to draw attention to discrimination through destruction:

> Rather, rioting appeared more as a desperate and concerted effort to compel political authorities to change not only their policies but also to reform the process by which decisions are made. (Feagin and Hahn, 1973: 27–28)

The use of violent protest to effect change in a context where access to organisations is limited and inequality is institutionalised into the fabric of the everyday urban community is important in understanding the outbreak of disorderly violence from civil unrest.[4] Particular trigger events can be vital tipping points for shaping protest and civil unrest in relation to violence. The bombing of the 16th Street Church in Birmingham, Alabama in 1964 could be seen as a tipping point for the outbreak of racial violence, as could the shooting and death of Martin Luther King in 1968, but local conditions of possibility were also important: policing tactics, the urban environment, levels of employment and education all feed into the actual events.

These riots brought wider attention to the need for change in the organisation of urban democratic living that sparked widespread changes in the treatment, management and governance of cities over the next fifty years. Planners and civil servants were often given the task of addressing the problem of a sick and deprived urban core in need of redevelopment, but at the same time the authority of government and its ability to exert influence over individuals was consistently eroded. Successive waves of regeneration reshaped the post-industrial city concurrent with the rise of neo-liberal ways of doing in democratic capitalist nations. The end result was a view that saw the phoenix of the entrepreneurial global city rise from the ashes of industrial urban decay into a new egalitarian urban order of free markets and shareholder citizens (see Chapter 5). This had some specific ramifications for the management of ways of acting in particular urban locations (Chapter 6). In this order the individual entrepreneur was liberated from the old class and race discriminations that were at the heart of urban rioting and disorderly ways of life. Ironically, this realignment has engendered different forms of civil unrest (see below).

Neo-liberal economic policies engendered a fundamental shift in the art of government that increasingly passed responsibility for economic performance to local coalitions of corporate and civil stakeholders, and individual citizens. Monitoring the success or failure of a coalition to meet its obligations is achieved by setting targets and key performance indicators against which the innovative entrepreneur is assessed. The city and its space took on a different role, rather than as public spaces managed in trust by government for the public, the spaces of the city have increasingly been conceptualised as assets to be deployed for specific purposes, to raise the performance of the city in socio-economic rather than democratic terms. As such, the shift in the management of public space has moved from sustaining social order in the Greek tradition to sustaining economic order. The public remains at the same time a contested space in which citizens are able to oppose the elite coalition, but this creates conflict with the increasingly privatised treatment of appropriate uses of more controlled commercial pseudo-public spaces. Extreme examples can be found in cities like Los Angeles, where a new bunker landscape emerged (Davis, 1998). The London Docklands were

---

4   The most prominent theories for explaining violence are (a) sociological theories of collective violence and social conflict, (b) a game theoretic model of rational choice and (c) socio-psychological theories of cognitive dissonance or frustration and aggression. All of these are relevant to wider discussion of violence, but none are holistic explanations for why these events occur.

regenerated in the heart of some of the most deprived urban areas of the country to give rise to a new deregulated financial empire, echoed in other global cities (Minton, 2009). The ethnic and economic riots of the 1960s–1980s were replaced by forms of highly policed and well-ordered or 'acceptable' political protest that protect these economic spaces from disruptive citizens. As such, one can propose a realignment of civil unrest broadly split into legitimate forms of political protest and criminally destructive disorder.

Disorder, Policing and Political Protest

Political protest is a spatial activity by its very nature. As noted by Zajko and Bléland (2008), the 'protest march transforms the street from a transportation corridor heavily regulated by government power into a venue for the public expression of contentious claims' (Ibid.: 721). The contestation of space highlighted above in relation to the American 'ghetto riots' shows that these were on the one hand an attempt to address social inequalities, and they can be read as an informal or potentially spontaneous form of political protest. At present, civil unrest as political protest has become far more formal and ritualised in institutionalised actions by organised coalitions, often attempting to make an ideological point – such as the coordinated anti-war 'protest marches' in cities around the world in February 2003. Such protest is not centred on destruction, rather on disruption of the orderly flow of day-to-day life though civil disobedience to bring a particular grievance into focus, call to account decision-makers and open public debate. Such contestation creates a situation of heightened tensions between the tasks of ensuring the orderly flow of everyday life, protecting the rights of citizens to voice dissent whilst ensuring that elites do not abuse power or exclude other coalitions (from ethnic minorities to political parties and non-government organisations). The very complexity of this process shows how much more open access has become through the diversification of perpetually lived organisations such as non-government organisations (e.g. Greenpeace) and issue-based global protest networks (the anti-globalisation movement). However, the formalisation of dissent as a protected right to protest is changing in the current geo-political context of urban security concerns.

The World Trade Organization (WTO) Ministerial Conference was held in Seattle in 1999, and diverse groups came together to protest against WTO policy around the world including People for Fair Trade/Network Opposed to WTO (PFT), the Direct Action Network (DAN), the American Federation of Labor-Congress of Industrial Organizations (AFL-CIO) and local groups such as the King County Labor Council branch, AFL-CIO (KCLC) and the Labor Employment Law Office (LELO) (Levi and Murphy, 2006: 252). The coalitions had diverse approaches to the topic and the methods of protest and the sheer number of protesters (estimated between 40,000 and 50,000) in this coalition of interest groups meant that the predetermined policing tactics – arresting those engaged in civil disobedience – were not fit for purpose. The resultant cancellation of the first day's events by the WTO led to a firm response by the state and city police, use of militarised tactics (chemical irritants and rubber pellets), the creation of a 'No Protest Zone' around the Central Business District (CBD) and clearing the streets of protesters for the duration of the WTO summit. This led to an intensification of protesters' resistance and stimulated further disorder which led to some violence, destruction of property and over six hundred arrests (with only seventy-seven charges later laid) (Seattle Police Dept., 2000). Such a statistic shows the extent to which the tactical policing of the event drew close to, and perhaps crossed, the line of legitimacy for policing of dissent by the established rules, customs and traditions of democratic spatial governance for social ordering. This in itself, however, can be read in different ways. For the police, their obligation to protect the Seattle CBD, the delegates and the wider everyday users of the city streets was an operational concern. At another level, protecting the image of the organisation of law enforcement (as competent and capable) and the global city of Seattle (as a knowledge economy hub) required decisive action. For the protesters and many members of the local community, the build-up of police and the use of non-lethal weaponry caused widespread concern and the zoning of the city breached certain constitutional rights under dubious justification; furthermore, the enforcement of these questionable tactics broached several civil liberties (Herbert, 2007). Such pre-zoning tactics have since been in widespread use, perhaps most effectively during the global day of protest against the Iraq war in cities around the world (Mitchell and Staheli, 2005), but are now common practice in the policing of public protest. Indeed, Zick (2006) goes so far as to suggest that:

> the state has moved from *regulating* place to actually, in some cases, *creating* places for the express purpose of controlling and disciplining protest and dissent. This sort of spatial sophistication is a recent phenomenon. It represents a new generation of spatial regulations ... This is a substantial extension of the principle that the state may regulate the time, place, and manner of expressive activity. (Zick, 2006: 584)

The creation of exclusion zones and parade routes, but also tactics of open-air imprisonment of protesters known as 'kettling' and the granting or misuse of exceptional powers and terrorist laws for policing dissent, are increasingly common features of the landscape of protest. In the London tuition fees protests, campus and civil building occupations and refusal to follow predetermined and police-bordered routes led to a fierce crackdown by the police. Reports from those exposed to the policing tactics on the day suggest that comparatively calm protest was transformed by the 'containment' into an antagonistic situation which provoked protesters to give licence to violent actions by the police. The 'containment' typically lasted between four and eight hours, precipitating attempts to leave that were construed as violence, thus allowing the police to use violence to disperse the now riotous assembly (Younis, 2011). Equally, several problems have arisen in American cities from the 'occupy' movement where city spaces are reclaimed in protest against global capitalism. In Portland, as of 26th October

2011 the police used tear gas and flash-bang grenades to disperse the peaceful crowd (Collins, 2011); in California, a judge refused to prosecute arrests made during the dispersal of the Sacramento 'occupy' protest (Leach, 2011). Where the access to expression and information is open, it is the form of access to urban space that becomes contested – not the message but rather the time–space–place where it can be performed and thus 'heard'.

Whilst ethnic, theological, economic and cultural differences can all act as triggers for political forms of protest, it is a mistake to assume that all political protest is necessarily violent. Violence is frequently a consequence of tactical interventions by social ordering organisations (e.g. police, military). In the case of the American race riots and several of the political protests at major summits, global networks of protesters have confronted social order agents as representatives of the organisations that they protest against. Equally, the police are trained to deal with social disorder using strategies of containment and dispersal that do not stifle public expression or basic freedoms, rather curtail them temporarily to maintain order in a specific time–space–place. Regardless of the global or geo-political issues, it is in local spaces that such coalitions are most effective, and in local spaces where protests must occur. Mitra (1991) suggests that the local political coalitions in India are equally capable as larger non-government organisations, perhaps are even more effective. The reason for this is that when protest is supported by social order organisations, rather than aggressively policed, it can be integrated more meaningfully into local democracy. Such endeavours make for a less coercive alignment of the forms than those social orders that separate protest from institutionalised democratic participation. However, it is also noted that widespread reforms towards more neo-liberal, globalising capitalist beliefs, rules and norms within the social order, such as those highlighted above, even in the Indian model, have resulted in 'the use of force and "criminalisation" [becoming] increasingly present in the local political arena' (Mitra, 1992: 143). Equally, riots are only dispersed in developing and limited access democracies when it is in the interests of the dominant political coalition to limit the violence; when it is targeted at a minority group non-essential to electoral success, intervention in disorder is far less likely.

The global level offers many varieties and examples of geo-political protest, and at the local level many cases of contestation over the time–space–place of the city. As noted, it is often the local level where protest occurs, even if this draws on global issues. This is where the complexity of change in time–space–place for most individuals is experienced. At the level of the local community, protest is an act of political participation in the democratic process outside the institution of periodic representative elections. Protest can be disorderly and disobedient without being illegal, as the purpose of political protest is to circumvent or disrupt the orderly flow of everyday life to such an extent that those tasked with ordering everyday life must react to the argument placed before them. It is a way of lobbying the ruling coalition, to force them to hear an alternative perspective or even to demand that the concerns of the protesters be engaged with and acted upon by the dominant elite. Protest by its very nature is disorderly. It brings the paradoxical relationship of order and consent into contact, and thus conflict, with disorder and dissent. In seizure of the public city, alternative interpretations of the acceptable use of local spaces are forced into the everyday life of the city itself by the act of protest, in as simple a way as blocking a thoroughfare with singing, chanting, marching bodies. It is an inconvenience to the majority, but no more so than anti-social behaviour on the fringes of criminality (as discussed in the previous chapter). This is where the root meets the branch; political protest and forms of direct action that are taken in opposition to dominant coalition pose a threat to the orderly flow of everyday life, and as such require regulation. The spatial is brought into focus through the forms of intervention that emerge from policing tactics on the ground during an event, to the redesign of urban public space to 'design out' not just crime (as in CPTED) but also, intentionally or not, potentially the time–space–place of contestation and dissent are also threatened by those very changes that are intended to protect. This tension raises questions over the legitimacy of protest within such a system. In recent times many nations have enacted laws that blur the lines between acceptable civil disobedience, civil unrest, criminal disorder and security threat. The changing treatment of criminality discussed in Chapter 5 has widespread implications here as well, for political protest, organised dissent and anti-social criminality. However blurry the line may become, there are some clearly demarcated differences between what can be considered a political protest and criminal rioting.

Disorder as Criminal Rioting

In the above discussion of civil unrest, disorder has been treated implicitly as coming from a formal cause, emerging from the complex interplay of race, ethnicity, spatial distribution or disadvantage, and contestation enflamed by a trigger or tipping point *in statu na'scendi*. Such tipping points are most often local and time-limited, being tied to an event in the time–space–place of the city. It is a broad generalisation, but for the city in history such events were most often local in nature, tied to a specific suburb or social group. Larger-scale events, such as the machine breakers or 'luddites', the call for workplace regulation and fair wages, have a wider impact over time – emerging from broader social tensions that strain the interplay, they push the trajectory of events towards change by giving rise to new institutions (e.g. direct action, peaceful protest) and new organisations (e.g. the trade union); such changes can be linked to tipping points such as the Peterloo Massacre. Today, the potential is still present for a gathering of citizens to become a mob bent on disorder and destruction. However, the advent of the mass media, new information communication technology and social networks has changed the tempo, scale and effect of a trigger event.

Most of the major forms of civil unrest that have resulted in riot are tied to criminality in some way. However, as shown above, the framing of criminality in this context is often skewed in ways that reframe the activity and character of the offender and the space of the city that they contest. A protester can become a criminal by rezoning an area of the city to capture particular actions within a rebalanced interplay over time–space–place. Equally, the actions of protest can take on very different forms and provoke different responses; the legitimacy of the actions to control, repress or disperse the potential criminal rioters more often now depends on the framing of events *ex post facto* by social and political commentators in the mass media, but primarily in a legal setting.

Research into riots often focuses on these 'push' factors that drive people from civil unrest into disorder and, potentially, riotous assembly (Wilkinson, 2009). In Seattle, Genoa and other political summit meetings, policing strategies have later justified tactical decisions by highlighting the potential for civil disobedience to escalate into civil disorder. Walking this line is difficult, as police organisations are often criticised for allowing an assembly to gather, for contributing to trigger points that cause an escalation from disobedience to disorder to destruction and for not acting swiftly or strongly enough once the situation has escalated. Perhaps one of the most well-known minor police actions that lead to widespread conflict triggered the Los Angeles riots (1992) after the now infamous Rodney King incident – when the filming and broadcast of a young black male being violently arrested triggered rioting, during which protest descended into criminal destruction, indiscriminate racial violence and widespread looting, theft and property destruction. Similar incidents of conflict between local minorities and police can be identified as flashpoints in the Miami riots in 1980 and the Watts riots in 1960.

Despite being labelled as 'race riots', protest actions of this kind are different from formal political protest. When the spontaneous gathering of a crowd heightens tension between policing organisations and the public there is a layering of motivations within the crowd. Protest was directed at the organisation (the police) and institutionalised discrimination that Afro-American Angelinos perceived as inherent in the social order. However, some individuals and sub-groups thrive on the contestation itself, and the opportunity for profit inherent in civil disorder. Whilst some argue a social cause, protest an action or resist inequality, there are also those competing and concurrent opportunities for rationally weighing up the benefit of individual gain from criminal conduct within the conflict as it occurs (e.g. measures of the extent of policing, the costs of punishment, property ownership and the value of time). These considerations interplay with rational measures of gain for the community by protesters (e.g. improved social conditions and community stability, reduced racial segregation or relative poverty) in the decisions and actions of participants (Depasquale and Baker, 1998: 56). Widespread criminality can frequently surface not simply as a form of protest or resistance but as a consequence of circumstantial opportunities at that given time–space–place. Looting, the destruction of property and resources within the community suggests that the community cannot be treated as a homogenous group. Criminal rioting is thus distinct from political protest in a number of ways. Perhaps most significant is the intent of the action. Where protest may descend into violent conflict, destruction and criminality are not its purpose, nor the intent of the participants. Where criminal rioting occurs it is often more spontaneous, emerging from a trigger-point event and culminating in damage to the community undertaken for the personal profit of the individual. This poses the problem of intent during a disruption, a problem that is even more distinct when the riotous mob is treated as a homogenous group:

> [A]lthough we may assume in our interpretation of riot data that all members of a crowd are motivated by the stated goals of the so-called leaders, this may not be the case at all. Members of a crowd may come out to watch a public festival, or to defend a community symbol such as a mosque or temple, but then the actions of one or two rioters who shout political slogans and start throwing stones change the legal and social construction of all these individuals' actions to those of rioters in pursuit of a common cause. (Wilkinson, 2009: 331)

This is another problem of the 'push' factor approach to the study of riots. In the English riots of 2011 there is some evidence of the intent and purpose behind the rioting being harnessed from social networking, a feature of the disorder that has perhaps started to show another example of how deeply entrenched in everyday urban life such technologies have become during these events. A peaceful protest march on August 6th was organised by the family of a local police suspect (29-year-old Mark Duggan), who during a police action was shot and killed in the Haringey, London, local authority area. Following this rally, several groups of youths in the area stormed a police line set up to contain protesters; due to the sheer number of people mobilised – partly through social networks communicating the events and a degree of disorganised planning – the police were outnumbered and the line was overcome, resulting in widespread destruction of property and looting in Haringey. Over the next four days this pattern was repeated in other areas, and eventually in other cities, as social networks and the mass media broadcast the stretched police force, demonstrating the reduced risk to those undertaking looting, spikes in social network usage either precipitated or followed an increase in disorder in several other cities, and copycat riots targeted the commercial centres and police stations in fourteen other local areas of London, Birmingham, Liverpool, Manchester and numerous small and medium towns and peripheral urban areas in the South, Midlands and North-West. The tensions in specialist policing tactics which have recently emphasised political protest were arguably not best suited to curtailing a criminal riot. Once exposed, the lack of a strong response encouraged other entrepreneurial criminals to engage in low-risk acquisition by looting. However, events also changed over the four-day timeframe of the riots, as did the perception of rioters during that four-day period.

There were at least five deaths around the country linked to the rioting. In particular, the death of three young men in Birmingham from a 'hit-and-run' resulted in public calls from the family for an end to rioting, swinging community opinion and the focus of media attention away from the shooting of Duggan and social inequality as potential causes, onto social disorder and the human cost of the disruptions. Significant community measures were taken by minority groups; in one instance a group of Sikhs formed armed blockades of their own to protect religious buildings and residential streets. Anecdotal evidence suggests that such community response combined with the formal police response – which whilst slow starting was strong once mobilised – increasing the rates of arrests and the real threat of draconian penalties, and was aided by the broadcast of CCTV footage in the mass media as well as widespread public and political outrage. The 'push' factors for the violence are familiar, including the flashpoint event between community and police, widespread economic inequality and spatial segregation in low income areas. However, there are less familiar points to be considered. In the previous chapter the incremental exclusion of marginal interpretations of the entrepreneurial time–place–space of the city were highlighted, including anti-social and undesirable behaviour. Those less able to access the full range of choices made available through the entrepreneurial and post-industrial city are more likely to find themselves on the fringe of the beliefs, rules and norms underpinning this concept of the city and of urban everyday life. There is an inherent tension here in the use of a familiar language of 'sickness' that needs to be 'cured' and a 'broken society' that needs to be 'fixed', led by a combination of moral responsibilisation, a rallying cry to traditional social values and the threat of strong sanctions polished with an organisational overhaul of key social order organisations (Goodman, 2011). Where civil unrest and protest act as push factors on social change, so do the factors at the heart of rioting, resulting in attempts to redress the balance of the interplay between beliefs, rules and norms at numerous levels. The effect of these events, regardless of cause, is potentially long-lasting; where preventative policing measures (e.g. the blockade or 'kettling') are insufficient to quell unrest, more coercive measures may be used (e.g. the baton charge, incendiaries and chemical agents), leading to further flashpoints or the appearance of brutal repression by policing agencies in the attempt to maintain and restore order or protect both community resources and private assets.

Securing Free-Market Urbanism or Safeguarding Democratic Urbanism?

The new insecurity is a common feature of the entrepreneurial city. It is not the intention here to bemoan social change as a negative trajectory, nor to glorify or romantically recast the community of the industrial metropolis. The broad trajectory of change is clear. There has been a turn away from managerial regulation by governments towards a free-market model of entrepreneurial organisations. This is also true of the time–space–place of the city and is exemplified by legislative, situational and design-driven approaches to the management of fringe acceptability as potentially dangerous (Chapters 5 and 6). The 'danger shift' has occurred in tandem with the wider use of security-driven laws by social order organisations, but also in political organisations. A particular vision of order has become formalised into the beliefs, rules and norms of everyday life. One could argue that the attempt to free individuals of the old social divisions by surrendering decision-making authority to the free market has encouraged a drift towards more severe social and spatial segregation, requiring more sophisticated typologies of risk, hazard and threat overlaid with draconian spatial management strategies. The pattern of interplay across the complex interdependencies suggests a trajectory of change that increasingly conflates the emergent spatial and processual techniques of control within neo-liberal regimes of social ordering. Questioning the techniques and mechanisms of government that are used to direct and discipline becomes even more important as the call of Virilio to 'wage war' on the architectural edifices of liberal modernity (Reid, 2006: 84) begins to be played out in the experience of the city, not just through political protest but through the blurring of distinctions on both danger and criminality. In this reading of the city there is an implied domination of urban territory by entrepreneurial capital, rather than by the regulatory mechanisms of government, but these combined and overlaid open up the conditions of possibility for a cascade of institutionalised fragility to permeate socio-cultural, juridical and spatial forms. It is this triumph of the financial and economic that shifts the balance of power away from social concerns toward the concerns of capital in this landscape of conceptual 'war on everything'. Just as the World Wars shifted the logic of social organisation and (re)conditioned the body politic – through the destruction of the city in Europe and Asia, massive slaughter, massive rebuilding, emancipation, Auschwitz, Hiroshima and Nagasaki – these influences contributed to the realignment of interplay towards the liberal and now neo-liberal trajectory of global capitalism. The 'war on terror' is one amongst many forms in flux as the realignment continues today on a different pattern and a different level (or scale) of territory. This scale is not now explicitly tied to sovereignty; it rather cuts across and interpenetrates both the local and the global. From the geo-political level of rhetorical 'wars' and military strategy, the destruction and rebuilding of the city is aligned differently. From the total destruction of cities in countries torn by war (Graham, 2010), there is also in the post-industrial cities of the West contestation over the everyday territory of the street, the playground, the car park, the convention centre, the office, the sports stadium and the shopping mall, the residential suburb. These landscapes are all being perpetually contested, secured and rendered resilient to the danger posed by disorder of any and all kinds.

To this end, the rest of this book looks to harness the (re)alignment of these forms as they roll out, highlighting what is carried forward, what is learned, and what informs the adaptation of resilience through potential changes to the management of danger. Understanding danger as disastrous hazards, anthropogenic risks and security threats is here drawn through an etymological and genealogical review of what we mean by 'resilience'. Rather than bemoaning the frailties of the existing system for dealing with danger, the next chapter will look at these tensions in more depth. This helps us to start unpacking the (re)alignment of forms discussed above and carrying forward the current trends of enquiry into policy and process, thus contextually embedding the reading of resilience in the beliefs, rules and norms that inform how danger is dealt with. Some potential opportunities to increase positive change are highlighted and further potential for negative change is also noted. As in Chapter 4, the focus is concentrated again on necessarily broad topics – disaster, war, (dis)order and the city, but this time drawing these topics through the contemporary attempt to secure the resilience of the city.

Chapter 7
The Struggle for Resilience: Interplay and Urbanism

Our greatest glory is not in never failing, but in rising up every time we fail.
                                                                Ralph Waldo Emerson

Applying Genealogy and Interplay to Resilience

Throughout the book, the term resilience has been used consistently to refer to both the positive potential for a transformative adaptation and opening of access resulting from exposure to stimulus, and for the potentially negative resistance that emerges from sticky and unyielding institutions or organisations that can prevent positive change from occurring, even unto regression to a less open alignment of social order. The story of this book is an effort to tease out this meaning in theoretically informed but empirically grounded analysis, tracing the rising awareness of a more nuanced and complex systemic interdependency embedded in different ways in different contexts throughout the contemporary social (dis)order. The categorisation of dangers has been discussed, as have the various alignments of risks, hazards and threats as potential dangers to the democratic city. This attention will now be turned to the concept of resilience. Addressing resilience here, rather than earlier, positions the rise and rise of resilience in contemporary thinking roughly at the point in our story where it has come to take on a new significance. Resilience is a rhetorical tool and metaphor that encompasses the process of change as exposure of complex, dynamic and adaptive systems to uncertainty. It acts as an umbrella under which individuals, institutions and organisations define concepts, perceive space and other people and react to them. Resilience is about learning from exposure, but it is not as simple as such a presentation of the concept suggests. To build on both the abstract and the concrete elements of the genealogical approach undertaken throughout this book the concept of resilience will be unpacked in more detail. Having defined resilience, this chapter will then mobilise that approach to the realignment of attempts to deal with the disasters defined in previous chapters. Finally, how these affect, and might affect in the future, the time–space–place of the city will be discussed, before offering some summary thoughts on the direction of future research in the final chapter.

Resilience as a Generative and Emergent Metaphor

Recent attempts to develop a genealogy of resilience have often emphasised the importance of ecological science and systems theory (see, for example, Walker and Cooper, 2011). It is necessary to go deeper and further back to place this form of generative knowledge in its proper context. Thinking of how resilience has become influential as a concept requires a deeper understanding of its meaning. An etymological approach to the term thus informs the genealogy of its use in research, and the subsequent adoption of the emerging metaphor into political and policy rhetoric for dealing with disaster.

The Latin root of resilience has a number of variations, most prominent being the post-classical Latin *resilientia* which imbues a sense of avoidance which can be identified as early as 1540. More commonly understood is the 'action of rebounding', emerging slightly later. Recent research has tied resilience to Latin as *resilio* (see Klien, Nicholls and Thomalla, 2003) or as the Latin root of the French derivative *resiliere* (see, for example, Paton and Johnston, 2006). In the English common tongue, resilience appears in Francis Bacon's Sylva Sylvarum evoking a repercussive 'resilience of echoes' (1659) as a characteristic of sound. The common sense of the term in English has come to refer to resilience as a characteristic of 'things', but also of ways of thinking, doing, acting as characteristics or traits of individuals, institutions and organisations.

Resilience as a characteristic of material 'things' emerges from the engineering sciences in the nineteenth century, with reference to the efficiency of a material for taking strain. In this sense it refers to the obdurate qualities of materials when recovering from stress, most commonly wood and steel in the building of ships (Thompson, 2011 [1877]). In the twentieth century, research developed the engineering sense of resilience in different ways almost simultaneously in both ecology and psychology. Ecological resiliency emphasises the engineering resilience of the eco-system alongside the buffering capacity of the eco-system's ability to persist in the face of perturbation, drawing a sense of its ability to maintain robust functions (Holling, 1973). Psychology has framed resilience in terms of the positive adaptation of those who undergo exposure to harmful stimulus, originating in child psychology (Garmezy, 1971; 1973). These disciplinary roots all build on the original concept differently. However, they all position the definition of resilience as a characteristic that changes both itself and the subject in question as a result of stimulus, and this stimulus is often framed as a potentially destructive or negative influence on the original state. Resilience as such arises again in two further evolutions that inform the central characteristics of the concept in its relationship to dealing with disasters. The ecological definition can be linked to the psychological framing in both institutional and organisational contexts through its common features.

For example, in the 'evolutionary' approach that has come to build on Hollings's earlier work, the sense of maintaining robust functions has evolved into the adaptive capacity of socio-ecological systems. These systems are seen as interdependent in complex ways, rather than hermetically sealed from each other by virtue of the Enlightenment rationale that elevates the human above the ecological or the 'natural' world. Acknowledging the interdependence of biospheres and ecological systems (Levin, 1998) but also in terms of 'panarchic' socio-ecological systems (Gunderson and Holling, 2002) positions the process of interplay as a series of nonlinear, dynamic and complex adaptations. Resilience is not, as such, a quantifiable 'thing', but a means of assessing adaptive capacity through (a) the latitude in a system – as the point beyond which recovery becomes impossible, (b) the resistance of the system to change, (c) the precariousness of its current state and (d) the dynamics of cross-scale interactions between the components.

As seen in many of the examples through the previous chapters, the interplay of forms of thinking, doing and acting in synch with the external ecological hazard agents, as well as internally generated social conflicts from anthropogenic sources, mean that these systems are contextually contingent on the conditions of possibility within which a scenario emerges in a particular time–space–place. This is far closer to the messy unpredictability or uncertainty underpinning logics of risk, hazard and threat than traditional or classical approaches to individuals, institutions and organisations as limited or subjugated by structural hierarchies, and allows for a more nuanced understanding of interplay as an ongoing process. Extending the socio-ecological systems theory, interplay is the process by which a disturbance to a socio-ecological system stimulates the unpredictable reorganisation of both the ecological and social elements, thus allowing both to mitigate the potential impact of a disruption.

Table 7.1   A taxonomy of resilience in research

Discipline	Characteristics	Source
Engineering	Return-time / RECOVERY Material EFFICIENCY	Thompson (1877) Holling (1973)
Ecology	Buffer capacity / PERSISTENCE Maintaining ROBUST FUNCTIONS	Holling (1973)
Psychology	Patterns of POSITIVE ADAPTATION Mitigating RISK / adversity for healthy development	Garmezy (1971) Garmezy (1973)
Socio-ecological	Adaptive Capacity INTERPLAY of disturbance and reorganisation	Schrader-Frechette and McCoy (1993) Gunderson (1995) Gunderson and Holling (2002)
Business	Coping capacity ANTICIPATION of potential RISK Mitigation / PREVENTION	Wildavsky (1984, 1988) Sheffi (2005)

Somewhat surprisingly, a similar implicit meaning of resilient thinking has emerged in the private sector in areas of business risk management, quality management and in the insurance industry approaches to business continuity. In this sense, rather than adopting nonlinear 'panarchy' as a steering principle, the logic emphasises the coping capacity of an organisation under stress. Through the lens of risk management the resilience characteristics of the organisation can be enhanced through proactive anticipation and planning, allowing the organisation to anticipate risks and mitigate or prevent the event from causing disruption to the orderly flow of capital and the daily operations of the organisation (see, for example, Sheffi, 2005). Table 7.1 gives an overview of these approaches showing the common themes running through the various characteristics of resilience in each approach. Whilst these offer subtle variations on recovery, efficiency, persistence, they also evoke common themes of exposure to danger and the positive trajectory of adaptation that comes from proactive fore-knowledge, adaptive capacities and a flexible sense maintaining robust functions under duress.

In emergency management for dealing with environmental and biological hazards the evolution of resilience has emerged out of a review of the form and function of statutory obligations of governments to be prepared for the worst, rather than to simply respond and recover from a disaster after the fact of its occurrence. Reviews were occurring in this field throughout the 1980s following the obsolescence of the cold war military model of Civil Defence, the wider establishment of models of civil protection across the blue lights (fire, police, ambulance) and specialist organisations (such as FEMA in the USA). Into the twenty-first century, with numerous occurrences of widespread and large-scale environmental, biological and security disaster events, the need for a more comprehensive system of dealing with potential disasters received widespread attention and became a key focus for reform in many countries. To name but a few, these disasters ranged from the Asian tsunami, foot-and-mouth disease in the UK, the World Trade Centre attacks and anti-capitalism riots at major political conference events around the world. A renewed focus on identifying the existing capabilities for response and recovery have been aligned with widespread adoption of international standards for risk anticipation and assessment as core functions of government, and the adoption of the disaster cycle approach to the prevention of, preparation for, response to and recovery from disasters is now a core function, rather than a back-office function, of government.

Organisational Resilience

This has increasingly been adapted to align with the *organisational resilience* of governance for ensuring the orderly flow of commerce. Organisational resilience draws heavily on financial and economic business management, emphasised through the prevalence of quality management language and local and international quality standards models. These have seen rapid growth in the general principles and practices that improve service delivery and business continuity – see, for example, ISO 31000, risk management, and ISO 22300, societal security. It also draws on an approach to the implementation of these standards in organisational settings heavily influenced by risk management, going so far as to treat politicians as 'societal risk managers around issues such as security, health and the environment. They pose as the people who will protect us from our fears and regulate the world accordingly' (Durodie, 2005: 17). It is, however, important to note that organisational resilience is an *outcome* of improvements in other practical areas of doing that emerges from rethinking the concept of resilience as a central aspect of the organisation – be that a corporation, a government department, a small business or a nation-state. The disaster cycle runs throughout the rethinking of organisational resilience. As such, risk management, business continuity planning, quality assurance and quality standards are managerial capabilities, or tools in the box labelled 'resilience'. These tools enhance the capacity of the organisation to adapt under stress, thus reaching the goal of 'being resilient'.

The organisational resilience approach does appear to suffer in some areas from a preoccupation with organisational structure and the need to measure the performance of management and operational systems (Dalziell and MacManus, 2004), as well as creating some generic sweeping categories (Bell, 2002) that really only add to confusion over how the concept should be applied in practice. Where there are benefits of this approach one can clearly trace the systemic enhancement of core functions as capabilities (i.e. techniques and mechanisms) used to think, do and act in ways that are more resilient and to prepare for the worst. As the field of enquiry grows, more research is beginning to push towards understanding organisational resilience in broader terms, such as the 'ability to respond to and deal with disruptive events' (Sullivan-Taylor and Braniki, 2011) and the systemic interdependencies that require an honest situational awareness, a comprehensive understanding of vulnerability and embedded adaptive capacity to 'effectively manage crisis' (Seville et al., 2006: 4), thus building flexible capabilities into the ways of working – as forms of doing – at all levels, but a one-size-fits-all approach using organisational resilience as the catch-all phrase limits the potential positive benefits from allowing the distinct fields of resilient working and research to interplay in more dynamic ways.

As the resilience metaphor was rolled out in organisational terms this emphasised a 'bounce-back ability' typical of engineering resilience approaches. By emphasising technical and mechanical properties of systems and processes the outcome of organisational resilience is one that places the main focus on formalising and sharing best practice for risk management – as either mitigation, anticipation and/or assessment – then response and recovery – dealing with disaster on the front line if it happens – then increasingly a broadening of this into areas of prevention and preparedness; only once core profit-making functions and statutory service delivery obligations have been assured do other areas begin to get more attention. Further, where there are strategic politics at play within organisations there may be coalitions that seek to keep business continuity decisions off the strategic agenda in areas where there is not a need to provide continuous production (e.g. utilities – water, electricity, gas). In such cases, disruption of the orderly flow of commerce and economic repercussions can be easily quantified. In other areas of the private sector there is far less willingness to engage in the costly development of comprehensive risk management, business continuity and organisational resilience (Wilson et al., 2010).

The main capabilities developed have thus been limited, initially at least, to those experts in the private or civil services directly involved in delivering ubiquitous resources or services, or to those making profits from real or imagined crisis (see, for example, Klein, 2008). Meaningful organisational resilience of this type requires multi-agency partnerships between these groups and provides assistance to the private sector for enhancing the management of business continuity in the delivery of critical infrastructural service, such as utilities and food. As such, it can operate as a closed system with highly controlled and limited access to key information. However, as these systems tend to incorporate a requirement for ongoing and perpetual testing and review, the resilience project in many governance partnerships must become an endless and ongoing process rather than a set policy framework. It must also engage an ever-widening community of participants given the growing systemic interdependencies inherent in global capitalism. Resilient societies demonstrate the characteristics of resilience through more than a series of policy partnerships and best practices. They learn and adapt from the experience of planning and also from exposure to disruption. More importantly, in the rush to meet perceived statutory obligations to protect the privatised utilities there is perhaps some danger that the public are omitted from the decision-making process, and thus forced into a passive role as the consumers of services or the source of danger rather than stakeholders and participants in the resilient society.

Community Resilience

Parallel to organisational resilience is another tradition that has developed, but with a very different emphasis. The emphasis is here on a wider framework for mitigating psychological as well as financial impacts of events and seeking to embed a sense of awareness into the population for their own role in becoming more resilient through *community resilience*. This is again increasingly contested, but seeks to bring together the critical capabilities of experts with the adaptive capacity of engaged citizens for minimising any perturbation caused by a disaster event, real or imagined, through embedded preparedness. Vitally, it has been shown that 'national level adaptive capacity is dependent on social infrastructure and the accountability of institutions more than on the level of economic activity' (Adger et al., 2004: 1). This assertion demands attention in decision-making on changing the focus of policy and action from private sector and organisational capabilities to programs that are focussed on the public and community. Of course, this is not straightforward. There is a lack of agreement about what we mean by 'community', though a usefully broad definition is offered by Norris et al. (2008), suggesting:

> Not always, but typically, a community is an entity that has geographic boundaries and [a] shared fate. Communities are composed of built, natural, social, and economic environments that influence one another in complex ways. (Ibid.: 218)

Drawing more directly from the socio-ecological systems approach, the contrast of ecological and community resilience often mixes metaphors in interesting ways but only evokes some general need for learning, diversity and transformation, but with no cutting edge to the rhetoric (Gunderson, 2010). There is also a psychological element to the community resilience that can help give more focus to the field, something than can perhaps be if not quantified then at least grasped, and programmes developed to address the apparent need. If treated as linked to the psychological model of positive outcomes from exposure then psychological support can be offered to the community. Psychological research making reference to New York suggests that psychological resilience as a factor can in fact be predicted, making reference to gender, age, race/ethnicity, education, level of trauma exposure, income change, social support, frequency of chronic disease, and recent and past life stressors as factors that can be addressed, or even mitigated (Bonanno et al., 2007). Whilst the individual or group can be affected psychologically, and can pull together in the wake of an event, this is more than a simple cognitive agent, it evokes the sense that community can mobilise its internal capabilities and inherent capacities to reduce the negative impact and even create positive outcomes (Paton and Johnston, 2001).

So far, in practice, this has been oriented towards assisting the preparedness of the citizen, and enhancing the resources available to make people more resilient. Such might include developing improved information for insurance companies – which can then provide better coverage and premiums to customers for a faster recovery – or providing more comprehensive public information – on the risk in the area or on government policy or perhaps on the resources to have or the decisions to make at what point of a disaster event – this does still in many cases treat the citizen as a passive recipient of services rather than a resource in and of their own right. An aware citizen knows where a flood plain is or a high-risk bushfire area starts and ends, they know if they need sandbags and fresh water or canned food. They know when to stay and when to go and how to access public information in the event of a disaster. The key challenges are how to develop better information and databases of citizen needs to be delivered, and to make them more aware and thus responsible for their own actions should the worst occur. More information is increasingly asked of citizens on disability, or medical requirements, and the citizens themselves need to be more aware of the risks of the world around them, not as paranoid or fearful neurotic citizens, but as engaged and prepared active participants in a more resilient society. This requires an integration of the forms that interplay around individual, community and organisational resilience across areas of risk, hazard and threat:

> In this context it is not risk per se that is managed. Rather this is achieved by making choices regarding the losses (vulnerability) and gains (resilience) that could prevail within a given community. That is, risk reflects how hazard characteristics interact with those individual, community and societal elements that facilitate a capacity to adapt (i.e., increase resilience) and those that increase susceptibility to experiencing loss (i.e., increase vulnerability). (Paton, 2006: 305)

Returning again to Norris, community resilience can then be broken down into measurable capacities along the following lines:

> Economic Development – the level and diversity of economic resources, the equity of their distribution, and efforts to reduce risk and social vulnerabilities to hazards.Social Capital – the aggregate of resources linked to social networks. A variety of important capacities are included under the umbrella of Social Capital, including effective organizational linkages, social support and social influence, sense of community, place attachment, and citizen participation. Information and Communication – communication skills and infrastructure, trusted sources of information, responsible media, and narratives that instil meaning and hope.Community Competence – capacity for collective action and skills for solving problems and making decisions, which stem from collective efficacy and empowerment. (Norris and Stevens, 2007. *From Research Towards Policy: Applying Genealogy to Practice*)

The research approaches offered above begin to show the benefits of integrating the numerous discourses that are forming in the research across disciplines relating to resilience, from disaster research, hazards and risk, business management and social sciences. By building on research this genealogical appraisal shows that there are, and must be, strong links between interdisciplinary research and drawn from evidence-based policy (Coaffee et al., 2008; Walker and Cooper, 2011). Implementing resilience is, however, not unproblematic. There are problems in the perception of resilience as 'old wine for new skin' (O'Brien and Reid, 2004; 2005), implying that it is nothing more than a metaphor, a political exercise in repackaging what experts have been doing all along. Others might look at this as intrusion upon their traditional work and expertise, or endangering funding and organisational structure through problematic reform. In policy, resilience has become a metaphor that covers all hazards for all purposes, but in practice it must still be broken down if it is to be operationalised and implemented effectively. This tends to occur through specific tasks as capabilities and/or capacities amongst the diverse organisations throughout the disaster cycle, each tasked with different aspects of institutionalising the characteristics of resilience into workable best practice in complex organisational frameworks and partnerships. Some attention should be paid to how this is, in different ways, changing forms of doing across diverse interests if we are to meaningfully engage with the idea of interplay in this context.

Critical Infrastructure Protection and 'All Hazards'

At the conceptual level of strategic government policy and practice, 'all hazards' is a concept used to frame the structures, strategies and resultant practices for the management of a crisis event. All hazards is now used in many countries to encapsulate the entire typology of danger across security threats, natural hazards, biological and socio-technical risks and social disruptions. The concept of risk runs through all potential crisis events, though in practice it is used primarily as a framework for, first, the anticipation and typological categorisation of security threats, environmental hazards and anthropogenic risks, and second, the provision of metric assessment tools for the prioritisation of work to improve the capabilities to respond to and recover from events. This builds on the adoption of another cyclical model of actions – one example is found in the American model of comprehensive emergency management through four stages of activity (EMS, 2005). In the Australian comprehensive approach to all-hazards management this is echoed in the four stages of Prevention, Preparedness, Response, Recovery (PPRR) (Rogers, 2011a). Again, in the UK model the cycle is broken down even further into six stages (Coaffee et al., 2009), with similar components and actions linked to each area as 'capabilities' within a wider framework of 'resilience' (see Table 7.2).

Table 7.2   Different government models of the stages in all-hazards management activity

USA	Australia	UK
Mitigation	Prevention	Anticipation Assessment
Preparedness	Preparedness	Preparedness Prevention
Response	Response	Response
Recovery	Recovery	Recovery

Again, the local specifics for the treatment of disaster in this area are linked to the institutional cultures and organisational frameworks of governing, but there has been widespread reform in this area since the late twentieth century given the increasing scope, scale and frequency of disaster events and increased insecurity often linked back to terrorism. Whilst the reform in this area requires a fundamentally more open relationship between military agencies and public order and safety agencies, there has been for the most part a separation of policy in security and emergency in the pre-emptive areas of anticipation, assessment, prevention and planning, but far more explicit relationships in areas of response and recovery, be the disaster the result of bombing, flood, fire, disease, etc. The practical capabilities mobilised in response and recovery cut across all agency interests, whereas the pre-emptive areas of intelligence and policing are distinct from those required for planning and prevention of natural disasters, or this at least appears to be the case in the majority of agency restructuring and public information. What crossovers do exist we shall return to in the final chapter. For now, the nature of the natural hazards and the all-hazards approach is not so much to bring together security and emergency, but rather rationalise and embed the capability to cope and the capacity to adapt to any danger faced, should the worst happen.

This in and of itself poses significant enough a reform in the practices of social ordering within the institutional framework of governance organisations to be of key concern for the discussion, the more so as a result of the shifting institutionalised metaphor logically underpinning the ongoing transformation for the treatment of disaster through 'resilience'. The development of the disaster cycle shows up differently, but all of them incorporate these elements in some form as a cycle of activity linked to capabilities or capacities of organisations and resources. A key feature of this has been the initial development in the first phase of hard resilience in terms of critical infrastructure resources – to protect the basic functions of utilities from electricity and oil to food and water – of response capabilities – from disaster-specific planning for fire, flood, bomb, pandemic flu, CBRN (chemical, biological, radiological, nuclear), cyber security to technological integration of communications systems across agencies – of recovery capabilities – from site clearance to decontamination to mass mortuaries and family/community assistance. Then the second phase of process improvement has generally targeted softer resilience areas of a pre-emptive nature. This can include the expansion of preparation – wider testing of plans and scenario/table-top/field multi-agency exercises, conferences to share expertise and consultation, developing public information kits – as well as prevention activities – community engagement and more public education of behaviour that will stop dangers from human accident (such as bushfire) or ignorance on both sides of the divide (such as religious and cultural sensitivity training and investment in community and social cohesion initiatives). Throughout the whole process there is a constant self-referential checking and process improvement emphasis on getting better at every level, which evokes the meaningful implementation and embedding of adaptive capacity into the flexible capabilities of all those who have a vested interest in being more resilient. If anything, this enhances the importance of understanding systemic vulnerabilities in the forms of thinking and doing used to deal with ecological disaster alongside anthropogenic and socio-technical crises across all hazards in the urban environment.

Dealing with Disaster: Applying Interplay Through Resilience

This understanding of what resilience means and how it is increasingly operationalised in practice highlights the danger of schematically applying the core concept to specific areas without first understanding the underpinning logic at work in the development of its meaning. What the remainder of this chapter will extend is the sense of interplay between complex systems that overlap in unpredictable ways, charting linkages, intersections and interpenetrating aspects of the core topics drawn out in the previous chapter and looking at the challenges of managing those across diverse socio-historical conditions. This draws together the genealogical understanding of social order over time–space–place with the conceptual etymology of resilience.

The Interplay of Ecological Hazards with Urban Institutions and Organisations

Research on disaster and development by the United Nations has noted that urban habitations are increasing in size. In fact, the UN has the percentage of population living in an urban setting increasing in all of the top 30 most populous countries, projecting that a minimum of half the population in those nations will live in cities by 2050.

This means that the urban is expanding in every region of the planet, none faster than in the developing world (see Figure 7.1).[1] This unprecedented rate of urbanisation can be referred to as a transformation in the global ecology, one often accompanied by social or political revolution as the expansion of institutions reaches into the organisational fabric of everyday urban life in some fragile, basic and even mature natural states. If (as suggested above) there is no universally acknowledged definition of what constitutes a disaster event, then there can be no definitive demarcation of the tipping point between different types of disaster at the international or global scale; the implications of cascade effects *ex post facto* can, however, be very informative in exactly this way after the event – in terms of vulnerabilities exposed and lessons to be learned.

---

1   There are some problems with the sweeping statements that are made using broad statistics as a context for how prevalent disasters are. Given the widespread problems of replicability, generalisability and comparability inherent in many datasets collected across international boundaries by a host of organisations there are limited uses for this kind of data. For discussions of such dubious statistics, see Quarantelli (2001). For case studies of urban disaster, see Pelling and Wisner (2009).

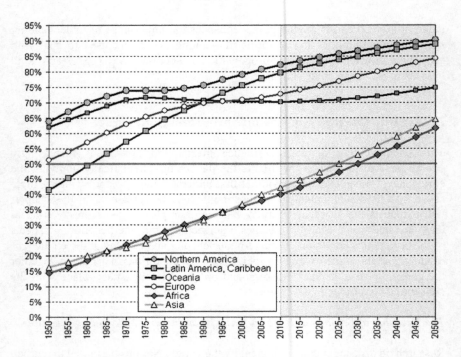

Figure 7.1   Urban population by major geographical area (by percentage of the population)

Source: UN (2010).

In densely populated urban environments the danger of disruption is perhaps more apparent, at the least more amenable to probabilistic metrics and economic measurements for the potential impact of loss of life (from number of those killed to the support of friends and relatives), critical infrastructure damage (from investment in appropriate defences to the maintenance of utilities *ex post facto*), economic cost over time (e.g. loss of GDP or FDI).

The range of potential impacts has yet to establish the cascading interplay between systemic failures across these forms comprehensively, however all-hazard approaches to resilience are certainly beginning to move in that direction (see the next chapter, and Blaikie et al., 1997; Hewitt, 1997; Comfort et al., 1999; Ozerdem, 2003). From the perspective of definitions, an event becomes a disaster when pre-existing causal components are aligned with an incident to create a systemic failure with disastrous consequences; one might say that hazard and vulnerability come together through and within time–space–place to result in a disaster. Whilst these events affect both rural and urban areas, it is consistently the urban areas that present the highest human and economic cost.

Perhaps a strong example of the interdependent interplay of forms through ecology, environment, hazards and the city is Hurricane Katrina in the USA. Hurricane damage has repeatedly caused problems along the Gulf of Mexico. The southern parishes of Jefferson and Orleans (Louisiana) have particularly been repeatedly exposed to severe damage from over nineteen flood and eighteen hurricane events between 1978 and 2000. Until Katrina, the most severe was Hurricane Betsy in 1965, which hit the city head on and left 50 per cent of the city underwater and 60,000 residents homeless (King, 2005). Following Betsy, extensive flood protection levees and mitigation works were carried out, including the 1968 National Flood Insurance Act, easing the burden of and access to flood protection insurance (not covered in most standard policies by the private sector). This stimulated expansive property development in the high flood risk areas, much of which was largely inexpensive housing for low and middle income households. The effect of this strategy of economic urban growth through 'safe' development set up an unusual and deadly irony:

> As the experience of New Orleans illustrates, federal policy has had its intended effect of facilitating and sustaining development in hazardous areas. The paradox is that in trying to make the most hazardous parts of New Orleans safe for urban expansion, it had the unintended effect of contributing directly to the devastation of Hurricane Katrina. It did that by increasing the amount of development possible in low-lying, flood-prone areas such as New Orleans East; and, some contend, by providing levee protection and new drainage works to that area of suburban growth, the Corps and city diverted resources that could have been used to improve drainage, pumping capacity, and levees in older areas of the city. (Burby, 2006)

This chain of effects is not a traditional cascade, but it does show the vulnerabilities in the wider socio-economic interplay of organisational performance, the institutionalised commitment to economic growth in the political economy and the absence of government regulation, public information on danger or adequate infrastructural defences. The tradition of preparing for low-cost but high-frequency events created vulnerability to rare (once in 100 years or more) high-impact events (Kates et al., 2006). As such, the profit–loss logic of neo-liberal capitalism would not encourage the required investment in critical infrastructure, the regulation was not in place to require conformance to an adequate standard of environmental defence and the public informed before the event (often through the news media rather than designated disaster agencies) were either gone early, unaware of the danger or unable to evacuate. Such wider systemic vulnerabilities have since been the focus of massive reform in the structure of organisations such as FEMA and Homeland Security in the USA, but it is clear that over the 50 years between Betsy and Katrina a highly vulnerable series of interdependencies were allowed to develop, which when struck by an unlikely event resulted in massive damage and the exposure of those vulnerabilities at many levels and at a high cost, both human and financial.

Whilst storms and flooding are also major features of the Australian experience of hazard agents, perhaps the most typically Australian hazard agent is the bushfire. In Victoria, Australia, a similar level of familiarity and exposure to dangerous bushfires existed as in the exposure to hurricanes along the Gulf Coast in the USA. However, the vulnerability of the population in rural and peripheral urban areas has been increased in recent years by a combination of relaxed planning regulations, the trend of urban dwellers seeking retirement, holiday or commuter homes in newly developed areas (often vulnerable to bushfire) and the wider institutionalised competition for resources amongst agencies that had led to a system of emergency planning highly differentiated by local district and state priorities. This system has been repeatedly put to the test, and 11 major bushfire events have been recorded in the last ten years – equivalent in the first decade of the twenty-first century to the recorded major bushfires over the previous 100 years. These ranged in severity and destructive impact, the smallest covering 9,000 hectares and the largest well over 2,000,000. Bushfire events in Australia tend to inflict lower overall damage (i.e. loss of life, cost of repair) than storms and floods; partially as bushfires tend to originate well outside urban areas. However, once begun and gaining in intensity they can create unprecedented devastation.

The 2009 Black Wednesday Victorian bushfires focussed international attention on the emergency planning, response and recovery strategies in place in Australia. A severe heatwave saw temperatures rise to 46.4 °C in the state capital (Melbourne) over a prolonged period, and on 7th February, bushfires broke out across the state.[2] One hundred and seventy-three people were killed and total damage costs were estimated by the Royal Commission to exceed four billion dollars (AUS); whilst the state capital was threatened it was smaller towns and peripheral urban settlements that were worst affected by the destruction. The commission found that whilst the fire fighters on the day had struggled bravely and performed well in combatting the unprecedented scale and severity of the fires, there were also some shortcomings in the policy framework that underpinned wider public information and community safety. In total, the commission made 67 recommendations for reform. These included the need for a general improvement in inter-agency cooperation and decision-making in key organisations, improvement to publicly accessible fire safety shelters, and better public information on both the dangers of bushfire and the intent and content of the Bushfire Safety Policy. The Bushfire Safety Policy – known colloquially as 'stay or go', but with the full title *Prepare, Stay and Defend or Leave Early*

---

2   It should be noted that despite the destruction caused by the bushfires far more people were killed by the heatwave that preceded the fires than by the fires themselves. The fires however had a far greater impact on the financial cost of recovery, through the destruction of critical infrastructure and property, and received much more attention in media coverage, policy review and governmental oversight.

– was under scrutiny but found to be basically sound in principle, if applied poorly on the day. It noted that the differences between smaller-scale bushfires and severe 'firestorms' was not incorporated into the policy, and that each type of event required different operational emphasis – in the case of smaller fires targeting fire suppression, and in the case of major firestorms evacuation and public safety. Some organisational disputes resulted between the commission and the state government, highlighting the fact that these coalitions had different interests. Many of the recommendations – including the called for improvements in critical infrastructure (from providing bunkers and shelters to relocating electricity cables) – were expensive at any time, never more so than during the global economic downturn that preceded the global financial crisis in 2010–2011. Equally, improved public education and information is expensive and difficult in a multi-agency environment. Different political and organisational priorities and provisions have in Australia led to the recommendations of Royal Commissions in 1983, 2003 and 2006 being only partially adopted, raising further questions over the institutionalised process of Royal Commission enquiries themselves.

On an anthropological level of analysis there is some anecdotal evidence from front-line responders in the emergency services that rural Australians require different support to those from urban backgrounds. Rural residents who have long-term knowledge and experience of the environment and its dangers require far less information or direction from emergency services and are far more prepared than those used to living primarily in urban areas. The typical urban dweller by comparison has far less understanding of ecological dangers and higher expectations of both the emergency services and local/state/federal government in terms of service delivery – be that information, evacuation or other fundamental aspects of the emergency management system. The 'stay or go' bushfire policy essentially requires that the public are highly informed, aware, prepared and capable of being responsible for their personal safety during an incident. It requires the citizen to be proactive about safety, and to make informed decisions about the choice to mount a fire defence in person or leave the area. This policy does not, however, take into account the relative naiveté of the urban resident in comparison to the self-reliant stereotype of a rural 'Aussie battler'. The problems during the event with communicating the location, path and likely impact of the fire also contributed to a situation where those most in need of up-to-date information were unable to get it, thus many members of the public were uninformed or misinformed and unable to make adequate decisions. Whilst during the 'Black Saturday' bushfires the front-line service performed admirably, there were widespread systemic vulnerabilities exposed in the command chain as well as with the process of communication, between agencies and with the general public before, during and after the bushfires. As systemic vunerability communication technologies, critical infrastructure and operational processes did not mesh as well as hoped, whilst this made little difference to the destruction caused by the bushfire it can be linked to the loss of property and even life as a result of inappropriate expectations amongst both the public and government. In such cases where the public are not highly educated in what to expect from responders during an event and responders may be overwhelmed by the unprecedented scale and speed of events systemic vulnerabilities become apparent, especially where process-based rigidity traps are thus exposed. This could also be seen after the event, highlighting the organisational resistance to change and learning from the lessons of the event, in the institutionalised process of Royal Commission enquiry. This may have been a state sanctioned enquiry but it had limited impact in terms of real change in the treatment of bushfires.

These layers of interplay are present in our understanding of the ecological and environmental hazard, but equally this shows the active role of human agency, both in institutionalised ways of doing and in organisational structures, for hazard-driven approaches to disaster. Regardless of the focus of researchers on ecological agents, physical damage, vulnerabilities or development, there are lessons to be drawn for these examples. Clearly, the understanding of hazard agents can only go so far towards mitigation of danger, it is also required to incorporate improvements in the vulnerabilities exposed by an incident, as well as development and 'betterment' of existing beliefs, rules and norms associated with the event, or all are at risk that the same or similar systemic failures will be repeated. While it is the human element that is highlighted as in need of improved protection and better information, one must acknowledge the danger inherent in humans when discussing disasters. It is to the more human-driven disasters that attention is now turned in developing threats, beginning with war and the security of the city.

The Interplay of Beliefs, Rules and Norms in War

As noted above, the legacy of rebuilding the city after the two World Wars had a significant influence on the types of architecture emerging in the replacement of damaged or destroyed urban infrastructure. The rebuilding of many major cities substantially damaged through the combination of gruelling urban conflict on the ground and the emergence of aerial bombing tactics, required substantial investment. It is not clear whether the massive investment in infrastructure redevelopment from the Marshall Plan (some 13 billion US dollars across Europe) or general adoption of free-trade policies in European countries were at the heart of the subsequent surge in growth (Schain, 2001); indeed, the Eastern Bloc also experienced growth, albeit at a slower rate, and also engaged in widespread rebuilding. The argument that has been made, and is agreed with here, is that such economic aid succeeds in alleviating shortages that reduce pressure on the organisations attempting to secure the social order, but unless it is accompanied by institutional reform of the rules and norms for conducting everyday life it can only temporarily reduce pressure on the resources and systems under strain (see, for example, Bradford De Long and Eichengreen, 1993: 190–192). Regardless, the outcome for the urban infrastructure was widespread reform and the need for new strategies and designs to deal with urban housing shortages and infrastructure failures. In the Eastern bloc this was a blend of 'socialist realism' with palatial reflections of ancient traditions, a new modernism and the grim spectre of the 'international style' of rational, and later brutal, modernism. In Western Europe the 'international style' was adopted more quickly, in England for example the growth of 'New Town' planning projects and the succeeding urban idealism underpinning the new modernism. In both cases the range of pressures were mixed between the need to meet high demand for economically viable and affordable housing with a degree of speed, the rise of new techniques for the manufacture of developments and the rise of a professional approach to urban planning, with the stylised influence of Le Corbusier which cannot be understated in the alignment of beliefs in vogue at the time, and which informed the logic for many of the subsequent variations of modernism that came forth (Heynan and Henket, 2002). The spectre of modern architecture rose to fill in many of the gaps throughout the post-war urban landscape. Many of the prefabricated or mass-produced buildings spoke of a new rational and mechanistic interpretation of the human through these 'machines for living' in the 1950s and 1960s. The increasing suburbanisation and creation of new towns and urban satellites in many Western European cities also ran throughout the post-war democratic urbanism of the 1970s and 1980s, accommodating the flight of the middle classes from the increasingly monolithic and militarised 'landscapes of defence' (Gold and Revill, 2000) and encouraging crime prevention approaches that were enforced through architectural forms of 'defensible space' (Newman, 1972).

The influence of defence and the rational model for thinking about the individualistic human machines emerges throughout this period, in part from the misapplied logic of modernism and in part from rational choice theories of the Cold War. The theoretical approach underpinning geo-political strategy for the nuclear-driven Cold War from the mid 1940s until the early 1990s emphasised the maintenance of the core executive functions of government, alongside critical infrastructure as the main areas where a meaningful impact could be made by strategic defence in the face of the real or imagined threat of total devastation from a global nuclear war. The technological and organisational revolution in military affairs brings out the tensions of this shifting balance in the beliefs, rules and norms surrounding the conduct of war, the relationship of the state to the citizen and the implications for the everyday beliefs and values of conduct. A period of flux in the interplay enhanced by the internecine conflict of the twentieth century informed a dramatic shift in the understanding of everyday life, and the appropriate governance strategies required to manage it. A 'liberal way of war' emerged throughout the twentieth century (Dillon and Reid, 2009) in which the use of propaganda at home and abroad was normalised as legitimate realignment of the underpinning beliefs amongst the people of a given nation-state. During the Eisenhower presidency, the US undertook considerable efforts at 'cultural infiltration' in the effort to part the 'iron curtain' (Hixson, 1997). The revolution in military affairs, however, at first largely ignored the urban form, though the Cold War had influenced urban design through attempts to create more disaggregated planning with dispersed targets more resilient to nuclear assault, and through the high level of investment in subterranean bunkers underneath the fabric of the everyday city. The Cold War also influenced the trajectory of change in organisations of social ordering, for example the potential mobilisation of the police and a pseudo-military force in the face of potential communist uprising was a feature of security-driven training. The logic of reordering spaces and the decline of institutionalised requirements for regulation into the 1970s and 1980s were part of a wider institutional revolution in politics that reapplied such approaches to spatial management and military tactics into the fields of economic and social policies; again, this interplay has substantial influence on institutional and organisation framework through which time–space–place is first imagined in reflection of the beliefs of the time and then managed to establish certain rules and norms. It is useful at this point to look at the interaction between the people (as citizens) and state (as government organisations), if only briefly, in the context of conflict and war.

The broad term of 'people's war' has been used here to refer to the role of information in the alignment of beliefs, rules and norms in times of conflict. Specifically, this refers to the rise of negotiated propaganda as a means of increasing public support, realigning public perceptions to increase public support for military action or to control public morale. In this particular discussion this is presented through the lens of conflict, and times of intense stress linked most often to military actions. The World Wars saw the rise of information as a key weapon in the armoury of conflict. Misinformation as a tool in military campaigns is nothing new, but the technological innovations of radio and television incorporated an ideological and informational aspect to the revolution in military affairs that was long-lasting and is still ongoing. Before World War I, contemporary governments had displayed little interest in the potential of manipulating public opinion on this scale, for this purpose, such endeavour being the province of electioneering, religion, the wider public media, for example. However, by 1918 a 'great historical divide had been passed in the development of opinion manipulation' (Messinger, 1992: 2). This informed the tone of the interplay between government and the general public for much of the twentieth century, particularly in terms of the underlying 'truth' and 'rhetoric' surrounding justifiable reasons for inter-state conflict. It can be argued that the technological and organisational transformations were further reinforced by the realignment of beliefs, rules and norms through such mediums as propaganda during the World Wars; all the players in these conflicts partook of the techniques of information manipulation, perhaps none more so than Germany and America (Welch, 2000; Sproule, 2005). Public propaganda was by now well developed as a tool for information dissemination, often with racist undertones, not to mention the sinister implications of largely useless public defence strategies like 'duck and cover', or presumptive on access to the 'do-it-yourself' home bunker projects that themselves were ideologically charged with pro-American traditional values (Lichtman, 2006). Such layers to the social ordering penetrated the suburban fabric of the 'nuclear' family and the urban 'home front' at the heart of the American ideal. The nuclear threat became a driver of change and a new kind of threat across many levels:

> Frighteningly, unfamiliar, and profoundly disruptive, the bomb was an uncanny object, but only properly so when given a geography, a place of impact. From this location in time and space, uncertainty and displacement would spread, upsetting conventions of domesticity, homeliness, and planned order that are the opposite of city as ruin. (Farish, 2004: 93–94)

The spatial distinction between the centralised city and the satellite suburbs capable of independent functioning, and the citizen militia of family and home, were all part of the realignment of governance during this time as forms of both geo-political and bio-political warfare. Ideological and spatial defence appear equally important as features of the conflict alongside the threat of total devastation itself. The influence they have had on the trajectory of transformation is clear to this day. Whilst giving a somewhat oversimplified view of the Cold War this discussion shows clearly that there was more happening than a geo-political and military arms race to sustain security through the threat of mutual destruction. There was also a battle for the realignment of the beliefs, rules and norms underpinning the maintenance of a given social order, that of a liberal democratic capitalism. This battle was fought for the soul of the people, and was engaged through the attempts to control the trajectory of social change.

This discussion begins to show that realignment of the institutional forms of everyday life can be explicit through the information presented to people about conflict and how to deal with the consequences of danger, or implicit in the redesign of urban landscapes, specific buildings or spaces. Wider changes in the realignment of political, economic and cultural institutions have built over time a trajectory of change that acts today as a platform for wider reform in the organisational hierarchies of government, and thus governance. Military concerns have undoubtedly affected the form and function of architectural design, alongside artistic trends within the field of expertise. Taken together these contribute to a particular form of urban landscape, with particular management strategies and concepts of spatial use-value attributed to these locations. This steers the range of options available to those using those locations towards a particular conceptual framework. Such an alignment to the interplay of forms does not impose absolute limitations, but rather realigns the conditions of possibility for taking action towards a particular set of rules and norms founded on wider series of beliefs that interplay to create an anthropological plateau of lived experiences. In understanding the links between the urban order discussed in the previous chapter and the impact of changes to how we conceive of and deal with disasters, it is useful to look at another kind of potential disorder, one that originates with the individual and the community itself.

The Interplay of Security, Crime and the Public City

If the 'war on terror' is not a strictly legal war, determined as a war between sovereign nation-states, it must be treated as something else. One approach is to treat such a war in the same way as the war on crime (declared by J.E. Hoover's FBI in the 1930s), the war on poverty (declared by President Johnson in 1964), or the war on cancer (declared by President Reagan in 1999), and the war on drugs (declared by President Nixon in 1971) or the 'war on anti-sociability' (ambiguously declared by various British politicians during the premiership of Tony Blair). The war then appears as one of a host of rhetorical tools used to legitimate the actions of the ruling coalition. The target is not a hostile nation-state but a social problem or a problematic concept. The tool of rhetoric can be used to mobilise not only every available resource, but also public opinion – the balancing thus is refined around (a) a shift in beliefs to redefine the enemy in relation to the concept, (b) establishing new rules (using legislation to deal with the problem), and (c) the assemblage of new norms which result in a shift in the balance of everyday life across the body politic. This process of realignment is the interplay from which particular conditions of possibility (for danger or disorder) become manifest. By targeting the concept, the potential impact of danger can be minimised (Howard, 2002: 8). If, however, 'war' is framed as a militarised war abroad against dug-in guerrilla forces, or a war at home dealing with radicalisation of the citizenry in opposition to the incumbent government policy, the interplay becomes more complex.

The interplay can be given context through, first, the trajectory of socio-historical and geo-political conditions at different scales (our genealogical appraisal). It also incorporates the micro- or local-level dimensions of contestation. The institutional and organisational management of cities, communities and specific locations, and the actions of individuals or groups of citizens within those locations, were exemplified in the previous chapter. Building the assessment of security and resilience on these foundations one must ask how this changing context of geo-political insecurity can affect the time–space–place of the entrepreneurial city. What is it that we can draw from the real experience of interplay, and how can this interplay between the governance of (in)security be mapped onto the conditions of possibility for social change in the everyday life of the urban citizen?

So far, research of this type has tended to specialise, focussing on case studies of particular major events (and often on major global cities) in order to test different aspects of urban security and resilience. A good example of the interplay at work is the concurrent streams of urban gentrification research and the common themes in work on the fortification of the urban environment. Research on the sanitised global city offers examples of these trends, where the global post-industrial city is realigned for tourism (Judd and Fainstein, 1999), service (Allen and Pryke, 1994) or knowledge economies (van Winden et al., 2007). The streets and public spaces of the city are cleaned, cleared or entirely avoided by creating alternative pathways around the city either by transport networks or streets away from the street, and where public spaces remain they are redesigned to incorporate prevention by environmental design strategies further limiting the conditions of possibility required for disorder.

The dovetailing of crime and security strategies is now common place in areas of cross-border and international crime, drug crime, cyber crime and financial crime – those suspected of funding terrorism. However, this has become a common feature of policing everyday life through the situational, community and public order strategies intended to decrease radicalisation amongst the population, reduce opportunities for potential terrorism or to 'harden' potential targets beyond the capabilities of terror cells to penetrate. Such activities appear at times very similar to those actions taken to reduce anti-sociability amongst the population, reduce opportunities for potential destructive misdemeanours that affect the quality of urban environment, and harden everyday infrastructure to limit opportunities for such destructive anti-sociability. Since the 1980s, situational crime prevention has attempted to move focus away from the individual towards systems, behaviour sequences, ecology, defensible space, target hardening (O'Malley, 2003). The situational treatment of crime as spatial and temporal fits into the alignment of the city centre with entrepreneurial and neo-liberal strategies for rational management of the time–space–place of the city writ large. Through the influential work of scholars like Oscar Newman (1972) and the subsequent widespread adoption of Crime Prevention through Environmental Design Strategies (CPTED) it became possible to spatially fix and design out certain undesirable groups and activities. This same logic was used to help fortify certain areas of the city in the face of potential danger posed by extremist groups.

In the UK, the colloquial term 'the Troubles' is used to refer to the conflict between the Provincial Irish Republican Army (PIRA), republican splinter groups (carrying out attacks on loyalists), the loyalist splinter groups supporting British rule (carrying out revenge attacks on Republican groups) and the occupying British Military forces, intended to secure social order in hostile cities (e.g. Belfast).[3] This conflict also spread to the mainland through the 1970s, 1980s and into the 1990s with bombings in major cities around the UK, including the Houses of Parliament, several major London train stations, an attempt on the life of then Prime Minister Margaret Thatcher and numerous public houses and public events frequented by the military (e.g. Guildford and Birmingham pub bombs). In Belfast, a literal 'ring of steel' was erected around the city centre to limit the access of potential terrorists and enforce checkpoints for entrance and egress where people could be searched – a policy also supported intermittently by random stop and searches in the city centre in the early 1980s. These were also features of some residential barriers erected by

---

3   These troubles go back over many generations and are a feature of the Irish identity for many; given the complexity of the interplay that led to these conditions of possibility arising it is not intended to give a comprehensive history of terrorism in Northern Ireland. For more information on this a recommended text is Dingley (2009).

the Northern Ireland Housing Executive to ostensibly separate rival populations from each other (Jarman, 2008).[4] Around 83 of these barriers of different types are still present in the fabric of the city today, clustered around residential suburbs – regeneration of the city centre has led to those barriers being long since removed (Brown, 1985). During this time several areas of the City of London became fortified in more subtle ways using a similar rationale. London built gates at the entrance to Downing Street (limiting access to the Prime Minister's home) in 1989, followed by a 'ring of plastic' and a 'ring of steel', the first referring to the 'funnelling of traffic through rings of traffic cones', the second to the formalisation of these barricaded access points in 1993 which limited access and controlled traffic entering and leaving the central financial district (Coaffee, 2004: 204). The term 'ring of steel' is now generally used to refer to any technological barrier around a defined urban area, be it of physical barricades or automated systems and even if it is simply a part of the everyday operation of the infrastructure network. A good example of this is the use of Automatic Number Plate Recognition (ANPR) camera systems that monitor traffic flow. Whilst justified in London as a security infrastructural development these are now often used to monitor everyday traffic flow into congested urban areas, and can also be linked to driver registry databases and administer fines for illegal access, as in central Manchester, central London or crossing the harbour bridge in Sydney without an electronic permit (e-tag). Rings of concrete have been used to further fortify particular buildings of note, such as the Houses of Parliament or the Emirates football stadium in London, but increasingly there are efforts to render this form of fortified security 'invisible' as a part of the urban fabric to temper the insecurity that fortification engenders in the everyday life of the population (Briggs, 2006; Coaffee, 2009). The permanence of new security infrastructure of this type is another interesting facet of the function creep in the situational fortification of the global city. Whilst much of the urban security infrastructure is developed explicitly to secure a specific location permanently, there is another tier of security-driven development that comes from temporary security infrastructure and the major event. These events can be diverse, but the examples of party political conferences, major conventions and major sporting events are often a stimulus to the economy of the locale, region and nation in previously unexpected ways. Research on events has often focussed on major sporting events (e.g. the Olympic Games) as well as high-profile protests (e.g. G8, G20 or party political conferences). Outcomes from this work prove that such events bring major investment into the city, but also bring new real and imagined risks of potential disorder and of potential attack – these events being perceived as high-profile targets for potential terror attack. Investment in facilities requires security apparatus to protect the performers, the crowds, the reputation of the city and its lead organisations (from sponsors to professional associations to

---

    4   It should be noted that the barriers were unsuccessful in reducing the rate of attack, simply resulting in a change of tactics to smaller, more destructive devices, and also had a negative effect on commerce and trade in the city centre (Brown, 1985: 3).

social order agencies to civil government). Organisations of social order also need to be able to actively police the crowds for potential risks, identify threats and be prepared for the worst. This becomes a delicate balancing act in the interplay of competing requirements.

It is clear that there are major economic benefits to building a reputation as a city capable of hosting a major conference or sporting event, but there is also evidence suggesting that economic stimulus of this nature is short-term limited to construction and tourist industries, and the subsequent lifespan and economic contribution of such developments is far from assured (Whitson and Macintosh, 1996). Direct investment into the required infrastructure of conference facilities gives entry into a global marketplace of convention tourism (Weber and Chon, 2002), as does the sporting event to cultural tourism. In both cases the purpose of the infrastructure is to increase economic flows through the region and cater to the specific event; but the lifespan of the infrastructure continues *ex post facto* as a community resource and as a site for future events – such as the adoption of the Sydney Olympic Park for major music festivals. The construction of facilities is only one part of such major developments. There are also often links to major critical infrastructure works through transportation 'megaprojects' which often have 'strikingly poor performance in terms of economy, environment and public support' (Flyvbjerg et al., 2003: 3). The concerns over potential social exclusion of those who do not have the means, inclination or ability to access these developments dovetail rather neatly with the discussion of pseudo-public spaces, consumer landscapes and fringe acceptability amongst disadvantaged or disenfranchised groups of citizens in the previous chapter.

The legacy of this realignment of the urban landscape with neo-liberal entrepreneurialism in the urban landscape is such that a balancing act becomes central to the successful governing of the city. In Cape Town the problems of such a neo-liberalising strategy have shown cascade effects through strategic containment and fortification of the city through urban renewal, exacerbating 'social instability by reproducing aggressive forms of policing associated with the *apartheid* era' (Samara, 2010). The balance between the economics, the security, the reputation of the city/nation-state, the long-term stability and maintenance of the product and the consequences of failure or disruption must be maintained, whilst providing for a diverse urban population. In such circumstances there are tensions between high-profile white elephant mega-projects which attract investment and tourism over the longer term and local small-scale social projects that benefit marginalised or disadvantaged members of the community. There are also tensions with the development of a secure urban landscape that further excludes the locally disadvantaged from the new fortified urban landscape of economic tourism and consumption. Further to these developments we may often see that temporary security measures brought in for a particular event may then be retro-fitted into the security offering of the city as a whole, and new security legislation having unintended consequences in the use of new policing powers in areas that are peripheral to the intent behind legislation.

For example, when legitimate political protest has the potential to become disorderly, disruptive and even destructive, these tensions become explicit. The interplay of war with the urban landscape has been an ebb and flow of responses to different stimuli and concerns. To return to the theoretical language used earlier, any form of disorder is a direct challenge to the authority of organisations and elite coalitions, but what is considered to be within the remit of the rhetorical war on a concept is very different from a war between nation-states in the traditional post-Westphalian sense. Disorder and public protest in the post-industrial/entrepreneurial/global city are a far cry from the forms of urban warfare, fortification and division that are experienced along the Gaza Strip. The same rhetoric cannot be applied in both senses where public order is so dramatically different; however, we are increasingly seeing convergence between the policies, processes and infrastructure of social order. The concepts underpinning any distinctions made between the *threat* of war and the *risk* inherent in disorderly protest are of vital importance to understanding the role of security in the city. The remainder of the chapter will look at the changing context of terrorism in early twenty-first century and the changing understanding of civil unrest through public protest and urban rioting, before looking in brief at the shift in how governments attempt to deal with these two problems in the final chapter.

Towards Securing Meaningful Resilience

One might think of a sliding scale across which the impact of events may be experienced. At the upper level one might see the global effects of climate change. Across international borders, large-scale events such as the Chernobyl nuclear meltdown affected many nations. At the multi-regional level, disasters such as the chemical pollution in Bhopal affected many urban and rural regions of India. At the local level this can be drawn down to include, on one hand, the destruction of the urban environment by flooding or fire, the disruption to the flow of everyday life by widespread public disorder, and the impact on those individuals affected by such disasters (the victims of the catastrophic); yet on the other it can be also expanded into a different area by discussing personal responsibility of the individual, for example through the carbon footprint of the individual (linking back to the global), the act of littering or vandalism on a city street and the impact of such events on the local community. Such impact can, and must, be incorporated into how we understand the role of personal agency into understandings of resilience, as should the level of personal knowledge an individual has of the dangers they might face, or even the fear they feel from the perception of a given danger to their everyday life – such as living near a chemical plant or power station or living in an area with high crime rates and widespread anti-social behaviour. How such choices are informed by institutionalised personal beliefs, values or formal rules gives us a sense of the complexity inherent in analysing the role of institutions – both from the top-down and from the bottom-up – but it also helps us to identify which aspects of such institutions are changing, carried forward and transformed in the societal analysis of resilience.

At the global level the complexity of global ecological catastrophe must be linked back to both the scientific evidence now established for adaptation to climate change (Pelling, 2003)[5] alongside the adverse effects of anthropogenic dangers emerging from socio-technical and industrial sources, a subject increasingly important to the study of disaster (Helmer and Hilhorst, 2006; van Aalst, 2006). Such concerns affect organisations and institutions equally but in different ways. Whilst global environmental catastrophe remains a high-impact/low-risk event – to use the generic language of risk assessment metrics – it is not likely to cause the eradication of civilisation (as discussed in Chapters 3 and 4). The impact can, however, still have long-term effects on the ability of a country to function as a member of the international political community and global economy or on a corporation to compete in the global marketplace, with cascading effects on the individuals employed by these organisations, in how they think, do and act day-to-day. The evidence from high-impact natural disasters shows that a form of societal collapse is possible in the developed world, at the local level in the wake of Hurricane Katrina but also across regions as shown by the UK riots. More vulnerable developing nations are equally at risk of cascade effects that can arise from natural hazard events, as noted by Bissel (1983) in relation to poor conditions in disaster recovery centres affecting health and the spread of disease in the wake of a hazard agent – a problem that appeared again in Haiti following the 2010 earthquake, as one of many examples.

Increasingly, the need for thinking of potential disaster across local, multi-regional, national and global scales has been driven to the forefront of discussion. It is clear that the globalising influence of democratic capitalism has not increased control over the natural world; equally, the frequency and severity of environmental and biological disasters may be increasing. It is now far more likely that a global disaster event will be of ecological origin rather than military, perhaps for the first time since the end of the Cold War, but the spectre of social disruption through civil unrest is equally a growing concern as economic equalities continue to spread. It must also be noted, however, that given the complexity of interdependencies between the natural world and industrial capital these potential dangers are intertwined, also that comprehensive analysis requires that political, economic, cultural and experiential factors be brought together. The cascade effects of a disaster can have widespread repercussions, as we saw with the oceanic earthquake that stimulated the Japanese tsunami – the disaster stimulated an anthropogenic crisis in the nuclear power stations. Such industrial risks can also be seen as man-made socio-technical dangers; in an increasingly urban civilisation these systemic interdependencies are a significant concern if the critical infrastructure that allows the everyday to continue undisturbed is to be protected.

---

5   See also Vale and Campanella (2005).

What is certain is that when organisational resilience is made central to the development of flexible capabilities for dealing with disaster this only really deals with the disaster agent. Specifically the disaster agent in terms of its manifestation in damage measured in terms of economic cost – e.g. for replacement or betterment of infrastructure, insurance costs and impact on GDP. Where the human cost is measured in loss of life, critical infrastructure investment can be passed off as mitigation and prevention work, which it is, but not in terms of human security or broader societal resilience, rather it maps onto the rational neo-liberal ethic of governmentality, a poietic policy framework of risk management, process implementation and quality standards – as well as cost-driven resource management focussed on business continuity – that at best obscures community, and at worst reduces the human element to metrics of measurable financial costs from a primarily economic political rationale. Such work may be undertaken with the best of intentions; for example the need to reduce the loss of life to the lowest possible levels or to ensure the orderly flow of commerce, itself an implicit indicator that everyday life has not been disturbed. Where community resilience is developing we get a different but no less blinkered picture from much of the research, if such research is taken in isolation from its potential impact on policy and decision-making. This complexity can however be pulled back together and it is to this effort that the final chapter is addressed.

Chapter 8
Conclusion

If we are facing in the right direction, all we have to do is keep on walking.

Buddhist saying

The Idea Revisited

This book began with an attempt to offer some new ideas; some big ideas, yes, but made up of many smaller pieces. The argument was set up as an attempt to show (1) that the rhetoric of resilience in politics, policy and practice is of growing importance, and (2) this importance can be enhanced and meaningfully grounded in a project of spatial history. By building this preliminary work as theoretically informed and empirically grounded, the book has shown how resilience can be thought of, how we know what to do when we want to be resilient, and how we act out resilience in different ways at different times. This interrogation shows one potential way of creating closer resonance between 'top-down' political and economic views and more cultural, quotidian and experientially oriented 'bottom-up' analyses, though such crossovers will need further discussion and clarification in the future development of this approach. In the outline of the book (Chapter 1) the problems of taking too narrow an approach to risk, security, hazard or crisis were discussed. Part I of this book has explained one pathway to widening our focus without losing the sharp edge of enquiry by offering a reapplication of genealogical methods. This engages with the complexity of interplay between systems but does not seek to place any one topic at the centre of the process of change. This theory and method was then applied to the underpinning logic and purpose of gathering together in settlements and cities, how complex interplays of beliefs, rules and norms constitute complex systemic ordering through interdependent forms. These forms are layered over, under and throughout our life experience and are drawn upon both consciously and unconsciously in the making of our world, moment by moment. Returning to the central theme of this book this can be used as a theoretical foundation to then imply that the transformation and adaptation of institutions and organisations (especially in in natural states) requires a reading of resilience that offers more than a political and economic analysis, or a security and emergency focus; though certainly the rise of emergency, crisis and catastrophe, real and imagined, are the lens through which resilience has gained its current renaissance as a focal point of research.

In a book of this size it was not deemed useful to try and cover the whole of human history, so examples in Part I were largely limited to examples that pre-date the shift towards modernity so heavily debated elsewhere. Part II tried to use the same toolbox to assess the trajectory of change in the neo-liberal and entrepreneurial city. By unpacking the institutions and organisations underpinning the increasingly insecure urban everyday some tensions have been highlighted in the current trajectory of that change. Tensions have been noted in the categorisation of dangers and the cascade effect of such rational models of thinking into other areas of governance, spatial design, regulations and management of locations and the treatment of demographics of citizens whose presence does not always map neatly onto the concept of the entrepreneurial city.

These are all wider systemic concerns that can be sifted finer, indeed it is hoped that this method of analysis can inform more refined attempts to blend genealogy with a rhythmanalysis more true to Lefebvre's intent than the use of his theory was able to realise in this work. The reading of rhythm here has used only a reworking of circadian embodiment that aligns with the bio-political production of subjects suitable for the entrepreneurial city, not as an anthropological flaneuristic or voyeuristic reading of experiential space (seen in some other attempts to apply the study of urban rhythms). It was used as a way into the quotidian aspects of time–space–place, not as a pure analytical method. In the discussion there has not been perhaps as much anthropological reflection on experience as one might have hoped for, and this is something that can perhaps be addressed in other and future work. What is clear is that the challenges and dangers discussed in the previous chapter have stimulated a new wave of change in the policy and practices linked to dealing with crises, disasters and catastrophes of all types. The history of the present developed here has extended that framework for understanding institutions and organisations of ordering through the features and characteristics of access in the urban democratic and entrepreneurial order. In doing so, the diverse potential dangers to social order have been identified and drawn through a broad genealogic taxonomy, ranging from ecological and environmental hazards – fire, flood or other agents – to the variegated anthropogenic threats – warfare or industrial hazards – and the blurred boundaries of anthropogenic risks – extremism, fundamentalism and civil disorder.

Becoming Something Else

Through the approach developed in this book the impact of change is rendered *in statu na'scendi* – hence 'in the process of becoming something else' [*poietic*], to show how appropriate and applicable across the field the theory has become for informing resilience and the disaster cycle. Examples of the diverse approaches to the problem of both *defining* and then *ensuring* security and the increasing reference to a metaphorical and practical resilience to diverse risks, hazards and threats link global trends to local spaces and changing experiences of the city over time. Through this lens the topical issues of the tightening of security practices and changing governance structures for the regulation of difference and otherness in everyday spaces of the city (see, for example, Coaffee et al., 2008) in both exceptional as well as everyday contexts can be brought together with discourses of citizenship and liberalism, neo-liberalism and democracy (Rose, 1999; Harvey, 2005). The critical addition of this approach to the debate over discipline and security is the means by which such a new light may be cast on issues of the explicit 'hardening' of urban space; adoption of new security practices in diverse urban publics; changes to the regulations and rules of public conduct in new legislation and security powers; but also 'soft' securitisation practices such as the *use* and potential *abuse* of security legislation for policing and managing crises (from terrorist attacks to natural hazards); the growth of civil contingencies and security-oriented government and governance; and the interpellation of these strategies into the management of everyday urban spaces through blurring agendas of civil and criminal judgements, even disciplinary powers linked to 'quality of life' crimes and civil disturbance (from anti-social behaviour to race or labour disputes to both direct action political protest and criminal rioting). Despite the implied separation of discipline and security in many analyses, they are again frequently blurred and interconnected today.

Such concerns can be seen in previous work on the increased exclusion of minorities (e.g. young people) from democracy and public life (Rogers and Coaffee, 2005; Rogers, 2006); security-oriented interventions in ethnic minority communities (Fekete, 2004); the use of automated technologies in policing civil and minor offences (e.g. digital plate recognition and speeding) (Coaffee, 2005); the growth of algorithmic and biometric surveillance technologies (Introna and Wood, 2004); the creation of rings of steel in economic centres (Coaffee, 2003; 2004); as well as border control and immigration policies (Flynn, 2000; Graham, 2004) and the growth of 'militarised urbanism' in 'cities under siege' (Graham, 2010) as well as the influential 'risk society' discourse.[1] These purposive disciplinary realignments in the technologies of government (in policy *and* practice) often fall within the broad expansion of integrated emergency management (IEM) strategies, as well as the shifting ethos of embedding resilient 'ways of working' into the everyday governmentality of democratic societies (Coaffee et al., 2008). This embedding operates as a form of '*encastrement*' similar to the discipline implied by the organisational emphasis of military camps evoked by Foucault (Foucault, 1995 [1975]: 171–172) but is far more subject to mediation, not as the encroachment of security as discipline into the world (though aspects certainly reflect that view) but also as the engagement with security and discipline by all as active participants in change. Policies and practices from the top down act as

---

1   I have intentionally omitted re-treading old battlelines regarding the 'risk society thesis' (Beck, 1992; 1999) and its evolution in this book. For a comprehensive coverage of this debate readers can refer to Adam et al (2000). It is not excluded entirely however, many similar themes run through this work compatible with discussions of risk, but I find it is often useful to allow those currents to remain underneath the discussion rather than for the canonical argument over interpretation to stifle to wider contributions made from the emphasis on resilience offered here.

operative processes for increasing resilience (in its broadest sense as the ability to bounce back, or even *forward* towards a new, more stable, state) and become iterative through the cyclical tactics of process improvement and risk assessment; thus evoking both total quality management and both 'all-' or 'any-hazard' approaches to danger.

These have also been framed from the bottom up as both implicit and explicit interventions in everyday urban spaces. Discussions of 'gentrification' (Lees et al., 2007), 'revanchism' (Smith, 1996) and 'urban security' are conceptually conflated in the perception of danger as a social problem to be (risk) managed. When framing such concerns alongside the perpetual state of exception (Agamben, 2005), cultures of fear (Furedi, 2007b) and the embedding of everyday resilience into the practice of secure democratic governance (Coaffee et al., 2008), this raises the impact of security on everyday life for the everyday citizen as a focal point of debate. Using the methods begun and explored in this book it may be possible to reflect in a different way on the directive ethos underpinning human agency within a disciplinary democracy by rethinking our analysis of everyday life. Drawing on the critique of the 'Third Way' programmes of neo-liberal governmental reformation, as both a policy framework and as a culture of government and democracy at large, it also links to discussions on the new urban (dis)order. Tensions emerge between the rational choice model of game-playing citizens and the calls for altruistic engagement from the community, for example following the UK riots of 2011. It is difficult to bring together the strategic political realignment of purposive security and the realistic impacts of change on the conceptual orientation of entrepreneurial managerialism affecting the everyday experiences of urban space and democratic society for the secure citizen in cities 'under siege' (Graham, 2010), but worthwhile as a direction for future study.

From the standpoint of methodology, the context of researching such tensions between lifestyle demographics, power, citizenship, space and culture requires interdisciplinary research design and the development of shared understandings of 'quality of life' between diverse groups of urban users through a form of 'street phenomenology' (Kusenbach, 2003) which can be developed to integrate the top-down and formal planning structure with bottom-up ethnographies of urban citizenship. Alongside this it may be beneficial to develop a more integrated understanding of both 'social' and 'spatial' capital (Soja, 2005) to assist in unpacking the tensions of a multi-layered spatial dynamic which occurs moment to moment through the various uses of public space – in this context, regeneration can be seen as the top-down managerial use, as the main activities of managers affecting these spaces are driven through such activity, as opposed to the bottom-up appropriation of space by alternative normative moralities of youth cultures and minority subgroups (Miles, 2003a; 2003b).

Applying Interplay to the Entrepreneurial City

A new urban aesthetic is implicit in the rules and norms of entrepreneurialism emerging from the conflation of urban danger, urban security and notional resilience to the challenges posed by the policy rhetoric legitimating a 'war on everything'. The need to reclaim urban space from dangerous urban 'others' – criminals and dangerous youth gangs – has clearly crossed over into the treatment of public protest, and a confused and contradictory rhetoric that blurs the distinctions between extremist, radical, dissident and criminal, often whilst claiming to protect the city from the dangerous protesters at the same time as claiming to protect the protesters from themselves. As entrepreneurial beliefs were normalised and formalised in government process they subsumed the rose-tinted Englishness inherent in the pre-industrial imaginary of community, altruistic public service and civility. Agrarian ideals implicit in the socialist ideological mythos of an urban industrial working class were subsumed by the 'soft city' of selfish strangers (Raban, 1998) and a governance of economic growth, not of public life. The result is a more secular, alienated, less engaged urban population represented by authorities that can only manage the entrepreneurial city through market-driven practice.

Increasingly, categorisation has penetrated our thinking, about the uses of location, about the types of disasters, about the legitimacy of different demographics in accessing spaces and services. Typologies of urban assets with specific use-values become a means to rationally manage the urban experience, mobilising the capabilities of citizens and the capacity of locations as economic resources. Community redefined has resulted in new symbolic strategies of cultural transformation that effectively mask the economic revitalisation strategies underpinning the rhetorical 'reclaiming' of the city (Cooper, 1998: 467–470). The categorisation of urban areas by socio-economic status is another example, characterising the assets and costs needed to mitigate and manage the risks and requirements of those communities through rational planning, and allowing the free market to fulfil community needs. This was initially manifest in the expansion of urban shopping centres and implicit privatisation of many previously public spaces, but has extended now to the 'sale' of whole suburbs to supermarkets under the guise of regeneration (Taher, 2009; Minton, 2010). Furthermore, the influence of the private sector as an elite coalition has increasingly drawn the corporation into public–private partnership to deliver projects through governance innovation such as Public Interest Companies (PIC) and Private Finance Initiative (PFI) that make judgments on regeneration projects on the basis of value for money rather than public benefit or use-value.[2] Such systems are rarely transparent to the eyes of the layman and value for money may not in

---

2 One might look at others examples of social enterprise as a counter to this through, for example, Community Interest Companies (CiC) which are regulated as not-for-profit delivery mechanisms of social engagement, see for example Community Resilience UK.

the longer term benefit the public as much as the investors when assessing the extraction of profit in comparison to the added value of projects to the quality of life in a given locale. The proffer of tenders by government on a project-by-project basis demands a deeper understanding of consultation practices. Who is being consulted, in what way and for what purpose? When looking closer, the framework of consultation is one that is problematic, yielding in form and function far higher benefits and outcomes aligned with corporate rather than public needs. The 'stickiness' of the representative democratic process when aligned with the entrepreneurial rules of the game has created a tiered system of access. It does not deny the public access to governance but rather repositions the stakeholder above the citizen in terms of targeted outcomes and measurements for success in ways that make behaviours not conducive to the norm more difficult; it also engineers acceptability implicitly through the technical disposition of democratic processes for inclusion as a valid citizen – legislatively through citizenship but also spatially through the architectonics of experience. Architectonics here refers to both the metaphorical sense of appertaining to a systematised knowledge but also to the superintendence of control through designed and managed locations. In both cases, citizens are increasingly less able to access decision-making in meaningful ways, and to effect change in the regeneration and management of the urban landscape through democratic practice. The powerful have more coherent and direct means of accessing decision-making in these increasingly impersonal 'open access' orders, which are by no means open to all. The end result suggests an implicit institutionalisation of a metaphorical revenge taken against those deemed responsible for the collapse of the urban order in an urban 'revanchism'. No area of categorisation is as explicitly exclusionary as the use of biometric security and racial profiling technologies, even when these are only mobilised at the border. The technological intervention of security into the everyday life of the city is an explicit bio-political effect on the conceptualisation of the city across scales, territory, network and individual experiences, perhaps exacerbated by the lack of consistent regulation, oversight of emerging surveillance networks and opacity of information protection laws (Ball and Murakami-Wood, 2006).

Contesting the Security of Cities, Networks, Space and Places

It is important to understand that the city is not one whole thing but rather many things to different individuals, coalitions and organisations. The city is, as such, contested. This contestation is part of the democratic process; indeed, it is an institutional characteristic of democracy to be free to struggle with and for power and to disagree and disobey some of the restrictions that are a part of everyday life. The current democracy is undergoing realignment, a feature of which is increasing regulation that implicitly, perhaps unintentionally, places limits on the access to the time–space–place of the city, but also to political, economic and socio-cultural institutions. The limitations placed on different forms of access place 'the right to the city' at the nexus of an entrepreneurial alignment of the city itself and the process of democracy. This may be assumed as an element of socially institutionalised values and beliefs, but it is clearly mediated through the organisational frameworks and coalitions of rule that steer the management and maintenance of governance towards economic goals. This poses problems for opening access meaningfully. Regulation is central to representational rule. The nature of this regulation is framed by the attempts of government to withdraw from the lives of citizens under the neo-liberal model, yet maintain social order in the face of widespread post-industrial growth pains in a globally urbanising civilisation. At the nexus of the problems in setting up forms-of-doing regulation is a struggle between the need for intervention in the realm of everyday life to secure the rights of citizen consumers and the need to incorporate more individual responsibility into citizens so they participate in the 'open access' democracy more meaningfully. The critique of this trend emphasises how the city is being (re)made for particular groups, coalitions or elites and implicitly excluding those on the margins of the economic, rational citizen model. It often appears that in the effort to institute the greatest freedom in 'big societies' an imbalance is created between the rights and the responsibilities of the citizen. A divisive nomic 'rightness' or 'acceptability' is increasingly embedded into the perception of and reaction to 'others' in the time–space–place of the city. This, when applied to the variations of user behaviour in specific locations gives us the context for studying the interplay between new regimes of regulation that are less inclusive and less democratic and the everyday life of the city.

There are concerns over the imbalance between the public right to access democratic spaces of the city and the encroachment of entrepreneurial service orientation of acceptable conduct in public time–space–place, but this is also drawn into the interplay of security within the urban landscape. In recent times we have seen comparable but different processes of blurred distinctions for the appropriate use of public, or semi-public, space come into conflict with national security or terrorism law. Increasingly there has been a blurring of distinctions around the appropriateness or legality of peaceful public protest and the potential for such protests to become violent or destructive as a result of individual or minority actions. Violence on both sides of the divide between protesters and policing organisations has occurred in the past at anti-globalisation protests in Seattle, Geneva, London and Tokyo. In 2007, anti-terror laws were used to regulate, and subsequently disperse, a peaceful public protest by environmental campaigners at Heathrow Airport. These laws are now a regular feature of standard policing tactics used for public protests, again used internationally in variable contexts though most frequently in extremes seen at anti-globalisation rallies that have come to be associated with international political summits such as the G8, and annual holidays, such as May Day in the UK. The boundaries of acceptability and public disorder are refined to preclude specific behaviours, and even bodies, in pseudo-public and commercial areas, as are the demographic boundaries of suspicion and appropriate conduct blurred with legitimate political dissent and radical ideology blurred with fundamentalism and extremist positions. Further, a resilient citizen is capable of recognising a potential security threat from a terrorist in a public space, and of distinguishing between freedom of speech and the glorification of terrorism in the public speaking of a religious leader or a political activist. It is in the latter of these areas that we begin to see some blurring in the implications of resilience in the democratic city.

Learning, Adapting, Transforming

It should be noted that this book is not intended as a one-shot all-encompassing or comprehensive treatise, and to read it as such is to misinterpret the wider aim of the project. It also makes some comparative cross-references across wide time periods to help illustrate the argument. Where development is not linear, such ebbs and flows in the process of change render the occasional analytical leap of faith not only purposeful but necessary. This is not seen as a problem here because the book is intended to act as a point of departure for further discussion, or even a springboard to encourage a novel change in thinking around the topics that are raised herein. Links are made between the political, juridical, social and spatial influences on everyday life and the notion that certain concepts take on an almost mythological role when the institutionalised form comes to underpin (bottom-up), and at times place limits upon (top-down), the customary operations of the everyday. I have already suggested above that there is a need to broaden the 'effect' of 'influence' made coherent as the *impact of change on everyday life*. The layers of impactful change can be seen as a wide set of forms which interplay, this incorporates relations and conditions as well as institutions and organisations. In particular, the definition of the term relations as mobilised here suggests that we are drawing together political, infrastructural, economic, historical, social, cultural, memorial (of memory), spatial, cultural, temporal and experiential forms of interaction between decision-making agents. Put simply, how people interact with each other day to day. The term conditions equally signifies a vast range of environmental, geographical, topographical and equally geomorphic factors deemed to be impactful forms affecting the operative understanding of everyday life. Institutions are commonly seen as 'rules' underpinning the patterns of interaction between individuals, but they are more than this – they are constituted reflexively by rules, by beliefs, and by norms. Institutions inform 'any form of constraint that human beings devise to shape human interaction' (North et al., 1990a: 4). These constraints emerge as shared beliefs, rules and norms informed by relative interaction and conditions of space and place, as well as organisational regulation of those interactions over time. The organisation in this sense refers to the coming together of individuals into a coherent group that may offer, impose or align the structure, regulation, or mediation of interactions. This group as such pursues both individualised and collective goals in a cooperative fashion. Through coordinated cooperation the organisation is capable of developing an internal coherence of institutional norms, beliefs and rules that might not always be in synch with the wider social group, but enhances the common interests of its membership. Both institutions and organisations can be 'sticky', that is they gain inertia and can become resilient in either positive or negative ways – either enhancing social order through their durability or in fact creating disorder through an inflexible resistance to adaptation – when effected by either internal or external changes across interdependent elements (resilience as interrogated in Chapters 7 and 8). The complexity of this interplay can open up access in egalitarian alignments of social order and broaden societal security, or it can regressively limit access to the benefits of broader membership in the body politic and create rigidity traps that lead to disorder when tested and broken by stress.

These definitions are intended to set up a framework that allows a (re)constitutive analysis of resilience that engages more directly with this complexity. Each chapter engages a little more with the interdependent complexity of social, cultural, political, juridical, spatial, etc. as an analysable interplay. This allows historicity and genealogy to be closer aligned with the patterns of adaptation and transformation over time; interplay is thus framed as the 'process of becoming something else' at the nexus of change. The diversity of relations and conditions at play and the form in which they emerge from and refer to each other is a starting point from which we can begin to trace what is carried forward in (dis)orderly and perpetual realignment. Developing the debate engages with more complex aspects of interplay – such as how relations and conditions inform the development of an institutionalised social order and the corresponding organisations that can both maintain and disrupt the (dis)order of everyday life. Understanding change as a 'process of becoming something else', as a sense of *poiesis*, is particularly important for unpacking the dynamics of this process. One might try and simplify this by saying broadly that change is perpetual; as such, resilience becomes a characteristic of the particular forms in different ways as they flux, adapt or transform into something else. The book has begun to look at where this concept of change has come from, and how it runs through different ideas of productive and creative transformation. I have drawn on the Aristotelian concepts of *poiesis* and *praxis*, where the former is seen as a producing activity or as a 'way' or '*form*-of-acting' and the latter as the knowledge of a 'way' or '*form*-of-doing'. The wider aims have not been purely theoretical, but to develop a practicable application of these theories through the analysis of the urban, resulting in a more grounded understanding of change in the resilience of the democratic city today.

The philosophical aspect of this project brings together the diverse interpenetrating forms to better understand the *arts of government*, the *technologies of government*, the *sense of being* and the *knowledge* itself as a link into broader existence of resilient ways of knowing, doing and acting. This theoretical framework can be used to focus a cogent, critical reflection on the relations and conditions in which particular tendencies and traits of social and spatial order have become institutionalised in organisational forms for ordering the world, and taken on an inertial influence on our everyday lives. As Lefebvre suggested:

> Within this frame of reference we will observe active differences, relations and
> conflicts. By determining them we will be able to define historical and social
> peculiarities without assuming the supreme (and always illusory) power of
> capturing the universal and exhausting 'being'. (Lefebvre, 2008 [1961]: 189)

To tease out the differences and conflicts inherent in the interplay of forms
developed in this book, inspiration is drawn from the theory of rhythms, developed
by Henri Lefebvre (2008 [1961]), and then grounded using elements of the
genealogical method described by Michel Foucault (1991). The suggestion made
is that by using the theories developed by these two critical thinkers as a point of
departure, the everyday experience of 'being' a citizen 'under the yoke' of neo-
liberalism can be connected substantively to theories of government, governance
and governmentality. When we look at authority and order in examples of urban
society we can tease out examples of how the social relations and environmental
conditions inform the creation of institutions and organisations. These institutions
and organisations are reflexive, and as such inform a deeper sense of the patterns
by which everyday life is negotiated. Where Lefebvre championed the everyday
and experience as central to understanding the negotiations of power, space and
time in modernity, Foucault championed the genealogies of the bio-political
influence by which power is able to structure experience and 'produce' those
who experience. Both offer a creative insight into the complex layers of interplay
affecting everyday life and can be used to tease out these processes of change over
time. The goal is thus to demonstrate the relevance of interplay between forms
to the changes we see emerging from the current focus on urbanism, through the
lens of urban space, but also through the wider sense of adaptation in the face of
uncertain times. This book highlights the drift in much social scientific enquiry
away from a focus on the theory, or the right way of doing things, towards the
creative production – be that of time, space, place or body – as an end product
of technical and mechanistic processes. The debate in this book is structured to
open up intellectual space for novel insights into the development of change as
adaptation in an urban context and has built into an appreciation of some of the
patterns and rhythms that underpin the resilience of the city over time.

The blend of genealogical and rhythmanalytical theories may not appear at
first glance to be of interest to policymakers, but it does have a bearing on some
of the problems faced in this area of government and governance. It is in the
first case a different approach to social theory, but underpinning this is a different
appreciation of how adaptive and resilient social order can be in the face of
potential disorder over large periods of time. This is as significant for reflections
on urban regeneration and design, resilient urban life and critical infrastructures as
it is for governance strategies for anti-radicalisation and community cohesion. The
result is to highlight how changes towards more resilient forms of everyday life
are reflexively linked to changes in the shape, form, regulation of spaces. This is a
relatively simple part of the problem being addressed, but it is made more complex
through the interdependence of that change on the institutionalised values of

individuals and groups, the way in which authority is mobilised to increase order in the democratic city, the unpredictable (and often disorderly) results that emerge from the interplay of social, economic, political, cultural and spatial forms. In the final chapters this has been extended to incorporate the broader conceptual reach of security and emergency in the resilient democratic city for the future. Whilst this is not directly connected to the narratives of a 'military turn' in urbanism or specific technophiliac reiterations of the urban (Graham, 2010), these features and trends in debate do filter through to issues of risk and resilience. Developing the links between different types of danger – risk, hazards and threats – as a cycle of order–perturbation–reordering must draw on a range of contextual conditions such as social relations, institutions and organisations in the wider discussion of what danger means for the democratic city. The step-change in policy from conflict-based understanding of a war on terror to more integrated emergency management and resilient practices for securing everyday life show that there is a process of change underway. This affects more than the integrated management of risks, it also affects the forces at play in the changing logic, language, systems and codes of resilient security. Wider strategies and tactics for management of a secure urban everyday life are beginning to engage more and more with the potential disaster as a cycle of interacting variables; these variables are the relations, conditions, institutions and organisations from which risks emerge and which mitigate and deal with the implications of disaster and with specific disastrous events.

Conclusions: Opening Access for Future Research

In this book, the argument has been made that the concept of resilience is of growing importance which should be grounded in a project of spatial history. One can see the attempt to show where the realignment has occurred in research from the emphasis on a productive *praxis* towards one of a creative and destructive, progressive and regressive *poiesis*. This has been linked to the study of forms to raise these concepts to another level, and to empirically apply them to the city in history and the city of the present as it becomes something else. In trying to clarify the shift in thinking, the process and method have sought to open up and reconstruct the theory in a way that offers avenues for future research into resilience.

It leaves the unenviable task of spelling out the final thrust of the argument. This is twofold. Categorisation is a means not an end. It is vital to be able to draw out key concepts and redeploy them within the analytical framework to better understand the process of change. In categorising risk, hazard, threat, or perhaps emergency, crisis, disaster and catastrophe one falls prey to the logic of limitation, creating rigidity traps that limit our ability to learn and adapt to new challenges. Rigidity represents a binding of oneself to the singular aspect of the object under study and a resistance to change, it institutionalises inflexibility in a particular alignment of forms. Under stress such approaches exemplify the negative resilience, as resistant to change – this may endure but is also vulnerable to total systemic collapse if the upper threshold of such resistance is breached. A more flexible and positive reading of resilience shows adaptation and transformation as a metaphorical 'rolling with the punches' with positive outcomes resulting from potentially negative imapcts. The negative is not to be feared, blame is less important than ensuring that the cost and impact are accepted and learned from in becoming something new, something stronger, something more resilient. Through the lens of resilience change can be shown as a permeable realignment of different forms of thinking, doing and acting in flux. By accepting change as a constant we gain insight into the relative interplay between our concepts, perceptive reactions and responses to a given moment. A given example of an object or subject, say a disaster and our way of planning to deal with danger, can be reconstituted as an attempt to embed adaptation, and therefore resilience, into our civilisation. Such endeavours cut across scales of analysis such as the body, the location, the territory or the network. They are at once productions in flux but also reflexive processes that are changing all the time. This is the very heart of complexity, interdependence and adaptation. It is 'panarchic' *in statu na'scendi*.

Resilience is a means used to tease out the features and characteristics of a given social order (or disorder) that grease the wheels of change, but it is the process of interplay that guides the realignment and trajectory of that change. Resilience is not an object of study but a processually subjective way of tracking the trajectory of change. Resilience is not a concrete and measurable thing, if not least because a truly utopian reading of a resilient society is one so resilient that no one notices when it has been disrupted. If resilience is processual in its abstract sense then perhaps the concrete side of the analysis is how this features as a characteristic of individuals, institutions and organisations with positive and negative consequences. Resilience can be a characteristic of positive adaptation and transformation. It can also be framed as negative stickiness and resistance to change through those same individuals, institutions and organisations. Identifying and assessing resilience can be useful for understanding the principles of latitude, precariousness, resistance and panarchy in social, economic, political systems as well as ecological ones. It can be useful for identifying systemic interdependency across scales and forms. It can be useful for looking optimistically at the potential for change in the face of a dark and darkening outlook during uncertain times. We must not stop here, this is a beginning not an ending. If we keep on walking and go beyond that which we comfortably know, we can use these tools to push beyond isolation when using concepts of rational choice, or politics and economy, of culture and society or security, order and disorder. We can ask better questions about the features and characteristics of social ordering and the adaptations implied in the current trajectory of change. We can and must ask if this is the kind of world intended when the markets were opened up; can we redress the balance of freedom and choice to realign and adapt once more this process of interplay? I believe we can; after all, it is always in the process of becoming something else.

References

Adam, B., Beck, U. and Van Loon, J. (eds) (2000) *The Risk Society and Beyond: Critical Issues for Social Theory*, London: Sage.

Adger, W.N., Brooks, N., Bentham, G., Agne, M. and Eriksen, S. (2004) *New Indicators of Vulnerability and Adaptive Capacity*, Tyndall Project IT1.11: July 2001 to June 2003.

Agamben, G. (1998) *Homo Sacer: Sovereign Power and Bare Life*, USA: Stanford University Press (trans. Heller-Roazen, D.).

Agamben, G. (2005) *State of Exception*, Chicago: Chicago University Press (trans. Attell, K.).

Akrill, J.A. (1978) 'Aristotle on Action', *Mind*, 137: 595–601.

Alexander, J.T. (2002) *Bubonic Plague in Early Modern Russia: Public Health and Urban Disaster*, Oxford: Oxford University Press.

Allen, J. and Pryke, M. (1994) 'The production of service space', *Environment and Planning D: Society and Space*, 12: 453–475.

Amin, A. and Thrift, N. (2002) *Cities: Reimagining the Urban*, London: Polity Press.

Andalo, D. (2005) 'Teenager wins legal fight against curfew', *Guardian Online*, http://www.guardian.co.uk/crime/article/0,,1532373,00.html (accessed: 01/07/12).

Anon (2002) 'Washington First case goes to European Court (Tuesday)', http://www.liberty-human-rights.org.uk (accessed: 13/08/2009).

Anon (2005a) 'Boy, 15, wins curfew legal battle', *BBC News Online*, http://news.bbc.co.uk/1/hi/england/london/4699095.stm (accessed: 01/07/12).

Anon (2005b) 'Liberty High Court Challenge to Government Anti-Social Behaviour Policy', http://www.liberty-human-rights.org.uk (accessed: 01/07/12).

Antonopoulos, A. (1992) 'The great Minoan eruption of Thera volcano and the ensuing tsunami in the Greek Archipelago', *Natural Hazards*, 5(2): 153–168.

Aradau, C. and van Munster, R. (2011) *Politics of Catastrophe: Genealogies of the Unknown*, London: Routledge.

Ashworth, G.J. (1991) *Fortification and the City*, London: Routledge.

Asthana, N.C. and Nirmal, A. (2009) *Urban Terrorism: Myths and Realities*, Jaipur: Pointer Publishers.

Atkinson, R. (2000) 'Measuring gentrification and displacement in Greater London', *Urban Studies*, 37(1): 149–165.

Babington, A. (1990) *Military Intervention in Britain: From the Gordon Riots to the Gibraltar Incident*, London: Routledge.

Bacon, F. (1659) *Sylva sylvarum, or, A Natural History in Ten Centuries*, London: William Lee.

Baeten, G. (2002a) 'The spaces of utopia and dystopia', *Geografiska Annaler*, 84(B): 3–4.

Baeten, G. (2002b) 'Hypochondriac geographies of the city and the new urban dystopia: Coming to terms with the "other" city'. *City* 6: 103–115.

Ball, K. and Muakami-Wood, D. (2006) *A Report on the Surveillance Society*, For the Information Commissioner, by the Surveillance Studies Network: Summary Report, September 2006.

Barry, A., Osbourne, T. and Rose, N. (eds) (1996) *Foucault and Political Reason: Liberalism, Neoliberalism and Rationalities of Government*, Chicago: The University of Chicago Press.

Batty, D. (2008) *Cities as Complex Systems: Scaling, Interactions, Networks, Dynamics and Urban Morphologies*, University College London. Centre for Advanced Spatial Analysis: Working Paper Series. Paper 131 – February 2008.

Beck, U. (2002) *Risk Society: Towards a New Modernity*, London: Sage.

Beck, U. (1999) *World Risk Society*, London: Polity Press.

Belinda, B. and Helms, G. (2003) 'Zero tolerance for the industrial past and other threats: Policing and urban entrepreneurialism in Britain and Germany', *Urban Studies*, 40(9): 1845–1867.

Bell, M. (2002) *The Five Principles of Organizational Resilience*, Gartner (Research), Publication Date: 7 January 2002. ID Number: AV-15-0508.

Berlin, I. (1990) *The Crooked Timber of Humanity: Chapters in the History of Ideas*, New Jersey: Princeton University Press (ed. Hardy, H.).

Bernaur, J.W. and Mahon, M. (1994) 'The ethics of Michel Foucault', in Gutting, G. (ed.) *The Cambridge Companion to Foucault*, Cambridge: Cambridge University Press: 141–158.

Bettinger, R.L. (1991) *Hunter-Gatherers: Archaeological and Evolutionary Theory (Interdisciplinary Contributions to Archaeology)*, London: Springer Press.

Bissel, R.A. (1983) 'Delayed-impact infectious disease after a natural disaster', *Journal of Emergency Medicine*, 1(1): 59–66.

Blaikie, P., Cannon, T., Davis, I. and Wisner, B. (1997) *At Risk: Natural Hazards, People's Vulnerability and Disasters* (2nd edition, 2003), London: Routledge.

Blair, T. (2000). Plenary. Labour Party Conference 2004, London, ODPM.

Blouet, B.W. (1972) 'Factors influencing the evolution of settlement patterns', in Ucko, P.J., Tringham, R. and Dimbleby, G.W. (eds) *Man, Settlement and Urbanism*, London: Garden City Press: 3–17.

Bohstedt, J. (1983) *Riots and Community Policing in England and Wales 1790–1810*, Cambridge, MA: Harvard University Press.

Bohstedt, J. (2010) *The Politics of Provision: Food Riots, Moral Economy and Market Transition in England, c.1550–1850*, London: Ashgate.

Bonanno, G.A., Galea, S., Bucciarelli, A. and Vlahov, D. (2007) 'What predicts psychological resilience after disaster? The role of demographics, resources, and life stress', *Journal of Consulting and Clinical Psychology*, 75(5): 671–682.

Borden, I. (2000). 'Thick edge: Architectural boundaries in the post-modern metropolis', in Borden, I. and Rendell, J. (eds) *Intersections: Architectural Histories and Critical Theories*, London: Routledge.

Boyne, S. (2004) 'Law, terrorism, and social movements: The tension between politics and security in Germany's anti-terrorism legislation', *Journal of International and Comparative Law*, 12: 41–58.

Bradford De Long, J. and Eichengreen, B. (1993) 'The Marshall Plan: History's Most Successful Structural Adjustment Program', in Dornbusch, R., Nolling, W. and Layard, R. (eds) *Post-War Economic Reconstruction and Lessons for the East Today*, Cambridge, MA: MIT Press: 189–230.

Branyar, L. and Skjølberg, K. (2000) *Why Terrorism Occurs – A Survey of Theories and Hypotheses on the Causes of Terrorism*, FFI/RAPPORT-2000/02769, Kjeller: Norwegian Defence Research Establishment.

Brenner, N. and Theodore, N. (2002) 'Cities and the geographies of "actually existing neoliberalism"', *Antipode*, 34(3): 349–379.

Bretagnolle, A., Daudé, E. and Pumain, D. (2003) 'From theory to modelling: Urban systems as complex systems: The complexity in urban systems: Theory model', *Cyber-Geo: European Journal of Geography, 13th European Colloquium on Theoretical and Quantitative Geography*, Lucca (Italy), 5–9 September 2003.

Briggs, R. (2006) *Invisible Security: The Impact of Counter-Terrorism on the Built Environment*, London: Cabe.

Brock, R. and Hodkinson, S. (2003) *Alternatives to Athens: Varieties of Political Organization and Community in Ancient Greece*, New York: Oxford University Press.

Brown, S. (1985) 'Central Belfast's security segment: An urban phenomena', *Area*, 17(1): 1–9.

Brown, T.S. (1998) 'Urban Violence in Early Medieval Italy: The Cases of Rome and Ravenna', in Halsall, G. (ed.) *Violence and Society in the Early Medieval West*, Woodbridge: The Boydell Press: 76–90.

Bryson, M. (1992) 'Riotous Liverpool', in Belchem, J. (ed.) *Popular Politics, Riot and Labour: Essays in Liverpool History 1790–1940*, Liverpool: Liverpool University Press: 98–135.

Buikstra, J.E. and Beck, L.A. (2006) *Bioarchaeology: The Contextual Analysis of Human Remains*, Elsevier: London.

Burby, R.J. (2006) 'Hurricane Katrina and the paradoxes of government disaster policy: Bringing about wise governmental decisions for hazardous areas', *The Annals of the American Academy of Political and Social Science*, 604(1): 171–191.

Burchell, G., Gordon, C. and Miller, P. (eds) (1991) *The Foucault Effect: Studies in Governmentality*, Chicago: University of Chicago Press.

Cameron, S. (2003) 'Gentrification, housing redifferentiation and regeneration: Going for growth in Newcastle upon Tyne', *Urban Studies*, 40(12): 2367–2382.

Castelden, S. (2005) *The Mycenaeans (Peoples of the Ancient World)*, London: Routledge.

Chaliand, G. (1994) 'Warfare and strategic cultures in history', in Chaliand, G. (ed.) *The Art of War in World History*, London: University of California Press: 1–47.

Chang, K.C. (1991) 'Ancient China and its anthropological significance', in Lamberg-Karlovsky, C.C. (ed.) (1991) *Archaeological Thought in America*, Cambridge: Cambridge University Press: 155–166.

Cheng, X. (2009) 'Changes of flood control situations and adjustments of flood management strategies in China', *Water International*, 30(1): 108–113.

Clarke, D.B. and Bradford, M.G. (1998) 'Public and private consumption and the city', *Urban Studies*, 35(5/6): 865–888.

Coaffee, J. (2003) *Terrorism, Risk and the City*, Aldershot: Ashgate.

Coaffee, J. (2004) 'Rings of steel, rings of concrete and rings of confidence: Designing out terrorism in central London pre and post 9/11', *International Journal of Urban and Regional Research*, 28(1): 201–211.

Coaffee, J. (2005) 'Urban renaissance in the age of terrorism: Revanchism, automated social control or the end of reflection?', *International Journal of Urban and Regional Research*, 29(2): 447–454.

Coaffee, J. (2009) *Terrorism, Risk and the Global City: Towards Urban Resilience*, London: Ashgate.

Coaffee, J. (2010) 'Protecting vulnerable cities: The UK's resilience response to defending everyday urban infrastructure', *International Affairs*, 86: 939–954.

Coaffee, J. and Murakami Wood, D. (2006) 'Security is coming home: Rethinking scale and constructing resilience in the global urban response to terrorist risk' *International Relations*, 20: 503–517.

Coaffee, J., Murakami-Wood, D.F.J and Rogers, P. (2008) *The Everyday Resilience of the City: How Cities Respond to Terrorism and Disaster*, London: Palgrave Macmillan.

Cochrane, A. (2003) 'The new urban policy: Towards empowerment or incorporation', in Imrie, R. and Raco, M. (eds) (2003) *Urban Renaissance? New Labour, Community and Urban Policy*, London: Polity Press: 223–234.

Coleman, R. (2004a) 'Reclaiming the streets: Close circuit television, neoliberalism and the mystification of social divisions', in *CCTV and Social Control: The Politics and Practice of Video-surveillance – European and Global Perspectives*, Sheffield University Centre for Criminological Research (SCCR).

Coleman, R. (2004b) 'Watching the degenerate: Street camera surveillance and urban regeneration', *Local Economy*, 19(3): 199–211.

Collins, T. (2011) 'Police, protesters clash in Oakland at Occupy camp', *Associated Press*, 26 October 2011 3:02 AM ET. http://www.ap.org (accessed: 27/10/2011).

Comfort, L. (2005) 'Risk, security and disaster management', *Annual Review of Political Science*, 8: 335–356.

Comfort, L., Wisner, B., Cutter, S., Pulwarty, R., Hewitt, K., Oliver-Smith, A., Wiener, J., Fordham, M., Peacock, W. and Krimgold, F. (1999) 'Reframing disaster policy: The global evolution of vulnerable communities', *Environmental Hazards*, 1: 39–44.

Cooper, D. (1998) 'Regard between strangers: Diversity, equality and the reconstruction of public space', *Critical Social Policy*, 18(4): 465–492.

Cuthbert, A.R. (1995) 'The right to the city: Surveillance, private interest and the public domain in Hong Kong', *Cities*, 12(5): 293–310.

Cutter, S. (2005) 'Pragmatism and relevance', in Perry, R.W. and Quarantelli, E.L. (eds) *What is Disaster? New Answers to Old Questions*, Philadelphia: Xlibris: 104–106.

Dalziell, E.P. and MacManus, S.T. (2004) 'Resilience, vulnerability, and adaptive capacity: Implications for system performance', *IFED*, Stoos, Switzerland, 5–9 December 2004.

Darvall, F.O. (1934) *Popular Disturbance and Public Order in Regency England: Being an account of the Luddite and other public disorders in England during the years 1811–1817 and of the attitude of the authorities*, Glasgow: Oxford University Press (reprinted in 1969, foreword by Angus Macintyre).

Davis, M. (1998) *Ecology of Fear: Los Angeles and the Imagination of Disaster*, New York: Metropolitan Books.

Davis, M. (2006) *City of Slums*, London: Verso.

Dayton-Johnson, D. (2004) *Natural Disasters and Adaptive Capacity*, OECD Development Centre Working Paper No. 237, Geneva: OECD Development Centre.

De Almeida, D.B. (2008) 'The 1755 Lisbon earthquake and the genesis of the risk management concept', in Mendes-Víctor, L.A., Oliveira, C.S. and Azevedo. J, *The Lisbon Earthquake of 1755: Revisited*, London: Springer: 167–185.

De Boer, J.Z. and Sanders, D.T. (2001) *Volcanoes in Human History: The Far-Reaching Effects of Major Eruptions*, New Jersey: Princeton University Press.

De Boer, J.V. and Sanders, D.T. (2004) *Earthquakes in Human History: The Far-Reaching Effects of Seismic Disruptions*, Woodstock: Princeton University Press.

Dean, M. (1999) *Governmentality*, London: Sage.

Defilippis, J. (1997) 'From a public re-creation to private recreation: The transformation of public space in South Street Seaport', *Journal of Urban Affairs*, 19(4): 405–417.

Deleuze, G. (1988 [1999]) *Foucault*, London: Continuum (trans. Athalone Press).

Depasquale, D. and Baker, E.L. (1998) 'The Los Angeles riot and the economics of urban unrest', *Journal of Urban Economics*, 43: 52–78.

DETR (2000) *Our Towns and Cities: The Future – Delivering an Urban Renaissance*, Urban White Paper.

Dillon, M. and Reid, J. (2009) *The Liberal Way of War: Killing to Make Life Live*, London: Routledge.

Dingley, J. (2009) *Combatting Terrorism in Northern Ireland*, London: Routledge.

Downey, G. (1955) 'Earthquakes at Constantinople and vicinity, A.D. 342–1454' *Speculum*, 30(4): 596–600.

Drayton, W. (2002) 'The citizen sector: Becoming as entrepreneurial and competitive as business', *California Management Review*, 44(3): 120–132.

Driessen, J. and MacDonald, C.F. (2000) 'The eruption of the Santorini volcano and its effects on Minoan Crete', *Geological Society*, London, Special Publications, 171: 81–93.

Driver, F. (1985). 'Power, space, and the body: A critical assessment of Foucault's Discipline and Punish', *Environment & Planning D: Society and Space*, 3: 425–446.

Driver, F. (1993) *Power and Pauperism: The Workhouse System, 1834–1884*, Cambridge: Cambridge University Press.

Durkheim, E. (1893) *The Division of Labour in Society*, Basingstoke: Macmillan.

Durodie, W. (2005) 'The limitations of risk management in dealing with disasters and building social resilience', *Tidsskriftet Politik*, 8(1): 14–21.

Dynes, R.R. (1997) *The Lisbon Earthquake in 1755: Contested Meanings in the First Modern Disaster (Preliminary Paper #255)*, Disaster Research Center, University of Delaware.

Dynes, R.R. (1999) *The Dialogue Between Voltaire and Rousseau on the Lisbon Earthquake: The Emergence of a Social Science View (Preliminary Paper #293)*, Disaster Research Center, University of Delaware.

Economist Intelligence Unit (2011) *The Democracy Index 2011: Democracy under Stress*, London: Economist Intelligence Unit.

Elden, S. (2001) *Mapping the Present: Heidegger, Foucault and the Project of a Spatial History*, London and New York: Continuum.

Elden, S. (2004) *Understanding Henri Lefebvre: The Theory and the Possible*, London: Continuum.EM-DAT, 'The OFDA/CRED International Disaster Database', www.em-dat.net, Université Catholique de Louvain, Brussels.

Emergency Management Solutions (2005) *All Hazards vs Homeland Security Planning. Disaster Resource Guide, September 2005*, USA: EMS.

Evans, G. (2001) *Cultural Planning: An Urban Renaissance*, London, Routledge.

Evans, G. (2005) 'Measure for measure: Evaluating the evidence of culture's contribution to regeneration', *Urban Studies*, 42(5/6): 959–983.

Farish, M. (2004) 'Another anxious urbanism: Simulating defence and disaster in Cold War America', in Graham, S. (ed.) *Cities, War and Terrorism: Towards an Urban Geo-politics*, London: Blackwell: 93–110.

Feagin, J.R. and Hahn, H. (1973) *Ghetto Revolts: The Politics of Violence in American Cities*, New York: Macmillan.

Fekete, L. (2004) 'Anti-Muslim racism and the European security state', *Race & Class*, 46(1): 3–29.

Ferguson, R. (2002) 'Rethinking youth transitions: Policy transfer and new exclusions in New Labour's New Deal', *Policy Studies*, 23(3/4): 173–190.

Flannery, K.V. (1972) 'The origins of the village as a settlement type in MesoAmerica and the Near East: A comparative study', in Ucko, P.J., Tringham, R. and Dimbleby, G.W. (eds) *Man, Settlement and Urbanism*, London: Garden City Press: 23–54.

Flusty, S. (2000) 'Thrashing Downtown: Play as resistance to the spatial and representational regulation of Los Angeles', *Cities*, 17(2): 149–158.

Flusty, S. (2001) 'The banality of interdiction: Surveillance, control and the displacement of diversity', *International Journal of Urban and Regional Research*, 25(3): 658–664.

Flynn, S.E. (2000) 'Beyond border control', *Foreign Affairs*, November/December 2000.

Flyvbjerg, B. (2001) *Making Social Science Matter: Why Social Inquiry Fails and How it Can Succeed Again*, Cambridge: Cambridge University Press.

Flyvbjerg, B., Bruzelius, N. and Rothengatter, W. (2003) *Megaprojects and Risk: An Anatomy of Ambition*, Cambridge: Cambridge University Press.

Fogelson, R.M. (1971) *Violence as Protest: A Study of Riots and Ghettos*, New York: Anchor & Doubleday.

Fordham, M. (2006) 'Disaster and development research and practice: A necessary eclecticism?' in Rodriguez, H., Quarantelli, E.L. and Dynes, R.R. (eds) *Handbook of Disaster Research: Handbooks of Sociology and Social Research*, New York: Springer (Kindle edition).

Foucault, M. (2003 [1963]) *The Birth of the Clinic*, London: Routledge (trans. Tavistock Press).

Foucault, M. (1970) *The Order of Things: An Archaeology on the Human Sciences*, New York: Vintage (1994 edition).

Foucault, M. (1972) *The Archaeology of Knowledge and the Discourse on Language*, New York: Pantheon (trans. Sheridan-Smith, A.M.).

Foucault, M. (1995 [1975]) *Discipline and Punish: The Birth of the Prison*, New York: Vintage.

Foucault, M. (1997 [1975]) *Society Must Be Defended: Lectures at the College Du France 1975–76*, New York: Picador (trans. Macey, D.).

Foucault, M. (1977) *Power, Knowledge and Selected Other Writings*, New York: Pantheon Books Ltd (trans. Gordon, C. et al.)

Foucault, M. (2007 [1978]) *Security, Territory, Population, Lectures at the College du France 1977–1978*, New York: Picador (trans. Burchell. G).

Foucault, M. (1979) *Power, Truth and Strategy*, Sydney: Feral Publications (ed. Morris, M. and Patton, P.).

Foucault, M. (1982) 'The subject and power', *Critical Inquiry*, 8(4): 777–795.

Foucault, M. (1991) See Burchell et al. (1991).

Friedman, M. (1962) *Capitalism and Freedom*, Chicago: University of Chicago Press.

Friedman, M. (1980) *Free to Choose*, New York: Harcourt Brace Jovanovich.

Fritz, C.E. (1961) 'Disasters', in Sill, D.L. (ed.) *Encyclopedia of the Social Science*, New York: Macmillan: 202–207.

Fuchs, K. (2008) 'The great earthquakes of Lisbon 1755 and Aceh 2004 shook the world. Seismologists' societal responsibility', in Mendes-Víctor, L.A., Oliveira, C.S. and Azevedo, J. (eds) *The Lisbon Earthquake of 1755: Revisited*, London: Springer: 43–65.

Fukuyama, F. (1993) *The End of History and the Last Man*, London: Penguin.

Fukuyama, F. (2011) *The Origins of Political Order: From Pre-human Times to the French Revolution*, London: Profile Books (Kindle edition).

Furedi, F. (2006) *Culture of Fear Revisited*, London: Continuum.

Furedi, F. (2007a) *Politics of Fear: Beyond Left and Right*, London: Continuum.

Furedi, F. (2007b) 'Meet the Malthusians manipulating the fear of terror: From climate change doom-mongers to population alarmists, every kind of fear entrepreneur is piggy-backing on the "war on terrorism"', *Spiked*, http://www.spiked-online.com/index.php?/site/article/907/ (accessed: 01/07/12).

Fyfe, N.R. (1995) 'Law and order policy and the spaces of citizenship in contemporary Britain', *Political Geography*, 14(2): 177–189.

Ganor, B. (2002) 'Defining terrorism: Is one man's terrorist another man's freedom fighter?', *Police Practice and Research*, 3(4): 287–304.

Garmezy, N. (1971) 'Vulnerability research and the issue of primary prevention', *American Journal of Orthopsychiatry*, 41(1): 101–116.

Garmezy, N. (1973) 'Competence and adaptation in adult schizophrenic patients and children at risk', in Dean, S.R. (ed.) *Schizophrenia: The First Ten Dean Award Lectures*, New York: MSS Information Corp: 163–204.

Garnsey, P. (1989) *Famine and Food Supply in the Graeco-Roman World: Responses to Risk and Crisis*, London: Cambridge University Press.

Garret, P.M. (2007) 'Making "anti-social behavior": A fragment of the evolution of "ASBO Politics" in Britain', *British Journal of Social Policy*, 37: 839–856.

George, A.R. (2003) *The Babylonian Gilgamesh Epic: Introduction, Critical Edition and Cuneiform Texts*, Oxford: Oxford University Press.

Giacomelli, L., Perrotta, A., Scandone, R. and Scarpati, C. (2003) 'The eruption of Vesuvius of 79 AD and its impact on human environment in Pompeii', *Episodes*, 26(3): 234–237.

Gilbert, C. (1998) 'Studying disaster: Changes in conceptual tools', in Quarantelli, E.L. (ed.) *What is a Disaster? A Dozen Perspectives on the Question*, London: Routledge (Kindle edition, 2007).

Gilbert, P.H., Isenberg, J., Baecher, G.B., Papay, L.T., Spielvogel, L.G., Woodard, J. and Badolato, E.V. (2003) 'Infrastructure issues for cities – countering terrorist threat', *Journal of Information Systems, ASCE*, March: 44–54.

Gold, J.R. and Revill, G. (eds) (2000) *Landscapes of Defence*, Harlow: Pearson.

Goodman, P. (2011) 'Cameron post-riots speech in full', http://conservativehome. blogs.com/thetorydiary/2011/08/cameron-post-riots-speech-in-full.html (accessed: 01/07/12).

Gottdeiner, M. (2000). 'Lefebvre and the bias of academic urbanism: What can we learn from the "new" urban analysis?', *City*, 4(1): 93–100.

Graham, S. (2004) *The Cyber Cities Reader*, London: Routledge.

Graham, S. (2010) *Cities Under Siege: The New Military Urbanism*, London: Verso.

Graham, S. and Marvin, S. (2001) *Splintering Urbanism: Networked Infrastructures, Technological Mobilities and the Urban Condition*, London: Routledge.

Greenberg, N.A. (1961) 'The use of poiema and poiesis', *Harvard Studies in Classical Philology*, 65: 263–289.

Grove, D. (1972) 'The function and future of urban centres', in Ucko, P.J., Tringham. R. and Dimbleby, G.W. (eds) *Man, Settlement and Urbanism*, London: Garden City Press: 559–574.

Gunderson, L. (2010) 'Ecological and human community resilience in response to natural disasters', *Ecology and Society*, 15(2): 18.

Gunderson, L.H. and Holling, C.S. (eds) (2002) *Panarchy*, Washington: Island Press.

Hackworth, J. and Smith, N. (2000) 'The changing state of gentrification', *Tijdschrift voor Economische en Sociale Geografie*, 92(4): 464–477.

Hall, P. (1998) *Cities in Civilisation*, London: W&N.

Hall, T. and Hubbard, P. (1996) 'The entrepreneurial city: New urban politics, new urban geographies', *Progress in Human Geography*, 20(2): 153–174.

Hall, T. and Hubbard, P. (1998) *The Entrepreneurial City: Geographies of Politics, Regime and Representation*, Chichester: J.W. & Sons.

Hansen, M.H. (2000) *A Comparative Study of Thirty City-State Cultures: An Investigation Conducted by the Copenhagen Polis Centre*, Copenhagen: Kongelige Danske Videnskabernes Selskab.

Harvey, D. (1989) 'From managerialism to entrepreneurialism: The transformation in urban governance in late capitalism', *Geografiska Annaler. Series B, Human Geography*, 71(1): 3–17.

Harvey, D. (1991) *The Condition of Post-modernity*, Oxford: Blackwell.

Harvey, D. (2005) *A Brief History of Neoliberalism*, Oxford: Oxford University Press.

Hayek, F.A. (1973) *Law, Legislation and Liberty: A New Statement of the Liberal Principles and Political Economy. Volume I: Rules and Order*, London: Routledge.

Hayek, F.A. (1976) *Law, Legislation and Liberty: A New Statement of the Liberal Principles and Political Economy. Volume II: The Mirage of Social Justice*, London: Routledge.

Hayek, F.A. (1979) *Law, Legislation and Liberty: A New Statement of the Liberal Principles and Political Economy. Volume III: The Political Order of a Free People*, London: Routledge.

Hebdige, D. (1979) *Subculture: The Meaning of Style*, London: Routledge.

Hegel, G.F. (2010) *Science of Logic*, Cambridge: Cambridge University Press [trans. Di Giovanni, G.].

Helmer, M. and Hilhorst, D. (2006) 'Natural disasters and climate change', *Disasters*, 30(1): 1–4.

Herbert, S. (2007) 'The "Battle of Seattle" revisited: Or, seven views of a protest-zoning state', *Political Geography*, 26: 601–619.

Hewitt, K. (1983) *The Interpretation of Calamity from the Viewpoint of Human Ecology*, London: Allen and Unwin.

Hewitt, K. (ed.) (1997) *Regions of Risk: A Geographical Introduction to Disasters*, Harlow: Addison Wesley Longman.

Hewitt, K. (1998) 'Excluded perspectives in the social construction of disaster', in Quarantelli, E.L. (ed.) *What is Disaster? Perspectives on the Question*, London: Routledge: 75–93.

Heynan, H. and Henket, H.J. (eds) (2002) *Back From Utopia: The Challenge of the Modern Movement*, Rotterdam: OIO Publishers.

Hixson, W.L. (1997) *Parting the Curtain: Propaganda, Culture, and the Cold War, 1945–1961*, New York: Palgrave Macmillan.

Hjorth, D. and Bjerke, B. (2006) 'Public entrepreneurship: Moving from social/consumer to public/citizen', in Steyaert, C. and Hjorth, D. (eds) *Entrepreneurship as Social Change: A Third Movements in Entrepreneurship Book*, London: Edward Edgar.

HMSO (2003) *Anti-Social Behaviour Act 2003*.

Hodder, I. (2008) *Çatalhöyük 2008 Archive Report: Çatalhöyük Research Project*, http://www.catalhoyuk.com/archive_reports/ (accessed: 01/07/12).

Holden, A. and Iveson, K. (2003) 'Designs on the urban: New Labour's urban rennaissance and the spaces of citizenship', *City*, 7(1): 57–72.

Holling, C.S. (1973) 'Resilience and stability of ecological systems', *Annual Review of Ecology and Systematics*, 4: 1–23.

Hooke, G. (2000) 'On the history of humans as geomorphic agents', *Geology*, 28(9): 843–846.

Howard, M. (2002) 'What's in a name? How to fight terrorism', *Foreign Affairs*, 81(1): 8–15.

Hudson, R.A. (2002) *Who Becomes a Terrorist and Why: The 1999 Government Report on Profiling Terrorists*, Washington: The Lyons Press.

Ignatieff, M. (1979) 'Police and people: The birth of Mr Peel's Blue Locusts', *New Society*, 30 August, 1979.

Imrie, R. and Raco, M. (eds) (2001) *Urban Renaissance? New Labour, Community and Urban Policy*, Bristol: The Policy Press.

Introna, L. and Wood, D. (2004) 'Picturing algorithmic surveillance: The politics of facial recognition systems', *Surveillance & Society*, 2(2/3): 177–198.

Jackson, P. (1998) 'Domesticating the street: The contested spaces of the High Street and the Mall', in Fyfe, N.R. (ed.), *Images of the Street: Planning, Identity and Control in Public Space*, London: Routledge: 176–191.

Jarman, N. (2008) 'Security and segregation: Interface barriers in Belfast', *Shared Space*, 6(1): 21–34.

Jessop, B. (1997) 'The entrepreneurial city: Re-imaging localities, redesigning economic governance or restructuring capital?', in Jewson, N. and MacGregor, S. *Transforming Cities: Contested Governance and New Spatial Divisions*, London: Routledge: 25–39.

Jessop, B., Brenner, N. and Jones, M. (2008) 'Theorising socio-spatial relations', *Environment and Planning D: Society and Space*, 26: 389–401.

Judd, D.R. and Fainstein, S.S. (eds) (1999) *The Tourist City*, New Haven, CT: Yale University Press.

Kates, R.W. and Burton, I. (eds) (1986a) *Geography, Resources and Environment (Volume I): Themes From the Work of Gilbert. F. White*, Chicago: University of Chicago Press.

Kates, R.W. and Burton, I. (eds) (1986b) *Geography, Resources and Environment (Volume II): Themes From the Work of Gilbert. F. White*, Chicago: University of Chicago Press.

Kates, R.W., Colten, C.E., Laska, S. and Leatherman, S.P. (2006) 'Reconstruction of New Orleans after Hurricane Katrina: A research perspective', *Proceedings of the National Academy of Science of the USA*, 103(4).

Katz, P. (1994) *The New Urbanism: Toward an Architecture of Community*, New York: McGraw Hill.

Keane, J. (2009) *The Life and Death of Democracy*, London: Simon & Schuster.

Keeley, L.H. (1996) *War Before Civilisation: The Myth of the Peaceful Savage*, Oxford: Oxford University Press.

Killian, L.M. (1954) 'Some accomplishments and needs in disaster study', *Journal of Social Issues*, 10: 66–72.

King, R.O. (2005) *Hurricane Katrina: Insurance Losses and National Capacities for Financing Disaster Risk (CRS Report for Congress)*, Washington: Congressional Research Service. The Library of Congress.

Kinzig, A.P., Ryan, P., Etienne, M., Allison, H., Elmqvist, T. and Walker, B.H. (2006) 'Resilience and regime shifts: Assessing cascading effects', *Ecology and Society*, 11(1): 20.

Kipfer, S. (2002) 'Urbanisation, everyday life and the survival of capitalism: Lefebvre, Gramsci and the Problematic of Hegemony', *Capitalism, Nature, Socialism*, 13(2): 117–149.

Klauser, F. (2004) 'The consequences of video-surveillance on urban territoriality: A comparison between different spatial concepts of visual surveillance', *CCTV and Social Control: The Politics and Practice of Video-surveillance – European and Global Perspectives*, Sheffield University Centre for Criminological Research (CSSR).

Klauser, F. (2010) 'Splintering spheres of security: Peter Sloterdjick and the contemporary fortress city', *Environment and Planning D: Society and Space*, 28: 326–340.

Klein, N. (2008) *The Shock Doctrine: The Rise of Disaster Capitalism*, USA: Picador.

Klien, R.J.T., Nicholls, R.J., and Thomalla, F. (2003) 'Resilience to natural hazards: How useful is this concept?' *Global Environmental Change: PART B: Environmental Hazards*, 5 (1–2): 35–45.

Koc, M., MacRae, R., Mougeot, L.J.A. and Welsh, J. (eds) (1999) *For Hunger-Proof Cities: Sustainable Urban Food Systems*, Ottowa: International Development Research Centre.

Kofman, E. (1999) 'Citizenship for some but not for others: Spaces of citizenship in contemporary Europe', *Political Geography*, 14(2): 121–137.

Korieh, C.J. and Njoku, R.C. (eds) (2007) *Missions, States, and European Expansion in Africa*, London: Routledge.

Kusenbach, M. (2003) 'Street phenomenology: The go-along as ethnographic research tool', *Ethnography*, 4(3): 455–485.

Leach, A. (2011) 'California's DA office will not prosecute Occupy Sacramento arrests', http://www.occupytogether.org (accessed: 27/10/2011).

Lees, L. (2000) 'A re-appraisal of gentrification: Towards a "geography of gentrification"', *Progress in Human Geography*, 24(3): 389–408.

Lees, L., Slater, T. and Wyly, E. (2007) *Gentrification*, London: Routledge.

Lefebvre, H. (1974) *The Production of Space*, Oxford: Blackwell.

Lefebvre, H. (1978 [1966]) *The Sociology of Marx*, Middlesex: Penguin (trans. Guterman, N.).

Lefebvre, H. (1988) 'Toward a leftist cultural politics: Remarks occasioned by the centenary of Marx's death', in Nelson, C. and Grossberg, L. (eds) *Marxism and the Interpretation of Culture*, Urbana: University of Illinois Press: 75–88.

Lefebvre, H. (1995[1962]) *Introduction to Modernity*, London: Verso (trans. Moore, J.).

Lefebvre, H. (2004 [1992]) *Rhythmanalysis: Space, Time and Everyday Life*, London: Continuum (trans. Elden, S. and Moore, G.).

Lefebvre, H. (2008 [1951]) *Volume I – Critique of Everyday Life*, London: Verso (trans. Moore, J.).

Lefebvre, H. (2008 [1961]) *Volume II – Critique of Everyday Life: Foundations for a Sociology of the Everyday*, London: Verso (trans. Moore, J.).

Lefebvre, H. (2005 [1981]) *Volume III – Critique of Everyday Life: From Modernity to Modernism (Towards a Metaphilosophy of Daily Life)*, London: Verso (trans. Moore, J.).

Lefebvre, H. (2009 [1940]) *Dialectical Materialism*, Minneapolis: University of Minnesota Press (trans. Sturrock, J. – 1968).

Legg, S. (ed.) (2011) *Geographies of the Nomos: Sovereignty, Spatiality and Carl Schmitt*, London: Routledge.

Lemke, P. (2001) '"The birth of bio-politics": Michel Foucault's lecture at the Collége de France on neo-liberal governmentality', *Economy and Society*, 30(2): 190–207.

Lentin, R. (2008) *Thinking Palestine*, London: Zed Books.

Lepage, J.G.G. (2002) *Castles and Fortified Cities of Medieval Europe*, Jefferson, NC: McFarland.

Levi, M. and Murphy, G.H. (2006) 'Coalitions of contention: The case of the WTO protests in Seattle', *Political Studies*, 54: 651–670.

Levin, S.A. (1998) 'Ecosystems and the biosphere as complex adaptive systems', *Ecosystems*, 1: 431–439.

Lichtman, S.A. (2006) 'Do-it-yourself security: Safety, gender and the home fallout shelter in Cold War America', *Journal of Design History*, 19(1): 39–55.

Little, R.G. (2002) 'Controlling cascading failure: Understanding the vulnerabilities of interconnected infrastructures', *Journal of Urban Technology*, 9(1): 109–123.

Little, R.G. (2010) 'Managing the Risk of Cascading Failures in Complex Urban Infrastructures', in Graham, S. (ed.) *Disrupted Cities: When Infrastructure Fails*, London: Routledge.

Longrigg, J. (1980) 'The Great Plague of Athens', *History of Science*, 18: 209–225.

Luongo, G., Perrotta, A., Scarpati, C., De Carolis, E., Patricelli, G. and Ciarallo, A. (2003) 'Impact of the AD 79 explosive eruption on Pompeii, II. Causes of death of the inhabitants inferred by stratigraphic analysis and areal distribution of the human casualties', *Journal of Volcanology and Geothermal Research*, 126: 169–200.

McCahill, M. (2000) *CCTV and Social Exclusion, Surveillance and Society: Understanding the New Technologies of Surveillance*, University of Hull.

McCahill, M. (2003) *The Surveillance Web: The Rise of Visual Surveillance in an English City*, Cullompton: Willan Publishing.

MacLeod, G. (2002) 'From urban entrepreneurialism to a "revanchist city"? On the spatial injustices of Glasgow's renaissance', *Antipode*, 34(3): 602–624.

McNeil, W. (1999) *The Glance of the Eye: Heidegger, Aristotle, and the Ends of Theory (SUNY Series in Contemporary Continental Philosophy)*, New York: State University of New York Press.

Madanipour, A. (2003) *Public and Private Spaces of the City*, London: Routledge.

Mannheim, K. (1936) *Ideology and Utopia*, London: Routledge and Kegan Paul.

Marlow, J. (1969) *The Peterloo Massacre*, London: Rapp & Whiting.

Marx, K. (1974 [1867]) *Capital*, London: Aldine House.

Messinger, G.S. (1992) *British Propaganda and the State in the First World War*, Manchester: Manchester University Press.

Miles, S. (2003a) 'Consuming cities; consuming youth: Young people's lifestyles and the appropriation of cultural space', in Eckerdt, F. and Hassenpflug, D. (eds) *Consumption and the Post-Industrial City*, Oxford: Peter Lang.

Miles, S. (2003) 'Resistance or security? Young people and the "appropriation" of urban, cultural and consumer space', in Miles, M. and Hall, T. (eds) *Urban Futures: Critical Commentaries on Shaping the City*, London: Routledge: 65–75.

Miles, S. (2005). '"Our Tyne": Iconic regeneration and the revitalisation of identity in Newcastle/Gateshead', *Urban Studies*, 42(5/6): 913–926.

Miles, S. (2010) *Space for Consumption*, London: Sage.

Miles, M. and Miles, S. (2000) *Consuming Cities*, London: Palgrave Macmillan.

Minton, A. (2009) *Ground Control: Fear and Happiness in the Twentieth-Century City*, London: Penguin.

Minton, A. (2010) '"This town has been sold to Tesco." Are towns built by the UK's leading supermarket the future of urban development?', *The Guardian*, 5th May 2010.

Mitchell, D. and Staheli, L.A. (2005) 'Permitting protest: Parsing the fine geography of dissent in America', *International Journal of Urban and Regional Research*, 29(4): 796–813.

Mitra, S.K. (1991) 'Room to manuever in the middle: Local elites, political action, and the State in India', *World Politics*, 43(3): 390–413.

Mitra, S.K. (1992) *Power, Protest and Participation: Local Elites and the Politics of Development in India*, London: Routledge.

Mladek, K. (ed.) (2007) *Police Forces: A Cultural History of an Institution*, New York: Palgrave.

Molina, A.A. (1993) 'California's anti-gang street terrorism enforcement and prevention act: One step forward, two steps back?', *Southwestern University Law Review*, 44: 457–470.

Moore, H.E. (1958) *Tornadoes over Texas*, Austin: Texas University Press.

Mumford, L. (1961) *The City in History: Its Origins, its Transformations and its Prospects*, London: Harcourt Inc.

Musterd, S. (2003) 'The creative cultural knowledge city, some conditions', paper presented at the University of Kaiserlautern, October 2002.

Musterd, S. and Murie, A. (2010) *Making Competitive Cities*, Oxford: Blackwell.

Murray, W. (1997) 'Thinking in revolutions about military affairs', *Joint Force Quarterly*, July, 1997, Fort Belvoir: The Defense Technical Information Center.

National Advisory Commission on Civil Disorders (1968) Summary of report, NACDC.

Newman, O. (1972) *Defensible Space: Crime Prevention Through Urban Design*, London: Macmillan.

Nancy, J.-L. (2003) *A Finite Thinking*, Stanford: Stanford University Press.

Nietzsche, F. (1968) *Will to Power*, Random House (trans. Kaufman, W.).

Nietzsche, F. (1977) *A Nietzsche Reader*, London: Penguin (trans. and ed. Hollingdale, R.J.).

Nietzsche, F. (2003 [1913]) *The Genealogy of Morals*, Mineola: Dover Publications (trans. Samuel, H.B.).

Nippel, W. (1995) *Public Order in Ancient Rome*, London: Cambridge University Press.

Nolan, N. (2003) 'The ins and outs of skateboarding and transgression in public space in Newcastle, Australia', *Australian Geographer*, 34(3): 311–327.

Norris, F.H. and Stevens, S.P. (2007) 'Community resilience and the principles of mass trauma intervention'. *Psychiatry*, 70(4): 320–328.

Norris, F.H., Stevens, S.P., Pfefferbaum, B., Wyche, K.F. and Pfefferbaum, R.P. (2008) 'Community resilience as a metaphor, theory, set of capacities, and strategy for disaster readiness', *American Journal of Community Psychology*, 41: 127–150.

North, D.C., Wallis, J.J. and Weingast, B.R. (2005) *The Natural State: The Political-Economy of Non-Development*, NBER working paper.

North, D.C., Wallis, J.J. and Weingast, B.R. (2009a) *Violence and Social Orders: A Conceptual Framework for Reinterpreting Human History*, New York: Cambridge University Press.

North, D.C., Wallis, J.J. and Weingast, B.R. (2009b) 'Violence and the rise of open-access orders', *Journal of Democracy*, 20(1): 55–68.

O'Brien, G. and Read, P. (2004) 'Future UK emergency management: From discretion to regulation—panacea or long overdue reform?' *Proceedings of the International Emergency Management Society 11th Annual Conference*, 18–21 May 2004, Melbourne, Australia.

O'Brien, G. and Read, P. (2005) 'Future UK emergency management: New wine, old skin?', *Disaster Prevention and Management*, 14(3): 353–361.

Oc, T. and Tiesdell, S. (1997a) 'The death and life of city centres', in Oc, T. and Tiesdell, S. *Safer City Centres: Reviving the Public Realm*, London: Sage.

Oc, T. and Tiesdell, S. (1997b) 'Towards safer city centres', in Oc, T. and Tiesdell, S. *Safer City Centres: Reviving the Public Realm*, London: Sage.

O'Malley, P. (2003) 'Risk, power and crime prevention', in McLaughlan, E., Muncie, J. and Hughes, G. (eds) *Criminological Perspectives: Essential Readings*, 2nd edition, London: Sage: 449–468.

Ortner, D.J. and Putschar, W.G.J. (1981) *Identification of Pathological Conditions in Human Skeletal Remains*, City of Washington: Smithsonian Institution Press.

Ozerdem, A. (2003) 'Disaster as manifestation of unresolved development challenges: The Mamara earthquake, Turkey', in Pelling, M. (ed.) *Natural Disasters in a Globalising World*, London: Routledge: 199–213.

Paton, D. (2006) 'Disaster resilience: Integrating individual, community, institutional and environmental perspectives', in Paton, D. and Johnston, D. (eds) *Disaster Resilience: An Integrated Approach*, Illinois: Charles C. Thomas: 305–326.

Paton, D. and Johnston, D. (eds) (2006) *Disaster Resilience: An Integrated Approach*, Illinois: Charles C. Thomas.

194 *Resilience & the City*

Paton, D. and Johnston, D. (2001) 'Disaster and communities: Vulnerability, resilience and preparedness', *Disaster Prevention and Management*, 10(4): 270–277.

Parker, G. (1988) *The Military Revolution: Military Innovation and the Rise of the West, 1500–1800*, Cambridge: Cambridge University Press.

Pelling, M. (2003) *The Vulnerability of Cities: Natural Disasters and Social Resilience*, London: Routledge.

Pelling, M. and Wisner, B. (2009) *Disaster Risk Reduction: Cases from Urban Africa*, London: Earthscan.

Perry, R.W. (2006) 'What is a disaster?', in Rodriguez, H., Quarantelli, E.L. and Dynes, R.R. (eds) *Handbook of Disaster Research: Handbooks of Sociology and Social Research*, New York: Springer (Kindle edition).

Pettinato, G. (2000) 'Ideology and nomenclature of power in Sumer and Ebla', in Panaino, A. and Pettinato, G. *Ideologies as Intercultural Phenomena: Proceedings of the Third Annual Symposium of the Assyrian and Babylonian Intellectual Heritage Project*, USA: International Association for Intercultural Studies of the MELAMMU Project, Mimesis Edizioni.

Phillips, M. (2002) 'The production, symbolization and socialization of gentrification: Impressions from two Berkshire villages', *Transactions of the Institute of British Geographers*, 27(3): 282–308.

Philo, C. (2001) 'Accumulating populations: Bodies, institutions and space', *International Journal of Population Geography*, 7: 473–490.

Pintor, R.L. and Gratschew, M. (2002) *Voter Turnout since 1945: A Global Report*, Stockholm: International IDEA.

Poggi, G. (1990) *The State: Its Formation, Development and Prospects*, Stanford: Stanford University Press.

Pohl, J. and Hook, A. (2001) *The Conquistador: 1492–1550*, Oxford: Osprey.

Power, M.J. (1992) 'The growth of Liverpool', in Belchem, J. (ed.) *Popular Politics, Riot and Labour: Essays in Liverpool History 1790–1940*, Liverpool: Liverpool University Press: 38–68.

Quarantelli, E.L. (1987) 'Presidential address: What should we study?', *International Journal of Mass Emergencies and Disaster*, 5(3): 285–310.

Quarantelli, E.L. (ed.) (1998) *What is a Disaster? A Dozen Perspectives on the Question*, London: Routledge (Kindle edition).

Quarantelli, E.L. (2001) 'Statistical problems in the study of disasters', *Disaster Prevention and Management*, 10(5): 325–338.

Quarantelli, E.L. and Dynes, R.R. (1977) 'Response to social crisis and disaster', *Annual Review of Sociology*, 3: 23–49.

Raban, J. (1998) *Soft City: A Documentary Exploration of Metropolitan Life*, London: Harper Collins.

Raco, M. (2003) 'New Labour, community and the future of Britain's urban renaissance', in Imrie, R. and Raco, M. (eds) *Urban Renaissance? New Labour, Community and Urban Policy*, London: Polity Press: 235–249.

Rasler, K.A. and Thompson, W.R. (1989) *War and State Making: The Shaping of the Global Powers*, London: Allen and Unwin.

Read, D. (1958) *Peterloo: The Massacre and its Background*, Manchester: Manchester University Press.

Reeve, A. (1996) 'The private realm of the managed town centre', *Urban Design International*, 1(1): 61–80.

Roberts, C. and Manchester, K. (2007) *The Archaeology of Disease*, Ithaca, NY: Cornell University Press.

Rodriguez, U. (2006) 'The seductive comparison of shareholder and civic democracy', *Scholarly Works*, Paper 238. http://digitalcommons.law.uga.edu/fac_artchop/238 (accessed: 01/07/12).

Rogers, P. (2006) 'Are you normal? Young people's participation in the renaissance of public space – a case study of Newcastle upon Tyne, UK', *Children, Youth and Environments*, 16(2): 102–116.

Rogers, P. (2009) 'Youth participation and revanchist regimes: Redeveloping old Eldon Square, Newcastle upon Tyne', in Madani Pour, A. (ed.) *Whose Public Space? International Case Studies in Urban Design and Development*, London: Routledge: 51–68.

Rogers, P. (2011a) 'Development of resilient Australia: Enhancing the PPRR approach with anticipation, assessment and registration of risks', *Australian Journal of Emergency Management*, 26(1): 54–59.

Rogers, P. (2011b) 'Between nomos and everyday life: Securing the spatial order of Foucault and Schmitt' in Legg, S. (ed.) *Geographies of the Nomos: Sovereignty, Spatiality and Carl Schmitt*, London: Routledge: 182–199.

Rogers, P. and Coaffee, J. (2005) 'Moral panics and urban renaissance: Policy, tactics and lived experiences in public space', *City*, 9: 321–340.

Rose, N. (1999) *Powers of Freedom: Reframing Political Thought*, Cambridge: Cambridge University Press.

Rosen, G. (1993) *A History of Public Health*, New York: Johns Hopkins University Press.

Rousseau, J.J. (1987) *The Basic Political Writings*, London: Hackett Publishing Company (trans. and ed. Cresswell, D.A.).

Royle, E. and Walvin, J. (1982) *English Radicals and Reformers 1760–1848*, Brighton: The Harvester Press.

Ruggiero, V. (2003) 'Fear and change in the city', *City*, 7(1): 45–55.

Russell, J. (2009) *Liberty's Supplementary Evidence to the Joint Committee on Human Rights: 'Policing and Protest' – Private Property*, London: Liberty.

Sack, J.J. (1993) *From Jacobite to Conservative: Reaction and Orthodoxy in Britain, c.1760–1832*, Cambridge: Cambridge University Press.

Samara, T.R. (2010) 'Policing development: Urban renewal as neo-liberal security strategy', *Urban Studies*, 47(1): 197–214.

Schain, M. (ed.) (2001) *The Marshall Plan: 50 Years After*, London: Palgrave.

Schmitt, C. (2003) *The Nomos of the Earth: In the International Law of the Jus Publicum Europaeum*, New York: Telos Press.

Schrader-Frechette K.S. and McCoy, E.D. (1993) *Method in Ecology*, London: Cambridge University Press.

Seattle Police Department. (2000) *WTO After Action Report*, Seattle: The Seattle Police Department.

Seville, E., Brunsdon, D., Dantas, A., Le Masurier, J., Wilkinson, S. and Vargo, J. (2006) *Building Organisational Resilience: A Summary of Key Research Findings*, Christchurch, New Zealand: Resilient Organisations Research Programme.

Shaluf, I.M., Ahmadun, F. and Said, A.M. (2003) 'A review of crisis and disaster', *Disaster Prevention and Management*, 12(1): 24–32.

Sheffi, Y. (2005) *The Resilient Enterprise: Overcoming Vulnerability for Competitive Advantage*, Cambridge, MA: MIT Press.

Shields, R. (1992) *Lifestyle Shopping: The Subject of Consumption*, London: Routledge.

Schmitt, C. (2003 [1950]) *The Nomos of the Earth: In the International Law of the Jus Publicum Europaeum*, New York: Telos.

Shnirelman, V.A. (1982) 'On the paleolithic/mesolithic transition', *Current Anthropology*, 23(2): 224–227.

Sigurdsson, H., Cashdollar, S. and Sparks, S.R.J. (1982) 'The eruption of Vesuvius in A.D. 79: Reconstruction from historical and volcanological evidence', *American Journal of Archaeology*, 86(1) (Jan. 1982): 39–51.

Slater, T. (2002) 'Looking at the "North American city" through the lens of gentrification discourse', *Urban Geography*, 23(2): 131–153.

Smith, N. (1996) *The New Urban Frontier: Gentrification and the Revanchist City*, London: Routledge.

Smith, N. (2002) 'New globalism, new urbanism: Gentrification as a global urban strategy', *Antipode*, 34(3): 427–450.

Soja, E. (2005) 'Mesogeographies: On the generative effects of urban agglomeration', *TCP Annual Distinguished Lecture – Territory, Culture and Politics Research Cluster*, School of Geography, Politics and Sociology, University of Newcastle upon Tyne.

Sorkin, M. (1992) *Variations on a Theme Park: The New American City and the End of Public Space*, New York: Hill & Wang.

Southall, A. (1998) *The City in Time and Space*, Cambridge: Cambridge University Press.

Sproule, J.M. (2005) *Propaganda and Democracy: The American Experience of Media and Mass Persuasion*, London: Cambridge University Press.

Stanley, J.D., Goddio, F. and Schnepp, G. (2001) 'Nile flooding sank two ancient cities', *Nature*, 4(12): 293–294.

Stewart, L. (1995) 'Bodies, visions, and spatial politics: A review essay on Henri Lefebvre's *The Production of Space*', *Environment and Planning D: Society and Space*, 13: 609–618.

Strauss, L. (2001) *Leo Strauss On Plato's Symposium*, 1st edition, Chicago: University of Chicago Press.

Sullivan-Taylor, B. and Branicki, L. (2011) 'Creating resilient SMEs: Why one size might not fit all', *International Journal of Production Research*, 49:18, 5565–5579.

Swyngedouw, E. and Kaika, M. (2003) 'The making of glocal modernities: Exploring cracks in the mirror', *City*, 7(1): 5–21.

Taher, A. (2009) 'Tesco town planned next to 2012 site', *London Evening Standard*, 14th October 2009.

Tallon, A. (2009) *Urban Regeneration in the UK*, London: Routledge.

Tamineaux, J. (1992) 'Heidegger and praxis', in Rockmore, T. and Margolis, J. *The Heidegger Case: On Philosophy and Politics*, Philadelphia: Temple University Press: 188–207.

Thompson, E.P. (1963) *The Making of the English Working Class*, London: Free Vintage Press.

Thompson, J. (2011 [1877]) *Collected Papers in Physics and Engineering*, London: Nabu press.

Tierney, K.J., Lindell, M.K. and Perry, R.W. (2001) *Disaster Preparedness and Response in the United States*, Washington, DC: Henry (Joseph) Press.

Tracy, J.D. (ed.) (2000) *City Walls: The Urban Enceinte in History*, Cambridge: Cambridge University Press.

Turney-High, H. (1949 [1979]) *Primitive War: Its Practice and Concepts*, Columbia: University of South Carolina Press.

UN (2010) *World Urbanisation Prospects: Projections 2009 Revision*, Geneva: UN.

UNESCO (2008) *Project Concept Paper: Meeting of the Expert Advisory Group: UNESCO-IHP Project on Water and Cultural Diversity*, Paris, France (7–8 January 2008).

Vale, J.L. and Campanella, J.T. (eds) (2005) *The Resilient City: How Modern Cities Recover From Disaster*, Oxford: Oxford University Press.

Van Creveld, M. (1991) *The Transformation of War*, New York: The Free Press.

van Aalst, M.K. (2006) 'The impact of climate change on the risk of natural disasters', *Disasters*, 30(1): 5–18.

van Winden, W., van der Berg, L. and Pol, P. (2007) 'European cities in the knowledge economy: Towards a typology', *Urban Studies*, 44(3): 525–549.

Vasquez, J.A. (ed.) (2000) *What Do We Know About War?*, London: Roman and Littlefield.

Visser, G. (2002) 'Gentrification and South African cities – towards a research agenda', *Cities*, 19(6): 419–423.

Waldron, T. (2007) *Paleoepidemiology: The Epidemiology of Human Remains*, Walnut Creek: Left Coast Press.

Walker, J. and Cooper, M. (2011) 'Genealogies of resilience: From systems ecology to the political economy of crisis adaptation', *Security Dialogue*, 42: 143–160.

Walmsley, R. (1969) *Peterloo: The Case Re-opened*, Manchester: Manchester University Press.

Walsh, M.J. (2003) *The Conclave: A Sometimes Secret and Occasionally Bloody History of Papal Elections*, Norwich: Canterbury Press.

Weber, K. and Chon, K. (eds) (2002) *Convention Tourism: International Research and Industry Perspectives*, Binghampton: The Haworth Hospitality Press.

Welch, D. (2000) *Germany, Propaganda and Total War, 1914–1918*, London: Athalone Press.

White, R.J. (1957) *Waterloo to Peterloo*, London: Peregrine Books.

Whitson, D. and Macintosh, D. (1996) 'The global circus: International sport, tourism, and the marketing of cities', *Journal of Sport and Social Issues*, 20(3): 278–295.

Wildavsky, A. (1984) *Trial Without Error: Anticipation Versus Resilience as Strategies for Risk Reduction*, Centre for Independent Studies, Occasional papers: no. 13.

Wildavsky, A. (1988) *Searching for Safety (Studies in Social Philosophy and Policy)*, New York: Transaction Publishers.

Wilkinson, S.I. (2009) 'Riots', *Annual Review of Political Science*, 12: 329–343.

Wilson, D.C., Branicki, L., Sullivan-Taylor, B. and Wilson, A.D. (2010) 'Extreme events, organizations and the politics of strategic decision making', *Accounting, Auditing & Accountability Journal*, 23(5): 699–721.

Worpole, K. and Greenhalgh, L. (1996) *The Freedom of the City*, London: Demos.

Wright, A. (1986) 'The Evolution of Civilizations', in Sherratt, D.J.A. *American Archaeology Past and Future*, Cambridge: Cambridge University Press: 60–78.

Wright, Q. (1964 [1942]) *A Study of War*, (abridged edition), Chicago: University of Chicago Press.

Younis, M. (2011) 'British Tuition Fee Protest, November 9, 2010, London', *Interface: A Journal For and About Social Movements – Event Analysis*, 3(1): 172–181.

Zajko, M. and Bléland, D. (2008) 'Space and protest policing at international summits', *Environment and Planning D: Society and Space*, 26: 719–735.

Zick, T. (2006) *Speech and Spatial Tactics*, Faculty Publications, Paper 277, http://scholarship.law.wm.edu/facpubs/277 (accessed: 09/04/2008).

Zong, Y., Chen, Z., Innes, J.B., Chen, C., Wang, Y. and Wang, H. (2007) 'Fire and flood management of coastal swamp enabled first rice paddy cultivation in east China', *Nature*, 449: 459–462.

Index

Note: (*n*) indicates footnotes; **bold** page numbers indicate tables and figures.